Enlightenment

'When you asked me to be your wife, you said I was the first woman you had met to whom you felt you could reveal yourself. That is the seed from which our happiness will grow.' He nodded, and fixed his tremendous eyes upon her. She felt her words must ebb away and sat and looked at him in stillness. It seemed extraordinary to her that in less than a week she would be able to touch him. She could not imagine it at all.

SUE LIMB is a much-loved writer and broadcaster. For several years she has written a column in the *Guardian* as her alter ego Dulcie Domum. She adapted her novel *Up the Garden Path* for Radio 4, and later for television. Her previous books include *Out on a Limb*, *Sheep's Eyes and Hogwash* and *Passion Fruit*.

SUE LIMB

Enlightenment

ARROW

Published in the United Kingdom in 1998 by
Arrow Books

1 3 5 7 9 10 8 6 4 2

First published in the United Kingdom in 1997 by William Heinemann

Arrow Books Limited
Random House UK Ltd
20 Vauxhall Bridge Road, London SW1V 2SA

Random House Australia (Pty) Limited
20 Alfred Street, Milsons Point, Sydney,
New South Wales 2061, Australia

Random House New Zealand Limited
18 Poland Road, Glenfield, Auckland 10, New Zealand

Random House South Africa (Pty) Limited
Endulini, 5a Jubilee Road, Parktown 2193, South Africa

Random House UK Limited Reg. No. 954009

A CIP catalogue record for this book
is available from the British Library

Papers used by Random House UK Limited
are natural, recyclable products made from wood grown in
sustainable forests. The manufacturing processes conform to
the environmental regulations of the country of origin

ISBN 0 7493 2220 9

Printed and bound in Great Britain by
Cox & Wyman Ltd, Reading, Berkshire

For Jean and Linden Huddlestone

1

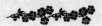

'Quick, Miss Jane! He's down in the valley now! Run, or you'll miss him!' The servant Hetty stood panting in the doorway. Jane looked up, startled, from her watercolour. 'My niece Kitty just came to the kitchen door with a basket of plums, Miss, and she told us he's down by the Lower Barn.' Jane leapt to her feet, seized her shawl and hesitated.

'If my mother – or Papa – ask for me, tell them I've gone for a walk!'

Jane rushed out, past her sister's door, and down the stairs. She knew Mary was deep in a novel, and would not stir for anything. Mary would not share her excitement either. Like everyone else in Gloucestershire, she had heard the feverish talk about Mr Harris, but Mary had only yawned.

'I'm sure he can't be so tremendous as the Count of Trevasso in *The Mysteries of Brunnenberg*,' she had said, turning languidly back to her book. Mary was more intrigued by Gothic tales of adventure in distant mountains than what was happening in the fields of her own parish. But Jane had heard of Mr Harris and his extraordinary powers with mounting amazement. She was now determined to see him for herself.

She burst out of the kitchen door and ran round to the terrace. Newington House stood aloof on a gigantic cliff, commanding immense views beyond the tumbling rocks and woods beneath, across the vast airiness of the Severn Plain to the Mendip Hills. In her state of exhilaration, Jane found something almost painfully piercing in the melancholy grandeur of the scene. Below her, the immense chasm of the valley seemed full of golden vapour. She hurled herself into the cloud of light, almost flying in her haste, plunging down the cliff path, below the glade, below the lake, down an immense and echoing valley, out of sight of her father's house, thinking, *In a moment I shall see him. I shall see him at last.*

She broke through a gap in a hedge, and stopped. There, in a field below, in the valley bottom, a vast crowd of people was assembled, their backs to her. They looked up at a solitary figure raised above them. The man addressing them was standing on a stile, wearing a long black coat. At Jane's appearance he looked up, and his white face seemed to flash. He had seen her arrival.

Though he was still several hundred yards away, Jane's sharp eyes devoured many details of his appearance. She could not yet hear any of his words, only the ringing cadences of his speech. His pale face and black hair roughly swept back gave him a haunted look, emphasised by his black clothes, which set him apart from the drab greys, greens and browns of his congregation – for a congregation it was, though outdoors. Mr Harris was an Evangelical preacher.

As Jane crept nearer she saw that his looks were striking. They suggested a portrait of a Tudor courtier or Puritanical spy. The face was not merely of exquisite beauty but mysterious, compelling, aloof. The eyes in particular had a hypnotic power, and as he completed the blessing and dismissed his congregation, he looked across at Jane for some moments, and she felt pierced by his look.

She had heard that Evangelical preachers could fix a hesitating soul with a look of scorching power, and now she felt it. When she had first heard that sermons were being preached in the fields, she had been amazed. Now she had seen it. Jane had often yawned through divine service at Ottercombe Church, finding it a tedious and somnolent ceremony. All over England, the most passionate preachers had forsaken the sleepy pulpits of tradition and taken their message of surging spiritual revival outdoors, to cry it to the air. Great multitudes of ordinary folk had followed. Their hearts had been touched, and they had begun to hope for better lives on earth as well as hereafter.

Now the congregation began to stir, and sigh and move off. Someone claimed the attention of the preacher and he climbed down off his stile, and was lost to view. Jane walked among the folk who had heard him preach. Many of them were in tears. From their smiles and sighs and scattered words she could tell they had been deeply stirred, and she sensed she had missed something extraordinary.

'Jane!'

She turned and recognised a neighbour, Miss Axton, who lived further along the valley in a small cottage with her brother, Humphrey. Miss Axton rushed up, wrung Jane's hand, and enquired fervently about the health of her parents and sister. With her small eyes, broad snout and wild cloud of hair, Miss Axton had the air of a pig in a wig, and Jane was fond of her and amused by her.

Mr Axton was a poet, some forty years of age, and his sister a year or two older. Jane and Mary had been taught to read by Miss Axton when they were little girls, and Mr Axton had ingratiated himself into John Lockhart's favour by the sketches he had made twenty years before, when he had travelled in Italy, and by his intelligent understanding of architecture and history.

'Did you ever hear such an inspiring sermon?' cried Miss Axton, wiping her eyes. 'My heart is still pounding. I wish Humphrey could have heard it! But he will not come.'

'I wish I had heard it,' admitted Jane. 'But I only came at the end. Hetty's niece came up from Woolton to tell us he was preaching in our valley, but I was too late. Still, at least I have seen him now.'

3

'Yes, you have seen his face – and he is such a handsome fellow. Not that his looks are significant. But his words! People talk of nothing else. He seems to know what one is thinking. He seemed to look straight into my heart, today. I shan't sleep a wink tonight, thinking of it.

'Will you walk along the lane and take tea with us, Jane? Humphrey will be delighted to see you again.' Jane very gladly consented, though she was disappointed, as they approached the stile where Mr Harris had stood, to find he had entirely disappeared.

'I don't suppose he will preach again hereabouts,' sighed Miss Axton, climbing into the lane. 'It's the end of the season. September. He will be leaving us now.' Jane felt frustrated. Her glimpse of Mr Harris had been too brief. 'He preaches up and down the West Country, on the circuit,' Miss Axton went on. 'This is his furthest north. And south as far as Devon in the summer, I believe. I think he spends the winters in Bristol. There are many Evangelists there. No doubt he will be going back there soon and we shall not see him again till April.'

Jane felt disappointed. 'Still,' she mused, 'I suppose his family must be very glad to have him to themselves.'

'He's not married,' confided Miss Axton with a wink, 'and to be honest I think this is part of his charm. The girls come from miles around to faint at his feet. I think I should faint myself, were I twenty and not forty. No, he lives with his sister, rather a formidable lady, with a very long face, like a shovel. Ah! Here we are. I hope Humphrey has not gone out.'

They walked up the path to the cottage and heard voices.

'Ah!' cried Miss Axton eagerly. 'There is somebody here.'

As they entered at the low door, a young spaniel jumped up to greet them, and though Miss Axton bustled straight through to the parlour to greet her unexpected guest, Jane bent down to caress the dog. 'Oh you darling!' she whispered. 'You beautiful girl!' The dog's head was firm and warm, the fur glossy with health, the tongue tremulous

4

and loving. 'You sweetheart! Oh I adore you!'

'Sir Thomas!' she heard Miss Axton cry. Jane grew apprehensive. Sir Thomas Burton owned the other great house in Ottercombe, but she had never met him. Newington House was known as The Manor, but Ottercombe Park, which Sir Thomas had for several years let out to a tenant, was thought of as The Mansion. Jane's father bridled at this supposed insult and had resisted an acquaintance with Sir Thomas, though without giving offence, as the Burtons were so often absent.

Two years ago Sir Thomas's tenant, an aged admiral, had died and Sir Thomas had embarked upon so extensive a programme of renovation as to excite the curiosity of the whole of Gloucestershire. He meant at last to bring Lady Charlotte home, after their years of residence in Bath, London and Dorset; but alas! before the house was ready, little more than a year ago, Lady Charlotte had suddenly died. There had been a hiatus of mourning, then work on the house had recommenced. The parish grieved for Sir Thomas, but rejoiced that he had resolved to make his home at Ottercombe despite his sad loss. Everybody looked forward to receiving him and to admiring his four fine children. Sir Thomas had three daughters and a son, all more or less grown up now, the youngest daughter some two or three years younger than Jane.

All this Jane knew and she got up with reluctance from the dog, knowing she would be required to be introduced to the master. She felt a little nervous, for the words 'Sir Thomas' had always carried about them associations of importance and style, wealth and connections superior to that of her own family; and beyond this intimidating grandeur she shrank from the desolate blow of his bereavement. She hesitated, therefore, dreading the moment a little.

'Come in, Jane, come and meet Sir Thomas,' cried Miss Axton and she knew she must endure it. She went into the parlour, where a pleasant-looking gentleman was standing by the hearth. She was puzzled. Could this be Sir Thomas?

He was in some ways very ordinary in his appearance, neither old nor young, and not especially tall, with solid shoulders. He had a countryman's weatherbeaten face and brown hair cut short in an informal style. His clothes were of a subdued green and his relaxed outdoor look, together with the presence of the dog, made him look more like Sir Thomas's gamekeeper than the man himself

He held out his hand, with perhaps more gentleness and grace than might have been expected of a gamekeeper. 'How do you do?' His eyes glinted. In the shadowy room they looked dark green. 'Miss Jane Lockhart – at last. I have wished to know you and your family for many years, Jane – if I may presume to call you so. What a great pleasure.'

He held her hand for a moment with an air of authentic delight and Jane thought how his warmth and strength contrasted with her father's coldness and formality. Next she was required to greet Mr Axton and exchange compliments and, these ceremonies concluded, she was invited to sit down and take tea.

As the Axtons busied themselves in removing cats and books from the chairs where their guests were to sit, Jane was surprised by the private thought that Sir Thomas could not be very far from her own father's age, which was forty-three. He seemed much younger.

'Do be seated, Jane. Take the old yellow chair.' Miss Axton whisked away several interesting sheets of paper upon which poetic fragments seemed to be scrawled.

'How very cosy your cottage is,' said Sir Thomas, looking about him with admiration. 'Don't you think so, Jane? What could be more delightful?'

'It must seem like a snuff-box after Ottercombe Park,' said Miss Axton. 'Now I'm going to be very impolite and ask when we may admire the new house. I'm so longing to see it!'

'Adelaide!' her brother rebuked her from the scullery, where he was filling the kettle. 'Sir Thomas has barely moved in himself. He will not wish to be troubled with visitors yet.'

'Quite the contrary!' cried Sir Thomas heartily. 'The very purpose of my visit is to invite you. My daughter Julia is to be married in early December and nothing would please me more than to welcome you to the celebrations – all of you, for I shall be exceedingly bad-tempered if I can't enjoy the company and bask in the congratulations of Miss Jane.'

Jane blushed, laughed and thanked Sir Thomas fervently for his invitation. She was enchanted at the thought of Julia Burton's wedding, though doubtful if her father would receive the invitation with the same rapture.

'I suppose the ceremony will be in Ottercombe Church,' said Miss Axton. 'Though it is so very small, it will hardly hold thirty souls. But it is so sweet! So antique. And if they marry in the morning there is half a chance Parson will be sober.'

'Adelaide is very severe upon Parson.' Her brother smiled nervously. 'Especially since she heard Mr Harris preach. I'm afraid few country clergymen could attain Mr Harris's exacting standards. How many ladies fainted today, Adelaide? Did you manage to cling to consciousness or not?'

'Who is this Mr Harris?' asked Sir Thomas, absent-mindedly caressing the ear of his spaniel, who sat before him on the rag-rug with her chin resting on his knee, staring with almost religious ecstasy into her master's face.

'Mr Harris is Adelaide's latest flame,' explained Humphrey Axton, folding up his long legs in his low chair until he looked rather like a grasshopper. 'I think

7

he's quite ousted the curate down at Hawksley, Mr Goodhew.'

'I never liked Mr Goodhew!' exclaimed Miss Axton indignantly. 'I could never seriously admire a man with a face like a bun.'

'Ah well,' her brother sighed, pursing his face up in a teasing style, 'Mr Harris has captured her heart and he's an Evangelist, so I'm bracing myself for an attack of seriousness. Ah yes. The housekeeping will be all serious now. I shall sleep between serious sheets and drink serious soup. And we'll only ever be permitted serious jokes, once a week, on Saturdays.'

'And what's Mr Harris's face like?' asked Sir Thomas. 'Serious? What is your opinion, Jane?'

'I thought him very handsome,' said Jane and blushed.

'Did you now?' observed Sir Thomas thoughtfully.

'Anybody would!' cried Miss Axton. 'You should judge him yourself, Sir Thomas. You must hear him preach, one day.'

Humphrey Axton seemed to feel that his sister had talked enough on spiritual matters, and at the first opportunity he seized the conversation and returned it to more satisfyingly profane subjects. 'So, Sir Thomas, how do you like Julia's choice? Will the young man make a properly obedient and respectful son-in-law?'

Sir Thomas sighed, and Jane noticed that his dog felt the sigh and stirred, as if she would smooth away all her master's perturbations of spirit, if she were not trapped in the body of a mere spaniel.

'Francis Lloyd is the gentleman's name,' said Sir Thomas. 'He seems to think of nothing but horses and cards and society, but I suppose he will suit Julia, as she likes that sort of thing. I imagine all young people do.'

'And where will they live?' enquired Miss Axton. 'Not too far away, I hope?

'Oh no. In town. They cannot endure the country.' Sir

Thomas sighed again and turned abruptly to Jane. 'Do you dislike the country too, Jane?'

'I've hardly ever spent enough time in a town to make a comparison,' she admitted. 'But I love Ottercombe.'

'It will be a treat for Jane to see Julia married, I'm sure,' cried Miss Axton.

'It will be a pleasure to meet her,' replied Jane.

'Of course, you have never met her, what a shame!' Miss Axton considered, for a moment, the curious absence of acquaintance between the two neighbouring families. 'Sir Thomas has been so long away. Though you must be Julia's age almost exactly. And she will be married so soon! Extraordinary! It seems only yesterday that we visited you in Bath, Sir Thomas, and she was playing with her dolls by the window-seat, I recall. And Henry made her cry by cutting her doll's lace with his toy sword.'

Sir Thomas smiled ruefully.

'Will he be able to get leave for his sister's wedding?' enquired Mr Axton.

'I'm not sure,' Sir Thomas pondered. 'The movements of the Navy are so uncertain. I have no hope of it.'

'What a shame!' cried Miss Axton playfully. 'For I'm sure Jane would have broken his heart, or else he would have broken hers, and that would have been diverting, you know.'

'He'd better not break Jane's heart,' said Sir Thomas with sudden vehemence, 'or I'll thrash him, for all that he's taller than me these days.'

'I wouldn't let him,' ventured Jane, though she thought that if Henry Burton resembled his father at all she would be more than happy to make his acquaintance.

'So. Miss Julia is soon to be married. I suspect it will not be long before we hear the same news about Jane.' Miss Axton had a certain mischievous spirit in conversation sometimes, which might have been crushed out of her had she had to endure the fatigues of motherhood. 'I wonder what sort of man you will marry, Jane?'

'I have no thought of marrying anybody,' said Jane firmly, hoping to deter further speculation.

'Has no one ever taken your fancy, my dear?' enquired Sir Thomas gently. His eyes danced, but modestly. She felt no offence in his question.

'Not till today,' Jane confessed. 'But I'm afraid I've fallen in love with your spaniel.' She leaned forward and caressed the dog's velvet ears which Sir Thomas had been touching all the while, and though the animal accepted Jane's hand with pleasure, Jane knew she would have preferred her master's touch.

'You have perfect taste,' said Sir Thomas with quiet approval beneath his jocular tone. 'Suzy is the best dog in the world and you're a clever girl to see it.'

'Jane has always been a clever girl,' gushed Miss Axton, though Jane was grateful for her barging in to the conversation just then. 'I think she will fall in love with a man of feeling, of understanding, of learning.'

'Oh nonsense, Adelaide!' cried her brother, eager to deprecate the attractions of literary men such as himself. 'Jane will marry a man of action, a soldier perhaps. Or a sailor. What do you think, Sir Thomas?'

Sir Thomas regarded Jane for a moment in silence. She felt his look steal over her shoulders like a delicate breath of air. Jane understood she was admired, for the first time in her life, by a man of taste and feeling, and was quite dumbfounded.

'We shall see,' said Sir Thomas. Soon afterwards he recalled an appointment with his steward, made his excuses and in a pleasant and relaxed style, took his leave. Moments after his return to Ottercombe Park he went to his desk and addressed a wedding invitation to the Lockhart family at Newington House. His encounter with Jane had made him regret that the acquaintance between their families had been so long postponed.

2

Mr Lockhart understood that to decline Sir Thomas's invitation was not possible. He must take his wife and daughters to Ottercombe Park and admire Sir Thomas's triumph. Despite his deep envy of his neighbour's effortless expenditure, however, Mr Lockhart was exceedingly curious to see how Ottercombe Park had been rebuilt. He was therefore prepared to endure the occasion as an opportunity for architectural study.

His wife, whose sociable nature had long been frustrated by her husband's solitary habits, was in raptures at the invitation.

Jane's sister Mary, however, was rather timid, and only really happy when she could lie on a sofa and lose herself in a book. 'I'm sure I shall say something foolish!' she lamented, 'and Sir Thomas's daughters will be so elegant. They are bound to despise us. They'll think my nose is too long. Look, Jane! I swear it's grown another inch since last night. I'm beginning to look like a heron.'

'Fishing for compliments!' cried Jane. 'Yes, just like a heron. And I look just like a bulldog. But Sir Thomas is very fond of birds and dogs and I'm sure when you meet him he will reassure you at once.'

And so it proved. Sir Thomas was so relaxed and pleasant as to dispel all anxiety. He seemed particularly happy to see Jane again.

11

'Miss Jane! Welcome to Ottercombe Park!' he beamed. 'Why, how very pretty you look, if I may say so.'

Jane knew it was only good manners, but Sir Thomas's tone was so easy and genuine as to make her feel immediately comfortable. She was introduced to his three daughters. Eleanor, the eldest, was married and in the latter stages of pregnancy, but seemed very well and in good spirits. Eliza, the youngest, was exceedingly pretty and very shy. The middle sister, Julia, was not so tall and fair as her sisters, but with her vivacious manners and stylish dress she made an elegant bride.

Jane was enraptured by the beauty of Ottercombe Park. The spacious hall was lit by hundreds of candles which sparkled in wrought-iron sconces and crystal chandeliers. A pair of life-size Moorish statues, turbanned in Chinese yellow and black lacquer, stood in two alcoves on either side of the great hearth, their lustrous pearl ear-rings more exquisite than anything Jane or her family were wearing.

The walls were panelled in pale gold and a delicate and beautiful frieze ran across the fireplace. Lofty Venetian looking-glasses reflected the dazzling scene in great quivering squares of light and it seemed to Jane that all the voices echoed about the high, dim ceiling like the sound of waterfalls.

They went in to dinner. The dining-room was of a most refined eau-de-Nil, and the silver candelabra and rose-bowls seemed to float on a sheet of liquid mahogany. The seating plan required that no members of any family were permitted to sit together. Jane looked around and saw that Mary was in conversation with the Burtons' youngest daughter, Eliza. It struck her that they resembled each other somewhat in colouring and hair-style, though Jane had conversed briefly with Miss Eliza just before dinner and had found her unexpectedly shy and entirely lacking any of Mary's wit.

Miss Eliza was, however, the youngest and perhaps the least robust of the Burton family. The eldest daughter,

12

Eleanor, was very amiable, though she seemed more sleepy in her manner than young Eliza. Jane had not exchanged more than a word or two of congratulation with Julia and had found her understandably distracted.

Jane was seated next to Parson Bridges, who fortified himself after the exertions of the marriage service with almost a whole goose and what seemed to Jane like a gallon of claret. She herself was too excited to eat much, feasting instead on the sight of so many interesting people. There was of course a crowd of relations, the bridegroom's family as well as the bride's. Only Henry Burton was absent. His ship was far away in the Mediterranean and Jane had learned from Miss Eliza that he was not expected to enjoy any leave until the following spring.

Mrs Lockhart was talking with animation to a young man whom Jane believed to be George Fortescue, Eleanor Burton's husband. Mr Lockhart was not seated so far away. Jane could catch the drift of his conversation with Miss Axton, the poet's sister, who had dressed her wild curls with daisies for the occasion and looked rather like a pig which has run through a haystack.

'I have always admired your quaint Gothic house,' Jane heard her father say.

'Oh, dear Humphrey would agree with you about that!' trilled Miss Axton. 'He is mad for anything Gothic. Indeed, I know I'm a great disappointment to him, for not being more Gothic myself. If only he could have had a quaint Gothic sister, I think he could have been a happy man.

'Oh yes! I should have been six feet tall, with beetling brows. And there would have been practical advantages too. For as it is, I'm so short I can't reach the sugar down off the shelf without performing a ridiculous little bounce, and, worst of all, once I start laughing about anything I find it almost impossible to stop. And that's not very Gothic at all! Ha ha!' Here Miss Axton put down her fork, to give herself up to her gales of laughter. Jane watched the painful effort with which her father attempted to offer at least an acknowledging smile. She felt ashamed of him and sorry for him all at once, and hoped no one else had observed the exchange.

She looked around the company and immediately found Sir Thomas's eyes upon her, offering such a friendly and perceptive look she almost felt he might have understood her embarrassment and wished to dispel it. She admired the manly grace with which he presided, noticing, it seemed, the merest hint of difficulty and providing all that was wanted for his guests' contentment.

'But above all, nothing is more delightful than a Gothic man. Don't you think so, Mr Lockhart?' Miss Axton's voice bubbled on amidst the wineglasses. 'And I have observed a very fine specimen of the genre. There is an Evangelical preacher hereabouts, a Mr William Harris, who exhibits very desirable Gothic architecture.' Jane's attention was instantly caught. 'He is so tall, his hair is almost veiled by clouds; so dark, it quite chills one's spine, and his skin has the kind of unearthly pallor that makes one long to feed him chicken soup and plum pudding! Ha ha!'

'I don't approve of Evangelism,' observed John Lockhart coldly. Jane flinched at her father's lack of courtesy, his inability to respond to Miss Axton's playful tone. 'I think so much emotion in public can be dangerous. Religious fervour can easily lead to political and social disturbance.' He sipped his claret with a frown.

'Not in England, Humphrey says. Only in France. And you know, many of the best families in the land are most interested in Evangelism.'

'Are they indeed?' Jane could see her father was struck by this possibility. He was always prepared to reconsider an idea he had found abhorrent if the best families in the land had shown some inclination for it.

'Oh yes – Lady Griffin, Lord Longville and the Marquis of Fairford's whole family are quite converted. Evangelism does not lead to mobs and riots in England, Mr Lockhart. It is more likely to lead to sober and modest citizens, family prayers, a quiet demeanour and the exercise of charity.'

'Indeed?' Mr Lockhart was reassured to discover that Evangelism could subdue rather than inflame emotion, though he was uneasy at the mention of charity.

'However, I don't think I could ever manage a quiet demeanour, for all Mr Harris's glamorous Gothic looks!' Miss Axton could not be serious for long. 'But a number of young ladies have been known to swoon at the climax of his sermons, so you must lock up your daughters, Mr Lockhart – Jane has seen him already and declares she thinks him very handsome. The enemy is not rakes and roués nowadays, but wild, charismatic clergymen!' Miss Axton gave herself up to a great salvo of laughter and Jane hastily looked away. She did not wish to catch her father's eye and supposed that when they got home she would be questioned closely about her attendance at the field preaching. Mr Lockhart needed no encouragement, even in jest, to curtail the freedom of his daughters.

After dinner there was dancing in the spacious hall so skilfully provided by Sir Thomas's architect. Violins and hautbois echoed in the airy vault and below, by the light of flaring torches and a thousand glimmering candles, the company gossiped and glanced, whispered and laughed, exulted and curtsied and, in Jane's case, simply wandered and gazed.

Jane declined all invitations to dance. She was too shy to attempt it, feeling sure she would trip or stumble. Listening to conversations was safer. She laughed with Miss Axton, was lectured about the kingfisher by Humphrey Axton, then found herself thrown together with the parson's wife, who complained of the heat, the noise and her dyspepsia, which, stimulated by the grand occasion, had increased its inconvenience to a heroic degree.

Next it was Jane's duty to be ignored by the parson, who preferred to discuss the joys of steeplechase with the groom's brother rather than exchange a single word with the insignificant girl at his side.

At this moment she felt a gentle touch on her elbow: a warm hand drew her away and Sir Thomas himself was before her. 'I think you've attended to the parson quite long enough, my dear,' he said. 'You must be quite fagged out, for his sermons about horses are even longer than the other sort. Come and sit with me for a while.'

He led her to a sofa beneath a pillar. Jane did not realise until she felt the relief of repose how tired she had become. Sir Thomas had recognised her discomfort before she knew it herself.

'I've only my youngest daughter unmarried now, Jane. And how do you think that makes me feel, eh?'

Jane was surprised at the question. She was not used to having her opinion solicited on the most common things, let alone topics of such a delicate, private character. 'I should think it makes you all the more concerned for her happiness.'

'You're right. There she is – Eliza. I think I saw you talking to her earlier?'

'Yes. We spoke before dinner. And I think Mary was seated near her. I saw them in conversation.'

'What did you think of her?'

'Think of her?' Jane felt confused. 'I thought her very pretty and agreeable.' She hastened to find a polite reply, though she felt it fell very far short of the compliment she would have wished to give. 'We did not talk for long and I've not had the chance to talk to her since.'

'She is shy,' admitted Sir Thomas with a sigh. 'And sickly.'

'She looks well enough.'

'Aye. But she is easily down-hearted. And she's going to feel lonely when Julia has gone.' Sir Thomas turned, now, to look directly into Jane's face. She was disconcerted to find herself scrutinised in silence for several seconds. 'I have formed a good opinion of you, Jane,' he announced suddenly. 'You have just the sort of understanding to be a helpful friend to Eliza. And your sister seems a sweet girl too.'

Jane blushed at these compliments, and caught sight at this moment of her father, who happened to walk across the room. Even he looked almost as if he was enjoying himself.

'And there is your good father. He's kept you too much to himself. Understandable. But he must not be so possessive. We must persuade him to share you a little. The house will be so quiet next week and poor Eliza will be pining for her Julia.'

'I would be so very pleased to see Eliza again. I can hardly say how much!' cried Jane.

'It's agreed, then. Delightful.' Sir Thomas took her hand and kissed it heartily, then turned to watch the musicians, who were packing up their instruments. The dancing was concluded and most of the company had drifted into the neighbouring room, where a light buffet supper was being served.

The last of the musicians left the hall and they were alone. A flower, fallen from some lady's hair, glowed on the flagstones.

'So, Jane, have you enjoyed yourself?' asked Sir Thomas.

'Oh yes! More than ever before, I think.'

'I have only one complaint about your behaviour.'

Jane felt a dreadful bolt of guilt that she had offended such a kind host. 'What have I done?' She trembled.

Sir Thomas laughed. 'Don't be upset, my dear. I am only teasing. I should have liked to see you dance, that is all. But I observed you refused all our young beaux.'

'I did not feel like dancing.'

'Well, next time we have the opportunity, I hope to see you dance. Indeed I am resolved to stand up with you myself, if you will do me the honour.'

Jane gladly assented. She wondered what it would be like to dance with Sir Thomas.

'However, there will be no immediate opportunity for dancing. Still, I feel that the quieter pleasures that await us in the coming weeks are no less inviting.'

Jane did not need to speak. The radiance of her face

17

signified her whole-hearted assent. She felt she had never met such delightful people as the Burtons, and she prayed that their determination to pursue the acquaintance would quite overcome her father's resistance.

3

The bride and groom departed and the weather changed. An aching frost gripped Ottercombe. Every tree sparkled. The great chimneys of Newington House devoured ton upon ton of cut and seasoned wood and Jane, lurking by the fire, wondered whether Miss Eliza might brave the cold weather, and call. It would be impertinent, her mother said, for Jane and Mary to presume to call at Ottercombe. They must wait.

A week passed and it seemed like a year. The uncertainty was especially trying to Mary's spirits. 'You see, Jane?' she fretted. 'I knew they would not like us. It's my fault, I told Miss Eliza the whole plot of the novel I was reading and half-way through I began to wonder if I was being tedious, although it was the most exciting bit, where Lydia was captured by pirates. But Miss Eliza's eyes did indeed go a little glassy. I expect I bored her to death and her father has given instructions to his gamekeeper to shoot me on sight.'

'You are a fool, Mary!' cried her mother, stitching a shift with almost military ferocity. 'I wish you had never learnt to read, for it has filled your mind with nonsense, and you are getting quite short-sighted and crook-backed from peering at your wretched novels. Put that one away, or I shall tell Hetty to burn it.'

Mary hastily buried the book beneath her skirts and took up her embroidery once more. Jane moved quietly to the door, hoping to escape to the kitchen in search of un-attended apple tarts.

'Where are you sidling off to, Jane?'

'Nowhere, Mamma. To put my room in order.'

'You liar! You're off to some mischief. Always slouching about and scowling. When I consider what I have produced!' She glared at her daughters. 'An hysteric, and a hoyden. I suppose I should be grateful that neither of you is a hussy. Although there's time enough for that.'

Neither Mary nor Jane contradicted her, which was a grave disappointment to Mrs Lockhart. She loved nothing so well as an argument and, since on this occasion nobody was prepared to indulge her, she amused herself for the next half-hour with a devastating critique of her husband's character.

Eventually Jane managed to escape and she was crossing the cold spaces of the hall as hastily as possible when she heard footsteps on the gravel outside. Somebody rang the bell and since she was almost standing by the door she did not wait for Hetty to come, but opened it herself – a habit for which her mother had often rebuked her. Sir Thomas and Miss Eliza were standing there, the girl much bundled up in furs and looking rather frail.

'Miss Jane!' He stepped forward and took both her hands in his. She felt his warmth through the leather gloves. 'We resolved to try to drive the cold out of our bones by a little rambling about the lanes and found ourselves by your father's gates – and thought we might call and enquire how you are?'

Jane assured him the whole family was well, made reciprocal enquiries and hastily invited him and his daughter to walk in.

They were soon made comfortable in the drawing-room by the fire and Jane, having informed Hetty of their arrival, sat with them while her family sped about the house seizing the combs and lace without which they could not feel able to appear. Jane was not particularly aware of her own looks. She was too pleased to see her visitors again and repeated to them how much she had enjoyed Julia's wedding and how ardently she wished all happiness to the handsome bride and groom.

At this moment John Lockhart came into the room and Sir Thomas rose to greet him. Jane's father was soon followed by her mother and Mary, whose curtsy equalled Miss Eliza's in timidity. Now she withdrew a little and listened to the conversation of her elders.

After due time had been devoted to the giving and receiving of compliments, the talk turned to seasonable topics, the effects of the profound frosts upon crops and animals, and the difficulties of travel in such weather.

'If we get a little mild weather after Christmas,' said Sir Thomas, 'I intend to take Eliza to Bath. My eldest daughter Eleanor is expecting her first child early in the New Year.'

'Ah!' cried the tender-hearted Mrs Lockhart. 'That will be some diversion for Miss Eliza, to have a baby to play with.'

'Indeed.' Sir Thomas looked at the fire for a moment. Jane felt he was preparing to say something more significant than the civilities with which they had all occupied themselves for the past half-hour. He knotted his fingers together, loosed them and ran them through his hair. Then he looked at his daughter and Jane saw in his glance a flash of anxiety.

'But I am afraid Eliza will lack companionship,' he went on. 'Eleanor will be unable to go about much. I was wondering . . . if Miss Lockhart and Miss Jane would care to accompany us? If you could spare them for a month or two.' Jane's heart leapt in astonishment.

Sir Thomas looked at Mrs Lockhart, sensing she would receive his invitation with greater enthusiasm than her husband. Surprise and delight flooded into her face, and she cried out in pleasure. 'Indeed, Sir Thomas, you're excessively kind! But how wonderful, girls, what an opportunity for you! I'm sure Mary and Jane will be delighted. Thank you for thinking of us. What a delightful notion. Is it not, Mr Lockhart?'

John Lockhart inclined his head. 'Too kind,' he acknowledged. 'But I'm afraid that my daughters will prove too much of a charge on your patience.'

'Not at all.' Sir Thomas smiled. 'I cannot think of any young women I would rather see in Eliza's company. And Eliza thinks so too.' Miss Eliza blushed and her father looked first at Mary, then at Jane. 'Nor can I imagine any companions more delightful for myself.'

'I would not have them a burden on your eldest daughter so near her confinement.' John Lockhart frowned.

'But we could help, Papa!' cried Jane. 'You know Mary loves nothing so much as babies.'

Mrs Lockhart was eager to press her husband to a public consent. 'Our daughters have had few playmates of any elegance or distinction.' She smiled, though her husband felt in her words a silent reproach which might be translated, in private, into the most ferocious rebuke. Mrs Lockhart's temper had grown, in the confinement and frustration of her marriage, into her most congenial exercise. 'I'm sure Mary and Jane would benefit greatly from Miss Eliza's society, do you not think so, Mr Lockhart?'

Her husband began to understand that he could not avoid giving his blessing to the expedition. His daughters were to pass the rest of the season in a city of surpassing elegance and diversion, with a family as agreeable as they were wealthy. John Lockhart resigned himself to the honour at last.

It occurred to him that having the girls away might offer the opportunity for him to set forward the work on the new window he wished to install on the east side of the house above the staircase. He resolved to write to his architect as soon as Sir Thomas could be persuaded to depart and fumed inwardly for another half-hour that his kind neighbour was so reluctant to leave the comfort of his hearth.

*

Christmas came and went, and then they watched the weather, for a mild spell was required to permit the journey, and as if some sympathetic divinity had understood their plans a thaw arrived at the perfect moment. Once more the grass was green and though it was now too muddy to be walking much at Ottercombe Mrs Lockhart exulted at the thought that her daughters would soon be floating up and down the fragrant pavements of Bath. She could not help feeling very jealous, however, and saying so.

'But why don't you go to Cheltenham, Mamma?' suggested Jane, packing her green silk gown in a rather careless and crumpled way. 'Especially if Papa is going to make the house uncomfortable by taking the window out.'

John Lockhart had furthered his plans for the new window. Once in the grip of an architectural enthusiasm, he could not be halted or even delayed, though his wife had pointed out the advantages of waiting until the warmer weather.

'What, go to your aunt's in Cheltenham?' Mrs Lockhart caught at the idea. 'Why, that is an excellent notion! You're so clever, Jane.'

'Very bad at packing, though,' laughed Mary, who, under the influence of the coming journey, had become more animated than usual. 'Let me fold that for you again, Jane, you are no more use at such things than a farmer.'

Anne Lockhart looked fondly at her daughters. The anticipation of their journey had improved their looks and their mother's temper. She was sure they would be admired, perhaps by some decent, respectable young men. Of course she hoped they would make good marriages. They were of an age, now, for such things to be considered, though both Mary and Jane had suffered from their father's remote and unsociable habits. Mary was more shy and childish than one would expect from a young woman of her years, and Jane . . .

Well, Jane was an odd, wild thing. But Mrs Lockhart was

23

sure they would benefit from Sir Thomas's attention and example. Mary might even return having attached a suitable young man. And at least Jane would have been prevented, for a few weeks, from running up and down the countryside looking like a scarecrow. As for herself, why, in a week's time she would be in Cheltenham, strolling in the Pump Room with her sister. She felt more grateful to Sir Thomas than she could express.

Jane's gratitude to the gentleman was also urgently felt. She had scarcely been to Bath since she was a child, though it was but twenty-seven miles to the south. Her father's habits of austerity and his dislike of society had not permitted many visits. And to think of going with Sir Thomas and Miss Eliza filled Jane's heart with a kind of rushing excitement.

The moment arrived. Sir Thomas was assisting Jane into her place. Her parents waved for a moment by the door, then the carriage turned, she saw the yew hedges wheel about, briefly glimpsed the stables and settled to a view of the park, as they were conveyed steadily towards her father's gates.

The chaise bowled through the gate and took the road down towards the valley bottom. Jane gazed out at the unfolding landscape with delight and soon recognised the field where she had seen William Harris preaching. The stile on which he had stood flashed past, empty. Where the congregation had stood there was now only a flock of sheep.

Jane felt a moment's unease. She one day hoped to hear William Harris preach and perhaps to perform some charitable acts, for it seemed to her sometimes that her life was so blessed with comforts she ought to exert herself for those who had little.

Jane wrestled with guilty feelings for ten minutes, but eventually the sense of mortification ebbed away, for Sir Thomas was continually pointing out new sights in the landscape and she could not help being enchanted by the scene. Her sister had admired Miss Eliza's gloves, and it seemed by the intensity of whispers and the fascinated scrutiny of each other's ribbons and lace that a tender intimacy was springing up between the two. Jane saw it with a smile.

Sir Thomas had noticed it too and gave her such a grateful look that her own pleasure was more than doubled. 'That's better,' he said quietly, settling back in his seat and looking across at her. Jane also sat back, with the deepest of sighs. She was going to enjoy herself: she could not avoid it. Charity would have to wait.

4

They drove down into Bath at the end of the afternoon. The bones of the great city seemed to emerge from a lagoon of blue mist; from above, it looked cold and still in the winter light, but as they plunged more deeply into the streets, they found only life and warmth and colour. Sir Thomas's daughter, Eleanor, lived on the southern side of town. To reach her house, almost the whole of Bath had to be negotiated.

Jane stared at the serpentine lines of coaches and chaises, and the numberless horsemen threading their way through the worst of the traffic. Crowds of people thronged the pavements and all were well-dressed. Mary and Eliza exclaimed in admiration at the splendour of the fashionable women.

'High heels are the rage again, look, Mary!' cried Eliza.

'And shoe-buckles are all small!' gasped Mary in some dismay, for hers were last year's and as big as a visiting card. She wondered wildly whether she could cut them off before they first went out, for she dreaded making a spectacle of herself.

She was immediately distracted, however, by the sight of a very fine lady in chequered silk, a green velvet cloak and a bonnet with gold feathers which nodded when she walked.

'Oh how delicious!' sighed Eliza.

'Most elegant,' agreed Mary.

'And the most curious thing of all', commented Sir Thomas, 'is that she might have been a lady's maid.'

'What! A servant?' Jane was astonished. 'Surely not!' Her mother's maids, Hetty and Jessie, did not aspire to elegance of dress – perhaps because they were both middle-aged.

'Ah yes, Miss Jane.' Sir Thomas smiled. 'Servants are quite as dashing as masters here. In gloves, hats, shoes, pockets, parasols, feathers and lace, it is hard to know which is the mistress and which the maid.'

'Well, that must be good,' pondered Jane. 'It might ... prevent their being discontented, I suppose.'

'You are thinking of what happened in France, I suppose?' asked Sir Thomas. Jane had not been, but she did not want to disappoint Sir Thomas so she nodded. 'Ah, but there was such poverty in France, my dear. Their peasants were but starving beggars, not like our sturdy yeoman families. We shall have no revolutions here in England. It is not in our nature.'

Jane was diverted by their arrival in a very grand street, lined on both sides by shops with dazzling glass windows displaying a vast variety of wares. Lamps were even now being lit in the smoky dusk to tempt the passer-by to linger and admire the silks, chintzes, the muslins and brocades, the sweetmeats and cakes, the silver and brass, the glittering crystal and china, the fans, the guns, the wigs, the pens, the fireworks, the leather portmanteaux.

One window was devoted to a great rocking-horse, almost as large as a real pony. Another offered a glistering pyramid of fruit. A coffee house sent out its delicious fragrance upon the evening air, a furniture maker's window revealed a day-bed of surpassing elegance, upholstered in golden stripes. Jane could not help being enchanted by the beauty, the skill, the ingenuity of it all. She felt she could spend a month here and never tire of looking.

They passed the sound of a violin; a dog barked, Sir Thomas sat forward and looked out keenly. The streets were lit by new gas-lamps: the effect was splendid. The chaise drew up beside a gracefully curved terrace of houses. Jane was assisted from her place and found herself welcomed by her host, George Fortescue, Sir Thomas's son-in-law, in the most genial manner possible.

They were speedily admitted to an exquisite drawing-room where Sir Thomas's eldest daughter, Eleanor, lay on a *chaise longue* before a great fire. She looked very well and happy, though it was obvious that her confinement could not be far off. Crystal lamps, shaped like dolphins, cast a pretty light from small tables and a pair of grand bronze horsemen threw curious shadows across the Turkey carpet. Everything was elegant, but comfortable and warm.

Jane was not intimidated by the Fortescues' establishment, for her own father collected furniture and antiquities, nor was she excessively shy, for Eleanor had the Burtons' easy manners and her husband said very little, but sprawled by the fire, smiling to himself and agreeing with everything anyone said with a gruff, 'Quite! Quite!' like the bark of a large but sweet-tempered dog.

Jane and Mary were accommodated in a fine, high-ceilinged room. A fire burned in the hearth, a maid brought hot water and helped them unpack their trunk, then they were invited to an informal but delicious supper down-stairs. They enjoyed a fricassee of chicken and a lemon pudding, but even before the meal was over their heads were heavy with fatigue.

'Miss Jane, the sparkle is gone from your eye. I can see you are ready for your bed,' Sir Thomas observed, and Jane and Mary were grateful to be excused at once.

Next day dawned clear and bright. Sir Thomas declared that he would accompany the young ladies to the Pump Rooms. Every face seemed happy and busy, as they passed along the pavements, every soul refreshed, and the shops offered distractions more voluptuous than ever.

Mary and Eliza were walking together arm in arm and Jane found herself strolling along behind them with Sir Thomas. This was a relief to her, for she had never been able to summon up the enthusiasm for dress which Mary required in a companion. However, having spent her early years under the guidance of a man for whom architecture was a passion, Jane was able to admire the crescents and terraces, porticoes and architraves, with some little knowledge.

'But your eye is more often caught by the architecture of the human face, I think, eh, my dear?' Sir Thomas smiled.

'Yes. When I see a beggar, I often amuse myself by thinking that if those features were a duke's they would be admired.'

'It is a curious thought. But you are not distracted by beauty, I think.'

Jane hesitated. There was something testing, at times, in Sir Thomas's observations to her and she was anxious not to appear stupid, for she knew she was not pretty and therefore felt under an obligation to avoid dull remarks.

'Distracted by beauty? Well, I could admire the looks of your daughters for a week.' Jane was at a loss, but instantly regretted the flattery.

'I thank you for their sakes. A father is always pleased to have his children admired, but it was not my intention to provoke a compliment.'

Jane felt awkward. She hated anything like a reproach from him.

'What I meant', Sir Thomas bowed to an acquaintance across the street, but his thoughts ran steadily on, 'was that I could not imagine your head being turned by a handsome, plausible rogue.'

'Oh no! Never.' Jane felt she could assure him quite fervently on this point. 'I don't think a man's looks are significant in the same way, for though of course a handsome man is to be admired, it would be his character which would attract me – or not.'

'Ah, that is some consolation.' Sir Thomas laughed. 'Then perhaps you will do an ugly old fellow the honour of taking his arm?'

Jane readily assented, for their walk was now uphill. She was tempted to contradict Sir Thomas's playful description of his own looks, for she had always thought him handsome, in a quiet English way. Though there was nothing really distinctive about him, every feature suggested a strength of character, and the expression of his eyes a quick and compassionate understanding. None of this could be said, however, so she fell silent.

'It is on my mind, I confess,' Sir Thomas resumed at length, 'because I very much fear the susceptibilities of my Eliza in that respect. A tall, swaggering fellow, with a flashing eye and a red coat perhaps, would make short work of the poor girl's heart I am sure.'

'If she has your shrewdness, it would not.'

'So, I'm shrewd, am I?' Sir Thomas stopped for an instant and looked down into Jane's face, which burned in agitation in case he was offended to be so described.

'In . . . in your understanding . . . of people . . .' she could only stammer and Sir Thomas, seeing that his tease had unnerved her, resumed his walk with a reassuring squeeze of the arm.

'You're too kind. I'm interested in people, as you are. That's all. But I don't think Eliza has much of me in her. She is all Charlotte. And Charlotte fell in love with people in a trice.' He paused for a moment, but presently continued, 'I cannot always be with Eliza. I think perhaps I shall go back to Ottercombe in a day or two and leave her here. But I only wanted to ask if you would be so good as to watch Eliza closely, and if there is the slightest sign of her being imposed upon by a handsome rogue, I would be most obliged if you would inform me at once.'

Here, then, was the intention behind Sir Thomas's leisurely conversation. Jane assured him she would spare no efforts to ensure that Miss Eliza's heart remained unbroken. She felt honoured that Sir Thomas considered her worthy of the trust. She was determined not to fail him.

They walked up and down so many streets that by dinner time they were exhausted, but it was a pleasant sensation. The afternoon was spent in reading newspapers and scanning the advertisements for the many plays, balls and diversions which offered themselves. Miss Eliza was musical and begged Sir Thomas to take her to a number of concerts. He gladly agreed and proposed also taking the whole party – excepting of course Eleanor – to the Theatre Royal, where one of Mr Sheridan's plays was being presented.

'It's my favourite,' said Sir Thomas. '*The Rivals*. You may find it a little old-fashioned, but it amuses me. There is a character in it called Lydia Languish who reads insatiably. She reminds me rather of Miss Mary.' They all laughed and Jane wished that, one day, some character in a play might remind Sir Thomas of her.

Several days of pleasure ensued. Charming people of all ages were introduced to the girls, but Jane noticed nobody offering unusual attention to Miss Eliza. She was sure her heart was untouched. As for herself, she was so dazzled by the pageants of human drama which unfolded in the streets, as well as the entertainments, that she had no time at all for the distractions of male beauty. Indeed, her chief delight was to stroll up and down the Royal Crescent, enjoying the views and being teased by Sir Thomas about her opinions on the landscape.

Sir Thomas did not return to Ottercombe after all, and when they had been in Bath some weeks celebrated with delight the birth of his first grandson. Mother and child were well, and the babe was to be called Thomas. With a doting father and mother, as well as an adoring grandpapa and young aunt, he was likely to be spoiled more quickly than most. Mary adored babies and Jane was intrigued by the infant's face, across which a thousand human expressions flashed, but without meaning or understanding.

31

Sir Thomas was an unusual grandfather, as well as a very youthful one, and would not leave little Tom to his nurse's charge, but stole him often from his cradle and played with him upon the sofa. He was happily employed in this way one afternoon when Jane happened to walk into the room. 'Come and admire my grandson again, Jane,' he cried, 'for I declare you have not said a kind word about him for at least half an hour.'

Jane was very glad to join him on the sofa and remarked that little Tom's expression, which was at that moment extraordinarily grave, suggested that Sir Thomas might have a philosopher on his knee.

'Charlotte had just that look, you know,' said Sir Thomas suddenly and a stillness came over him.

'Lady Burton lives on in him,' Jane suggested awkwardly, 'as she will in all her grandchildren.'

Sir Thomas received her faltering intuitions with grave attention. 'A glimpse now and then, perhaps.' He sighed. 'But thank you for your comfort.'

'Alas!' cried Jane. 'I'm sure I can be very little comfort in the face of such a loss.'

'You are a comfort to me, my dear,' he said quietly. 'You cannot guess how much.'

The baby, ignored suddenly, or perhaps sensing the change of tone, began to howl; the nurse ran in to remove him and tea was carried in. Sir Thomas stared at the fire. His hand, hanging loosely at his knee, fretted idly at the edge of the sofa.

'I think you miss your little dog Suzy,' suggested Jane gently. Sir Thomas looked startled, as if his very thought had been discovered. 'But not half so much as Suzy misses you, I'm sure.' Jane found herself thinking of the little dog, left behind at Ottercombe, longing for endless weeks for the return of Sir Thomas, waiting for the sound of the carriage wheels.

Sir Thomas looked at Jane for a few seconds in silence, and seemed about to make a reply, when a servant came in bringing a letter and he was obliged to open it. 'Why, this is tremendous news!' he cried, scanning it. 'My son Henry is in Portsmouth. His ship is in. He hopes to join us here in a day or two – now, my dear, you shall see a handsome man, I promise you.'

Jane and Mary were both intrigued at the idea of Henry Burton and next morning spent their walk quizzing Eliza about her brother. Sir Thomas had stayed at home to answer some letters.

'How tall is he?' asked Mary. 'And is his hair the same colour as yours?'

'Taller than Papa. About as tall as that fellow there – across the street – do not look directly, he knows we're speaking of him—'

'And the hair?' Mary was always exact in points of detail.

'Fairer than mine. The sun seemed to have bleached it last time he was home.'

'And his character?' enquired Jane gently. 'What are the worst and best points of his character?'

'His worst? – oh dear, I can't think – his best, let me see, he is friendly, very friendly . . . talks a lot . . . is very charming to old ladies . . . kind and generous. I can't think what his worst points might be.'

'With such a catalogue of virtues', Jane said with a smile, 'I can't believe that his vices can be very great.' She would have to find out his faults for herself.

Just as she was enjoying the prospect of meeting another of the Burton family, and thinking how agreeable were the members she had already met, an announcement caught her eye, posted by a nearby church. It gave notice that Mr William Harris was to preach there the following morning.

Jane felt a bolt of surprise and pleasure. 'Mr Harris!' she cried, stopping quite still on the pavement, so that a gentleman walking behind them collided with her amid many apologies. Mary looked puzzled. 'Mr Harris; you know,

Mary – William Harris who preached down in the fields at Woolton! Miss Axton was half in love with him.'

Mary had no recollection of the name, nor any interest in pursuing it. Jane, however, felt seized with a curiosity she could not dispel. They walked on, and Mary and Eliza still talked about Henry and the Navy, and the respective attractions of sailors and soldiers, but Jane sank into a recollection of that September afternoon when she had seen William Harris in the fields and heard all about him from Miss Axton. She was determined to hear him preach, if only she could get permission from Sir Thomas.

5

The Burtons' household was in a great bustle of excitement in anticipation of the arrival of Henry the Navigator, as his father called him. Jane took advantage of the family's agitation. It was much easier than she had supposed to ask Sir Thomas at a moment when he was particularly distracted if she might slip out to church for an hour.

'Why, of course, my dear,' said he, looking surprised for an instant. 'I'm sorry that I can't accompany you and Eliza won't sit still for a moment, waiting for Henry to come.'

'Oh, I'm sure Mary will come with me.' Jane was uneasy in her reassurances. This was the first time she had ever been less than candid with Sir Thomas. If Sir Thomas had known she was going to hear an Evangelical preacher he might have been perturbed. She had heard her own father express reservations on the subject.

But what about Mary? Jane felt the strongest possible instinct to go to church alone. Yet she had assured Sir Thomas that Mary would accompany her. She found her sister sitting by her looking-glass with one of the maids trimming her hair in the Grecian style. Curls hung down all around her temples.

'Look at this, Jane.' She smiled. 'Excessively ridiculous, don't you think? Not so much a hair-style as a menagerie. I'm like that Greek woman who had snakes instead of hair. The one who turned people to stone.'

'Oh, I don't think it's that bad,' said Jane. 'Not snakes.

More like jellied eels. A Cockney would fall in love with you directly.'

'Admiration is always welcome.' Mary laughed. 'But to be eaten alive would be going too far.'

'Seriously,' Jane ventured, 'it's too elegant for church, I think.' She saw Mary's frown in the glass.

'Church?' Mary did not sound enthusiastic. 'What for? We haven't been for weeks. Church is so melancholy. Oh dear! I can't face it – I know I'm damned. I've spent the whole morning by my looking-glass. I can't face God today. I'll do a lot of charitable things during the next few days and come with you next week.'

'I'm very happy to go alone,' Jane assured her. 'And it will be better if you stay here. If Henry arrives it would be a pity if we were both out.'

Mary looked relieved. 'Well, then, I'll stay here.' She smiled again. 'Since you've been so clever as to make it seem my duty.' Greeting Henry Burton was the very thing she was preparing for. 'Say a prayer for me, Jane.' Jane assured her she would pray most urgently for the curls to stay in place, put on her cloak and bonnet, and slipped out of the house.

It was not far to the church where William Harris was to preach, but every yard of the way seemed alive with beauty. The shop windows glowed. Jane smiled at the sight of a merry gang of children staring in at a pyramid of crystallised fruit. Their faces, as they gazed upon the in-accessible treat, were full of rapture.

Birds sang among the roofs. An old blind man played a violin at the street corner, another roasted nuts and the smell drifted beguilingly across the sparkling stones. The very railings glittered with peculiar, mathematical beauty and each tree carried in its bursting buds the hint of an energy that would break out, soon, into glory.

She found the church and, since she was early, obtained a place near the front. There was no talking among the congregation as they assembled. Jane was surprised, for at the little parish church at Ottercombe the atmosphere was more relaxed. The vicar's wife and the poet's sister often chatted agreeably throughout the service.

But here there was an air of hushed expectancy. Behind her was a continual sound of footsteps and the rustle of clothing as a vast crowd assembled. Jane permitted herself a single glance round and saw to her astonishment that every seat was filled, the gallery was overflowing and people stood four across in both of the aisles. All attention was focused intently on the pulpit and Jane was almost alarmed at the sight of so many eyes uplifted, like a shoal of fish poised in the ocean. Their stillness was unnerving.

A door at the front of the church opened and William Harris walked to the pulpit. At the sight of him, a sigh of expectation ran through the congregation. Jane felt a thrill almost of fear. He climbed into the pulpit and looked silently over the heads of his congregation. For an instant he regarded Jane, and dwelt on her for a moment, it seemed, with recognition.

He towered over his audience. He was in any case a tall young man and the pulpit raised him further. In any society he would have been thought handsome. Here his authority and the magnetic confidence of his manner made him an extraordinary figure even before he spoke.

In a ringing voice he pronounced some prayers, then led the congregation in a hymn. Jane was impressed by the great waves of sound which rose and fell, so many voices raised in unison. Congregational singing of hymns was not usual at Ottercombe, where Parson would intone metrical psalms in his erratic, cracked voice, while his flock dreamed, dozed or gossiped in an undertone. Here, Jane felt instead a surge of shared intensity, which moved her.

After the hymn the congregation settled into an expectation of Mr Harris's address. But they did not settle as her family did for Parson's sermon at Ottercombe, with fatigue and resignation. They leaned forward in their seats with an alert, avid stillness.

Again William Harris's eyes swept across his listeners. 'Which of us here will be first to die?' he cried suddenly in a soaring tone. 'One of us will be called to meet our Maker first. This afternoon, perhaps. It is not always the old that go, either. Some young person sitting here now may be snatched away before dark. Perhaps the first symptoms of your dissolution are already upon you.

'Have you noticed an ache in the ribs? A fluttering about the heart? A pain in the temple? That pain, so insignificant now, might be the beginning of your end.'

Jane's blood froze in horror. She had indeed noticed that her calves were aching recently. Perhaps she would be cut down now, this afternoon, by the sweep of an invisible scythe.

'I know what you are thinking,' Harris went on, and his voice dropped fathoms deep into a quietness, which made it buzz intimately like a whisper at every person's ear. 'That it cannot be your turn yet. But in a second we shall all be snatched away.'

Jane's mouth felt dry and she felt she must swallow, but the sound she made was distractingly loud. Not a soul moved. Nobody stirred or coughed. Hardly anyone seemed to breathe.

'But snatched away to what?' William Harris threw the question up into the air, tossing back his hair, casting his eyes towards heaven. His voice echoed among the rafters. 'To bliss? To behold those divine mysteries for which our souls so ache? To be taken to our Father's bosom, reunited with our dear ones, gone before? Or . . .' he turned his gaze down again upon the congregation, as if he saw each of them delivered up to their doom, 'to burn in hell fires, howling through the smoke, howling through the flames, blazing in agony for ever?' Jane began to feel she was rather too hot.

'The only certain thing is that we shall die.' William Harris fell silent again for what seemed an endless pause. Again his eyes ran over the rows of hypnotised listeners.

Jane felt his gaze approaching nearer and nearer to her, and when it arrived it seemed to ignite a great flash of heat, as if her bones had been struck by lightning.

'Somewhere on the calendar is the date of your death. The fourth of May, perhaps. The eleventh of December. Waiting for you, unsuspected at present but inevitable. None of us shall escape.

'And when we are called to make our account, what shall we be able to say? How will you answer, when your turn comes? When the Almighty asks what you have done here on earth?'

The congregation's eyes grew large at the thought and they did their best to cling to life for a few more precious moments. Jane felt herself almost swooning away. It had grown stifling in the church, despite the season, for so many people gathered together sweating in terror without the convenience of open windows or doors created a suffocating heat.

'Look into your conscience. You know how badly you have done. You have neglected good works and chosen diversion. You have turned your back on the poor and needy, and given yourself up to earthly delights.'

Jane felt herself blushing all over. She had meant to perform some charitable acts, but she had forgotten all her good intentions and lost herself in the intoxications of Bath. She had even enjoyed card games and concerts. There was something uncanny in his understanding. She felt he was talking directly to her, and only to her, and she was sure that everyone present knew; and she burned with shame at her careless selfishness.

'I say to you, it is easier for a camel to go through the eye of a needle, than for a rich man to get into the kingdom of heaven. There are those among us today who are not simple, poor folk. There are those who grew up attended by luxury. But I say to you, you shall knock and knock at heaven's gate, and all the world's riches will not get you in. Answer God's call, and your soul shall be free. Do God's work on earth and your arrival in heaven shall be welcomed with trumpets.

'Now is the moment of choice. Your salvation hangs on this instant. Your soul longs for you to set it free. Speak now. Stand up and be counted. Stand up for the poor and needy. Stand up and make Him smile. Your Father that is in heaven, make Him smile to see you stand up for His sake, who died for yours.'

This last challenge was flung across the listeners' heads in a ringing tone which seemed to hang in Jane's ears. A cold sweat broke out across her face and hectic palpitations fluttered in her breast. She felt a tingling in her fingertips and a terrible melting in her spine. Her head rang with his words. She knew she was going to faint and struggled feebly to her feet.

William Harris's face was looking down at her and his mouth was opening, but she heard nothing except the ringing. She staggered and felt herself sinking. Somebody helped her from the pew and half carried her out of the church through a door behind the pulpit. She heard the door close behind her. They placed her in a chair. She was aware of a woman's voice saying, 'Fetch a glass of water' and smelt cool flagstones, and the smell revived her.

She opened her eyes and saw a woman's face before her. The face was kind, but stern. It greatly resembled William Harris's, and for an instant, in her confusion of mind, Jane thought he had turned into a woman and that she must be dreaming.

'How are you, my dear?' the woman asked.

Another, older woman arrived, bringing the water, which Jane gratefully sipped. 'I was too hot,' she said, trembling.

'And the Spirit worked upon you,' said the younger woman, with such fierce conviction that Jane did not dare argue. It was strange to be in the ordinary world again. She could hear a blackbird singing outside.

Then a great surge of sound sprang up, so violent it startled her.

'Don't be alarmed,' said the woman, soothing her by stroking her arm. 'It is only the last hymn. My brother will come to you in a moment, at the end of service.'

'Your brother?'

'I am William Harris's sister. My name is Martha.'

Jane looked around the small, sober room with its stone floor. 'Is this the vestry?' she asked.

Miss Harris nodded. 'He will come to see you and pray with you,' she said. 'He will come and congratulate you and rejoice with you.'

Jane stirred uneasily in her seat. It was good of him to think of rejoicing with her, but she would just as soon have gone straight home. Her legs were still trembling, however, and her strength was utterly gone. It seemed she would have to accept William Harris's congratulations and rejoicings, though she felt very intimidated at the thought of seeing him in private. She was sure she would make some kind of spectacle of herself again. 'Could we open that door a little?' she enquired feebly. The smell of cool flagstones was beginning to overpower her. She longed for fresh air.

Miss Harris obliged her, and Jane saw as she rose how tall she was, and how like her brother, only some years older, for there were streaks of grey in her hair. As the door swung open, Jane was given a slanting glimpse of the churchyard and the smell of grass came in, reminding her of home. It seemed immensely dear to her now, and also somehow lost and distant, and a tear sped down her cheek at the thought and she wished she were back at Ottercombe.

The singing ceased. There was the sound of people leaving the church, the murmuring of voices. The door opened behind her and somebody came in. Jane's heart began to thud. She dared not look round, but kept her gaze fixed on the narrow glimpse of grass and twigs in the churchyard.

'How is the child?' She recognised William Harris's voice in its lowest, most intimate register. Something in her rebelled at being so described. She turned to face him, wishing she had the courage to declare that she was not a child. 'What is your name?' he asked.

'Jane Lockhart.' Her voice sounded weak and small.

'No, you are not a child, I see.' He took a chair and sat directly facing her. 'A young woman, and one of extraordinary courage and sensitivity. A child only in the sense that we are all God's children.'

She was unnerved again by his ability to know her thoughts, but encouraged by the sight of him sitting beside her, looking somewhat tired and human from his exertions, and smelling rather of sweat. His looks, however, were every bit as striking in repose. 'I'm sorry I felt faint,' Jane stammered. 'I hope I did not disturb the company. I would not for the world have wished to interrupt your address.'

'Your faintness was a sign of your strength,' he said, fixing his eyes upon her. 'When I stepped into the pulpit today, and looked across the congregation, your face alone among all the others shone out.'

Jane's trembling increased to a violent shivering.

'Close the door,' William Harris ordered. His sister rose to obey. 'She must not catch cold.' The smell of grass was shut out. 'Give her your shawl, Martha, and then leave us. I must speak with Jane Lockhart alone.'

Miss Harris draped her black shawl around Jane's shoulders. She did not quite like the smell of it. It reminded her of damp Bibles. But she was too polite to refuse. And in any case it seemed a trifle, compared with the mysteries which glittered in William Harris's black eyes. His sister went out and shut the door. They were alone. Jane's heart throbbed with agitation.

'I saw it all in your face,' he said. 'Yours is a great, prophetic soul. Now you have stood up for the Lord your soul shall be free. You will do great work in the land.'

Jane was dumbfounded at the thought of this impressive destiny. William Harris asked her about her family and, by steady questioning, she was encouraged to reveal almost the whole story of her life. Within twenty minutes William Harris knew that she was the daughter of John Lockhart of Newington House, and the guest, in Bath, of Sir Thomas Burton of Ottercombe Park.

William Harris knew Ottercombe well, of course. 'There is very great poverty in all the villages around Woolton,' he said. 'And you will have wondered whether there could be any justice on earth, or any compassion in heaven, when Sir Thomas's family could enjoy so much, while but a half-mile away, poor children starve in the dirt.'

Jane hung her head. At this moment, having to endure William Harris's gaze, she heartily wished she were poor. 'I'm ashamed', she whispered, 'of the luxury of my parents' house. But what can I do?'

'Look at me, Jane.' She obeyed. A sunbeam cut down through the air between them. She saw tiny motes of dust dance in it. As he spoke, they twirled in his breath. 'You have no need for shame now. You are intelligent, strong, compassionate, and you have dedicated your life to the Lord.' Some remote part of Jane's mind dared to question if she had absolutely and utterly dedicated it already, or whether perhaps complete dedication might be postponed for a day or two, while she became accustomed to the idea. But she dared say nothing. There was something frightening but pleasing in his words, which seemed to run all over her skin like the exquisite pain of cold water on a hot day.

'We study and read the Bible together on Thursday afternoons. We discuss how society may be improved on Tuesdays. We read the writings of learned men. We discuss the Rights of Man.'

'And when do you help the poor?'

The ghost of a smile passed across his face. 'Always. Every day, every hour. You shall have plenty of that sort of work, if it pleases you.' She was caught on his eyes. They seemed to draw her out of her body. She felt as if some vital part of herself was suspended on the air between them, whirling helplessly like a speck of dust in a sunbeam.

43

'Above all, however, you must understand that you were sent to help me. You see what I do to bring souls to Paradise. But I am weak and the work is hard. I need your support, Jane – you must allow me to call you Jane, for we are all brothers and sisters in the Lord.'

Jane nodded.

'Do you want to help me?'

'Very much.' She could not permit herself to wonder exactly how this destiny could be accommodated within the established habits and obligations of her life. It merely flashed across her mind as a flying doubt.

It was not too swift, however, for William Harris's observation. 'Your life has changed for ever,' he murmured, dropping his voice again into the low caressing mode, 'but you are young. You enjoy the hospitality of a rich man here. He is perhaps a good man too, despite the text I mentioned today.'

'Oh certainly! Sir Thomas is the very best man in the world.'

'You will not wish to alarm him, then. There is no need for extravagant declarations. You know what has passed here; I know; God knows. That is enough. We want to see you tomorrow at our rooms. We will read and discuss a text at three o'clock. If you can easily come, do so. But do not inconvenience your hosts. If we do not see you then, my sister will take the liberty of calling on you. Here is our address.' He handed her a card. They both stood up. Jane found that strength had returned to her legs.

Sombrely William Harris looked down at her. She stared back. There was something so very fascinating about his face and voice, she could have looked and listened for longer. But now she must go. She made her excuses.

'Would you like us to escort you back to your friends' house?' he asked. 'My sister would be happy to oblige.'

'No – no, thank you. I need some time to be by myself before I get back there.'

'Some time for reflection, yes.' He nodded. 'You are

right.' He escorted her to the door and she found herself in the street. 'Remember.' He still stood in the shadow of the porch. She stood outside in the strengthening sunlight. 'I depend upon you, Jane.'

She nodded, turned and walked off through the crowded streets.

Everything seemed changed. It was as if a glass screen had come down between her and the world. There was still a crowd of children staring into the confectioner's window, admiring the pyramid of crystallised fruit, but now the scene was resonant with some sinister significance. The children seemed intent on worshipping a false god. The buds of the tree bulged with a symbolic power: the railings seemed to pierce the air, taller and sharper than before.

At last she reached the Burtons' house and was admitted. She scarcely saw the servant who took her bonnet and cloak. She followed the sound of voices into the drawing room, as she knew she must, and saw Sir Thomas, all smiles, rise to meet her. A tall young man with golden curls and a crooked smile was presented to her.

'This, Jane, is Henry the Navigator,' said Sir Thomas proudly. 'And this, my dear Henry, is our Jane.'

6

Jane was able to express her great pleasure at the acquaintance and to hope that Henry's journey up from Portsmouth had not proved too tedious, though her mind was still distracted by her morning's excursion. She knew she must not alarm such kind hosts by seeming withdrawn or preoccupied, but at dinner she felt unable to eat much, or listen to the conversation with her usual alert attention. The face of William Harris kept returning to her imagination, and in her moments of repose she recalled his words and turned them over and over restlessly in her mind, as if they were a spell, or a prayer.

After dinner the young people played at cards, but Jane soon tired of it and went to sit apart, staring out of the window at the gathering dusk.

Sir Thomas joined her on the sofa and expressed the hope that she was well and happy. She assured him she was.

'And did you benefit, this morning, from an improving sermon?' he asked with a sly smile.

She blushed. 'Oh, yes. Indeed.' She could see that her blush had intrigued him.

'What was the text?'

'It was . . .' She hesitated. 'It is easier for a camel to pass through the eye of a needle than for a rich man to get into heaven.' At this moment, there happened to be a brief pause in the general conversation, so that Jane found her words were heard by everybody.

'This was the text of Jane's sermon today,' Sir Thomas informed the company. 'And I have to tell you, Jane, it is not one of my favourites.' He smiled and his family laughed. Jane only burned and writhed. 'I hope you are not going to recommend that I give away all my worldly goods before supper.'

'Oh, no. Of course not.'

'What church did you go to, Jane?' asked Eleanor, who was strong enough after her confinement to spend most afternoons in the drawing-room. Young Thomas had been given into the care of a wet-nurse. 'Who was the preacher? Georgie and I like the Reverend James Dawson, he is a dear old man and very learned.'

'Oh, quite! Quite!' barked her spouse contentedly.

'It was – Mr William Harris that I heard,' admitted Jane, not without some feelings of guilt and trespass.

'What! An Evangelical!' cried Eleanor. Amused glances were exchanged among the whole family.

Henry particularly seized upon the idea. 'Why, don't say you are going to become an infidel, Jane!' he cried. 'I have hardly met you, but I have already developed an ambition to dance with you at the first opportunity. But if you turn Evangelical on us you won't permit us any routs or balls.'

Jane deplored the subject of conversation. Anything else would have been preferable. 'I would never dream of forbidding you anything,' she said.

'Ah, but think what you'll have to give up yourself, my dear, if you go down that road,' said Eleanor. 'Your green silk dress will be quite abandoned to the moths for a start.'

'Aye,' agreed Henry, a tormenting light dancing in his eye, for he liked nothing so well as teasing girls and had been prevented from any such indulgence for months by his naval duties. 'You shall be condemned to black wool and a puritan collar, and you will always be telling your sister to comb out her curls and hide her beauties under some frightful religious cap or other.'

'Oh, don't turn Evangelical, Jane, I beg!' cried Mary, who

looked rather flushed and more animated than usual.

'How handsome was the preacher, though?' asked Henry mischievously. 'For some of these Evangelical fellows are damned good-looking creatures. Their sermons are packed with fainting females.'

Jane felt suddenly very hot, and wished she were not so close to the fire. She could not answer Henry. She merely shook her head and tried to smile.

'That's enough now, Henry,' said Sir Thomas. 'Don't torment my Jane. Be so kind as to divert us instead with an account of the island of Malta, or Cyprus – what you will.'

'Did you see Naples, though?' enquired George Fortescue, rousing himself from his habitual torpor. 'I went up Vesuvius, when I was there in '91 – 'twas a most amazing sight, one could look down into the sulphurous pit.'

Jane found this was a moment to escape. Making a quiet excuse, she left the room.

The cold air of the hall was welcome to her fiery cheeks, but a servant was passing through and Jane wanted privacy, so she ran up to her room. Here, though, a fire also blazed. She felt an overpowering desire for fresh air and tried to haul up the sash window, but it was stiff, and stuck. The more she wrestled with it the hotter she felt and the more desperate for air.

She was so busily occupied she did not hear a soft knock at her door. Sir Thomas walked in, saw her dilemma, was at her side in an instant and threw up the window. 'It is indeed exceedingly hot,' he acknowledged, turning to her with concern. 'Poor Jane! I will not let Henry tease you so.' He looked very carefully into her face. 'Nobody shall be allowed to offend you, my dear, while I am by.'

'I was not in the least offended,' Jane assured him. 'Only a little hot, as you say. It is so mild today.'

'Aye. Spring is creeping upon us. Look at the buds on that chestnut tree, at the corner of the street.'

Jane felt the air on her face. They stood together for an

instant looking out, saying nothing. After the trials of the day Jane found it a sweet moment.

'There is a ball at the Assembly Rooms tomorrow,' said Sir Thomas. 'Henry is wild for dancing and I think your sister would very much like it. Do you like to dance?'

'I do indeed.' Jane smiled.

'Well, I warned you at Julia's wedding party that I should like to see you dance one day. And here's our opportunity. I promise you, you will not lack partners – nor admirers.'

His eyes seemed to glow and Jane was grateful for his kind words. She thought how different her life would have been if she had enjoyed the attention of such a thoughtful and affectionate father. And yet she did not think of him as fatherly. He was more like a friend, perhaps. Or a brother. But no. That was not it either.

She gave up trying to understand what sort of feelings Sir Thomas aroused in her and simply enjoyed his company. Her most secret instincts were already gathering about a more glamorous figure. She had scarcely spent five minutes since noon without thinking of William Harris. Her attention had constantly been claimed by social duties, but whenever a few seconds of leisure had presented themselves the preacher's face had sprung back into her imagination with a delicious shock of pleasure.

'Are you restored to spirits now?' asked Sir Thomas. 'Shall we go down to the company again, or would you like to stay in your room? I could ask for some supper to be sent up to you.'

Jane was not at all tempted to return to the drawing-room. She longed for a couple of hours of solitude in which to admire her memories of the day. Only she wished Sir Thomas would not go away quite yet. To him alone, of all the people in the house, she would willingly turn her mind. His company was always refreshing. However, she confessed that she was rather tired, though not hungry, and would stay in her room for the rest of the evening and read.

Sir Thomas bade her good-night, took her hand and

kissed it. Still holding it for an instant, he gave her a serious look. 'There are many delights in the world, dear Jane,' he said quietly. 'I should like to think you will be able to enjoy them all.' He bowed and withdrew.

Jane wondered for a moment what he could have meant. Pretty soon, however, she gave up puzzling over Sir Thomas's cryptic utterances and gave herself up entirely to thoughts of William Harris. She lay for an hour by candle-light, trying to conjure up the preacher's face. She recalled his words, and with them the sense that her life had changed for ever and that he had offered her a glimpse of work and purpose which could transform her days on earth.

Eventually she slept. Some time later Mary came to bed, and Jane awoke. She felt her sister climb in beside her and roused herself so far as to bid her good-night. Mary, of course, was wide awake.

'Did you find him handsome, Jane?' she asked suddenly. Jane's mind was full of William Harris.

'Yes, I did,' she admitted. She could not help sharing her exhilaration. If her own sister could not be her confidante, then who could? 'I have to admit I admire him exceedingly. More than any other man I have met.'

'Oh, so do I!' cried Mary and Jane saw in an instant it was Henry Burton she was talking about. 'And then, he is so gallant and amusing – to think we shall dance with him tomorrow night! I can scarcely sleep, thinking of it.'

Jane was not sure she would sleep well either. Both girls did, however, soon fall into a slumber, though in the middle of the night Jane awoke suddenly and heard a blackbird singing in the dark. The sound was piercing, melodious and exquisite. It seemed to squeeze her heart and the mystery of it occurring at such a dead hour struck her with an almost supernatural thrill. She lay awake for a long time afterwards, tantalised and aching for the future.

7

The next day everyone but Jane could think of nothing but the ball. Sir Thomas, however, received a letter from his attorney and was occupied for the whole morning about his business affairs. Jane was almost grateful for his seclusion. It relieved her of the scrutiny of the only person in the household who might have noticed her agitation.

Mary was in a flutter, of course, about her hair and her dress, and Miss Eliza was exercising a frenzied delight at the return of her adored brother. Henry himself was obliged to patronise the hairdresser, for his naval service had left his looks too wild for an elegant public gathering. Eleanor and her husband were engrossed in a prolonged debate about whether she was well enough to go out and it seemed to Jane, whenever she attended to it, that Eleanor was winning the argument, as must usually be the case.

She did not manage to give it much attention, however. Her own dilemma was acute. William Harris and his sister would be hoping to see her at their rooms at three o'clock. She dreaded disappointing them and, indeed, disappointing herself, for she could hardly contain her impatience to see them again. But the hour of the meeting was not really convenient. At three o'clock preparations for the ball would be well advanced. She would be expected to be dressing by then.

If only William Harris's invitation had been for the morning! For some time Jane stared at the card, printed with their address – a house but two streets away, although not nearly so grand. She was so entirely at leisure at this moment, so unobserved by everyone, that a sudden impulse seized her. She would write a note offering her regrets and apologies, and walk round to the Harrises' rooms immediately. She would scarcely be away for five minutes.

She did not want to waste time puzzling too long about drafting the letter, though she found herself wishing her handwriting were more elegant, and her powers of expression more accomplished. But then, catching herself out in a vanity, she smiled. What did William Harris care for elegant script or fine words? Hastily she blotted her hectic scrawl and read it over: she regretted more than anything not being able to call today at three o'clock, but she was under the obligation of a prior engagement with her hosts. She wished very much to enjoy the pleasure of Mr and Miss Harris's company very soon.

For an instant she hesitated over the word pleasure. Was it the wrong word? Would it offend him? No, she must not think like this. She seized her cloak and bonnet and left the house. It was raining, but the feeling of it on her face was enjoyable. The wind caught at her clothes and buffeted her. She welcomed the sense of animation it brought. She had to make a positive effort not to run. Her body was full of energy and there seemed not enough opportunity to express her strength.

Here was the house. It was part of a narrow terrace, without any steps down to an area, or any pretension to balconies such as the Fortescues enjoyed. But to Jane's eyes it possessed an extraordinary distinction. Its very plainness suggested a secret glamour. She rang and was admitted. She had supposed the preacher and his sister would be out, but the servant immediately ushered her into a room where Martha Harris sat sewing.

On seeing Jane she rose up instantly and welcomed her with great cordiality. 'I'm just mending William's shirt,' she said, almost with a smile, though Miss Harris's demeanour was not effusive. 'He bursts his buttons off at times, with the vigour of his preaching.' She put the shirt aside, though Jane's eyes followed it. The idea of his shirt, and the burst buttons particularly, was strangely compelling.

'I'm sorry to intrude,' explained Jane, turning to the matter of her errand. 'I merely wished to leave you this note – I'm sorry that I cannot come this afternoon –'

'William will be disappointed,' said Martha, opening the letter, reading it and looking up again at Jane. 'He was quite depending upon seeing you again.'

'Is he at home?' asked Jane, looking about. 'Perhaps I could apologise and explain to him myself.'

'No, he's out,' said Martha firmly. 'He will be most distressed to find he has missed you.'

'I'm extremely sorry.' Jane felt the familiar descent into horrible guilt into which her father's disapproval had so often plunged her.

'He will understand, however, your obligations to your host. Is it a family commitment?'

'No.' Jane had hoped to avoid mentioning the reason for her absence, but Martha Harris's silence and enquiring look seemed to demand absolute candour.

'I'm going to the ball', stammered Jane, 'at the Assembly Rooms. Sir Thomas is taking us all. His son is just returned from the Mediterranean.'

'I see. Well, I hope it proves a pleasant occasion.' Martha's tone was cold. The contrast with her friendly greeting a few moments before could not be more obvious.

Jane was dismayed. She wanted more than anything to restore herself in Miss Harris's good opinion. 'I suppose you will not be there?' she enquired faintly, out of some instinct to present the ball as an event not entirely dedicated to corruption and debauchery.

'I shall not.'

This was terrible. Jane knew she ought to sit with Miss Harris another ten minutes at least to satisfy the expectations of civility, but she could not sit still under the pressure of such disapproval. She leapt up, begged to be excused, explained that the Burtons did not know she had come out and begged to be excused again. Then she hesitated. 'And when, do you think, may I have the pleasure of seeing you and your brother again?'

'Perhaps the day after. We always meet for prayers and readings at that hour.'

'Then I shall be glad to see you both. Good day!' Jane made her escape.

She suffered, for the next few hours, from an irritation of the spirits impossible to expel. Her secret expedition to the Harrises' house had succeeded only in damaging her account with the preacher's sister. No doubt her character had already suffered in his estimation as a result of his sister's description of their meeting.

'What are you going to wear, Jane?' asked Mary, who was trying a seventh way of putting up her hair. 'Your green or your blue?'

'Oh, I don't know. Whatever you think.'

'Perhaps you should wear white, for you are the younger and it would set off my grey silk very well.'

'Why don't we ask Sir Thomas?' Jane was staring out of the window, Mary into the glass.

'Sir Thomas? Why, what in the world would he care about it? I think you should wear your white muslin; it has a very pretty edging, and grey and white are elegant. Eliza is wearing the prettiest gown in primrose and we should not outshine her, you know.'

'I would not dream of outshining anybody,' snapped Jane. 'Even if I possessed the necessary distinction in my looks – which I do not.'

'Oh Jane! I think you are very pretty.'

'I don't want to be pretty!' Jane was surprised by her own ill temper. She was also aware that she was talking nonsense. She discovered, for the first time in her life, that she wanted very much to appear attractive and engaging,

54

but in the right way – without seeming to think of it at all. She was aware that instead she was not only condemned to her usual bad looks, but to the additional burden of being very much out of sorts.

Mary got up and came to her side. 'What's wrong, Jane?' she asked, putting her arm around her. 'Please don't be in a temper. I do think you are pretty, but I won't mention it again if you don't like it. I know I'm exceedingly tedious when I'm agitated about my dress. And I'm quite annoying myself by getting into such a state about Henry. You must be bored to death with it. Henry, Henry, Henry – I can't get him out of my head. Exorcism may prove to be the only answer. Perhaps your preacher could perform it.'

Jane realised how completely self-absorbed she had been for the past twenty-four hours, and with a great effort shook off all thoughts of William Harris. 'I'm sorry I've been so cross. You look lovely.' She turned to her sister and touched Mary's coiffure in admiration. 'I think so and I have heard Sir Thomas say so more than once.'

'Oh! Who cares what Sir Thomas says?' cried Mary. 'It is what Henry thinks that matters.'

Jane made her preparations for the ball with resignation. She managed, for her sister's sake, to take a greater interest in Mary's appearance and for herself she felt a certain satisfaction in the plain white dress. She would not go so far as to acknowledge that it was becoming, but she thought that if Miss Harris or her brother could have seen it they would not have found much in it to deplore. It was of an unadorned simplicity which suited her mood.

Sir Thomas admired his own daughter with a kiss. He held her at arm's length. 'My dear Eliza! You are like a little canary.'

'It is not canary yellow, Papa, it is primrose,' insisted Eliza.

Sir Thomas turned admiringly to Mary. 'Miss Lockhart! Grey! How excessively elegant! If Eliza is a canary, you must be . . .' He struggled with the demands of ornithology.

'A goose!' Jane could not help herself. As everyone laughed she realised it had been a long time since she had exercised her wit – more than twenty-four hours. She had forgotten how much she enjoyed it, how much it was a habit with her, to make others laugh.

'And Jane – you rogue.' Sir Thomas took her hand, but instead of admiring her dress he smiled into her eyes. 'With your wit, my dear, it matters little what you wear.'

Jane felt a stab of disappointment, but was annoyed with herself for feeling it. Sir Thomas's attention was immediately claimed by the footman, who informed him that the carriage had come round, and they were all caught up in the bustle of departure.

The streets were already sunk in the dim blue shadows of a winter twilight when they arrived at the Assembly Rooms, which blazed with light, warmth and music. Sir Thomas seemed to know everybody and introduced his party to all his friends. Jane, however, hardly marked them. Her customary interest in countenances and characters was quite suspended. Her mind returned again and again to a face that was not there.

She danced, however, with Henry Burton and found the exercise drew her out of her reverie enough to begin to notice the young man's character. There was a reciprocity, however, in this occupation.

'I understand your character, Miss Jane.' Henry grinned, squiring her down the set in elastic and flamboyant style. 'You wish to give the impression of philosophical detachment.'

'I certainly do not!' cried Jane. 'I don't care what impression I give.'

'Oh, yes you do – forgive me, but I understand you better than you do yourself. Most of the girls here care for nothing except to be pretty and amusing, but that is not enough for you. You must be pensive and sombre. You are in your Gothic mode, I think. You are not really at ease at a ball.'

'I like dancing very much and I am most grateful to Sir Thomas for bringing us.'

'Oh, tush! Spare me the etiquette, please, Miss Jane. You have never said a dull thing since I arrived till that.'

'I am afraid you have not been attending to me closely, then, if you have missed the hundreds of dull things I say every day.'

'Ah, you are wrong there! I have been attending exceedingly closely, indeed I have hung on your every word – not that you have vouchsafed many. No, you are in your Gothic phase. You would rather be idling in the moonlight upon the battlements of some enchanted castle.'

'My sister is the novel reader, Mr Burton. And she would idle a good deal more picturesquely.'

'You sister is a beauty, and a very sweet girl – I've quite lost my heart to her, as one is obliged to do, you know, to all one's sister's friends. But you present more of a challenge.'

'I don't intend any such thing.'

'Oh, you do! Come, come, you consider yourself apart from other girls.'

'Only inferior in point of looks and manners.'

'No, I'm sorry, you can scowl at me all you like, but you can't convince me of that for a moment. Besides, the proportions of the face, you know, aren't everything. It is the wit and vivacity of a woman's spirit which attracts.'

Jane found his courtesies irritating. She wished he would not talk, only dance; for as a dancer he was diverting and energetic. So, although she enjoyed dancing, she was relieved when the set came to an end and she could return to Sir Thomas's party.

Henry bowed as he handed her to her chair, and whispered, 'I shall now make love to your sister, since you are so cruel. But be sure I shall find some battlements tonight to throw myself off and then you will be sorry.'

Jane could not help laughing at this last idiotic riposte. She began to think that, in a different mood, she might perhaps find Henry Burton agreeable company.

As the evening wore on, she danced also with George Fortescue, who mercifully spoke little, for he needed every ounce of concentration to enable him to complete his manoeuvres without treading on everybody's feet. And then he was so solid and unyielding, Jane felt it was rather like dancing with a wooden door. But it was at least restful after Henry. Then a small, sandy-haired man applied for her hand. He was a friend of the Burtons', and smiled rather pathetically at her at every opportunity. His hand, moreover, was limp and his manner plaintive.

Jane was enjoying a moment of repose, and wondering if William Harris ever danced, when she found her hand solicited by Sir Thomas himself and was very glad to stand up with him. At last she felt suited in her partner. Sir Thomas moved gracefully, without any ostentation; he held her firmly with his customary strength and warmth. She felt herself begin to be at ease. In the moments of closeness she smelt his skin, a scent which was pleasant and very different from the lavish pomades of his son and son-in-law.

He did not trouble her with many observations, only looked kindly at her once or twice, until it was their turn to stand out at the bottom of the set.

'So, my dear Jane, are you enjoying yourself?'

'Oh yes!' Jane could assure him with perfect honesty now. 'I'm very grateful to you – most happy indeed to be here. I love dancing.'

'And you dance well. It has brought colour to your cheek and a sparkle to your eye. You look prettier than I have ever seen you, my dear, which is saying a vast deal.'

Jane blushed at the compliment, which more than compensated for his earlier omission. 'But Eliza looks quite wonderful. I think when she is finished growing she will be tall and elegant.'

'Your instinct is always to deflect attention from yourself, Jane. But I must repeat that I have never seen you looking so well.'

'It must be because I'm enjoying Bath so much.'

She smiled at him, and for an instant was oblivious of everything except his kindness and her gratitude. As she regarded him, however, somebody walked past behind him and looked over Sir Thomas's shoulder directly into her eyes. With a flash of horror she recognised William Harris. His pale face seemed to hesitate for an instant behind Sir Thomas's browner complexion, then disappeared, like an eclipse.

Jane's heart forsook its customary steadiness and was jolted into a stupid quivering. Sir Thomas, luckily, was distracted by the modulation of the dance. The moment had arrived for them to resume their progress up the set. He offered her his hand and she could only follow.

Somehow her limbs co-operated with Sir Thomas, but she felt on the point of swooning and had to drag herself through the set, aware only that William Harris was in the room, had recognised her and might, at this moment, be watching her. She only wished the dance to end and, when it did, to find her seat again.

Sir Thomas noticed her discomposure and sat down beside her in concern. 'My dear, what is the matter?'

'Nothing – thank you – I felt a little faint. It was the heat, I expect.'

'Shall I take you out? Would you like some air?'

'No, no.' Jane fanned herself vigorously. 'I'm much better now. I only wanted to sit still for a minute. I think I had better not dance again.'

'Are you sure you want nothing? Could I get you a glass of cordial?'

Jane acknowledged that this would be very welcome and after Sir Thomas's departure on this errand her eyes roved restlessly around the room. It did not take a moment to see where William Harris stood. He was taller than most of the other gentlemen present and the dark austerity of his garments contrasted most strikingly with the prevailing ostentation. He was accompanied by a lady and gentleman and engaged in conversation with them.

Mary arrived at her side, flushed from three dances with Henry Burton. 'Oh Jane!' she panted. 'There you sit all composed and contented; you have no idea of my excitement; it is so wonderful; I have danced so much! My head is almost spinning; I think I have never been so happy in my life. Where is he? Talking to that young woman. Lord! She is so much handsomer than I am. Henry is sure to prefer her. ... Oh! He looked across and smiled at me! What do you think he means by that? Oh Jane! It's terrible! I wish I could have some of your serenity.'

Here Sir Thomas arrived with the glass of cordial for Jane, saw Mary needed one as well and went away again. This left Jane to hear Mary's delighted monologue alone, but though she heard it she could not devote a moment of concentration to it. She was only aware of William Harris's presence across the room. She dreaded, and yet hoped, that he might be observing her.

8

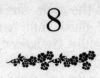

Above all, Jane dreaded the possibility that William Harris might approach her and that Sir Thomas would have to be introduced to him. She wanted nothing more than to talk to him, but not here. Even here she longed for something: a smile, a nod, an acknowledgement. Across the room the dark outline of his figure was very evident, but she dared not look directly at him. She inclined her head towards Mary, who was still talking, and pretended to listen.

Eventually Sir Thomas appeared with refreshment for Mary. 'Now, how are you all faring?' he enquired. Eleanor, who had insisted on coming but had spent the evening sitting and watching, was now beginning to be tired and wanted to go home.

'I think that would suit Jane too,' remarked Sir Thomas quietly. 'You're very fatigued, aren't you, my dear?' Jane nodded, although since she had recovered from the shock of seeing William Harris coming into the room she had felt wide awake and full of energy. It would be a relief to go, but also a keen disappointment. She had wanted above all things to see him again. Now he was in the same room, but she dared not look at him.

Mary and Eliza protested heartily at having to leave the ball and Henry declared he would stay longer and walk home. His father indulged him, for Henry had been too long away from amusements and there were several young ladies of his acquaintance present to whom he still owed a dance.

The others gathered up their shawls and fans, and turned to go. At this moment Jane's eye was caught by a dark movement across the room: she met William Harris's gaze and felt herself blush and her face buckle in an attempt at a gracious smile. He bowed slightly, then turned away. She left the room in the greatest possible confusion, relieved to have been acknowledged, but anxious that he had not smiled. But perhaps he was not the sort of man who smiled very often.

Soon Mary and Jane were in bed, but even the comfort of warm linen could not invite repose in two hearts so agitated by possibility and impossibility.

'Oh, Jane!' cried Mary. 'Who's he dancing with now, do you think? He said I was the handsomest girl in the room, but I'm sure it was only flattery, wasn't it? I expect he's dancing with that black-haired girl, Eleanor's friend's younger sister, Frances something – I can't recall her name, but she was horribly pretty. My only hope is that she might be bewitched and wake up tomorrow morning with a moustache, or a head like a donkey's.'

Jane insisted with perfect candour that she had hardly noticed the dark Frances, and urged Mary to believe Henry's protestations. 'You'll see, tomorrow, how he behaves towards you,' she suggested. 'The dark Frances does not have the advantage of living in the same house as Henry.'

'Tomorrow!' cried Mary restlessly. 'It's an age till then. You have no idea, Jane, what it is to be a little in love.'

Morning brought a foggy drizzle, which often hung over Bath for a whole day in the winter season. The position of the town, surrounded by a ring of hills, provided shelter for the mists, augmented by smoke from thousands of chimneys. On such days Bath seemed to be in a cold sweat. Vapour distilled on to the railings, and fashionable souls were less eager for their walk when the effect of wet pavements upon fine hems was considered.

Jane, however, was most anxious to go to the Harrises' house for the meeting at three o'clock. The difficulty of accounting for such an errand to Sir Thomas was overpowering. To go to church on Sunday might be considered the touching impulse of youthful enthusiasm, or even an excuse to show off bonnets or to cast an appraising eye over the young men present. It was understandable. But to go to a meeting to read the Bible and discuss sacred texts was dangerous. She knew what Sir Thomas would think. She suspected that he disapproved of Evangelism. She dreaded having to ask him for permission.

Mary had been encouraged by Henry's appearance, fresh and flirtatious as ever, to think of the day as a delightful one, drizzle or not. She and Eliza sat by the drawing-room fire, puzzling over attempts to read Henry's fortune in his palm, which necessitated a good deal of hand-holding and playful insults of a sort which Jane found particularly difficult to overhear.

She crept away to the library, pulled out a history of Hertfordshire and stared unseeing at the old maps. Here Sir Thomas found her an hour or so before noon. At his entrance she started and looked up guiltily. Her reverie had been so complete that she was hardly aware of being in the library at all. She had been supervising the installation of a paved floor in a poor family's hovel, while William Harris looked on approvingly.

The dream of charitable exertions with William Harris gave way to the solid reality of Sir Thomas. They were alone. Here was her opportunity. She must ask permission, now. But her spirit quailed at it. 'I'm sorry.' She got up hastily. 'I am sure you would like your library to yourself. My father always does.'

'No, no, Jane. Nothing could be more pleasing than to find you in my library. What are you reading?'

Jane had to look at the title of her book to discover what exactly it was that she had spent an hour and a half ignoring.

'A history of Hertfordshire?' enquired Sir Thomas with a quizzical look. 'Are you particularly interested in Hertfordshire, my dear?'

'I like . . . old maps.' Jane felt very stupid.

'Indeed? That's an unusual taste in a young lady. You should not be puzzling your head about old maps. You should be dreaming about some young fellow you met at the ball.'

'Do you think so? Why?'

'Because that would be natural and this is not. I don't like to see you too serious, Jane.'

This did not augur well for the Bible reading. Jane's spirits sank. She dared not mention it. She feared she would have to abandon the most urgent desire she had ever felt. For an instant she wished she could confess that she was indeed dreaming about a young fellow she had seen at the ball, but her agitation about William Harris was too profound, too serious somehow, to be so described.

'The fire's almost gone out. Are you cold?' He took her hand and frowned. 'You are indeed a little chilled.' He chafed her hands anxiously: the busy warmth of his own vigorous body soon communicating itself to her.

She felt better. 'You always have such warm hands, Sir Thomas.'

'You like that?' His look was sudden, playful.

'Oh yes. Above all things.'

'I shall make that my dearest aspiration in life, then. To keep your hands warm. I shall smoulder away in the corner like a disgusting old stove, hoping that when you come in from some walk in the frost you will be pleased to stand beside me for a moment or two.'

Jane laughed aloud, but was distracted from the joke by the appearance of an opportunity. 'Indeed, I do love walks in all weathers. It does not matter to me if there is frost, or even snow – as for this mist today, I love nothing more than a walk in the mist. It gives to everyday things a mystery.'

Sir Thomas hardly seemed to listen, however. She could see there was something else on his mind.

'Well, I'm extremely sorry to have to tell you, my dear, that I shan't be able to take many walks with you for the next few days. I have to go to London, there is nothing for it; it seems my affairs cannot be put in order without it.'

Jane's instinctive dismay at this news was tempered by a suspicion that without Sir Thomas it would be much easier to get out of the house. George Fortescue was often from home and when he was there scarcely seemed to notice or care what anybody did. Eleanor was preoccupied with her babe, and Mary and Eliza shared an intimacy of kindred souls from which Jane did not at all mind being excluded. There was only Henry to oppose or tease her. She would have to trust to her wits.

She expressed her hope that his journey would be pleasant and his business speedily concluded, and declared that she would look forward eagerly to his return. A tremor of embarrassment attended this speech, for she was so used to telling Sir Thomas exactly what she thought and felt it was particularly uncomfortable to be lamenting his absence in this way, while secretly busy with plans to take advantage of it.

Sir Thomas stirred the fire back into a blaze and stared into the flames for a moment. 'You recall what I asked you to do when we first arrived,' he said at length. 'I would be grateful if you would keep Eliza in your eye and protect her from impertinent advances.'

'With pleasure!' Jane had quite forgotten his original instruction, she had been so caught up in her own affairs. Her reassurances were therefore now more fervent with guilt. 'I shall see off any plausible rogues, Sir Thomas, I promise. I'll bark first, and if they don't heed that, I shall bite.'

Sir Thomas laughed and looked relieved. He grew sober, however, when the thought of his departure returned. 'I shall miss you very much, my dear,' he said, then suddenly got up and walked out.

Jane discovered quite soon that Sir Thomas was to leave

the next morning on a fast coach which, in dry weather, could complete the journey in under twelve hours. He therefore would be busy for the rest of the day making his preparations. Jane observed that Henry was paying the most emphatic attentions to her sister throughout dinner and she saw that Eliza was drooping with the effects of her late night. Both Sir Thomas's daughters retired to rest for the afternoon; Sir Thomas himself was closeted in his study. Jane judged that Henry and Mary might welcome a little seclusion and planned to make her escape after half an hour's idle talk in the drawing-room.

Mary and Henry were deeply engaged in assuring each other how ugly they were.

'As for your lips, Mr Burton,' cried Mary, almost in a paroxysm of laughing, 'you pout all the time, like the fat cupid on my father's sundial on the terrace at Newington.'

'Fat! Miss Lockhart, how could you? Such cruelty forces me to mention what I was too polite to remark on before: that your eyebrows resemble those of the screech owl.' For a third party to absent herself from such a conversation seemed more a necessity than a discourtesy.

Jane did not bother to tell them what she intended, or even to invent an excuse. At the conclusion of a half-hour she announced her intention of taking the air and walked boldly out of the house. The rain had stopped, but the mist was increasing as the afternoon light weakened. She was confident of being unobserved once she had turned the corner into the next street. But as she hastened through the thickening fog she almost ran into another person, stood aside with many apologies and looked up to find herself face to face with William Harris.

9

Both were speechless for a moment. Jane was astonished to see before her the face which had been so continuously present in her mind. His appearance seemed almost like supernatural conjuring: the operation of a spell. She was surprised that he, who was so used to expressing himself in public, did not speak at once.

She felt obliged to say something. 'I – was coming to your house,' she faltered. 'To the meeting.'

'There is no meeting today. My sister is not well.'

Jane expressed her concern at Miss Harris's indisposition and was assured it was nothing more than a sick headache, from which she often suffered. 'Ah. Then I suppose . . .' Jane hesitated. 'I should return . . .' She looked back towards the Fortescues' house, which had entirely disappeared in an encroaching fog.

'I'm going to the Apothecary', explained William Harris, 'to fetch some ginger. My sister finds an infusion of it helpful at such times. Would you care to accompany me?'

Jane hesitated, not sure whether to accept such an invitation would be prudent. Her extreme curiosity about William Harris's character, however, soon overcame her scruples. 'I should like that very much,' she acknowledged. 'I need to be out in the air. I'm too much indoors here.'

He made no remark. They set off towards the centre of the town. The Apothecary's shop was but four streets away, although the fog growing thicker and thicker had taken away all appearance of familiarity in the buildings. They heard the footsteps and occasionally the voices of other people, but could not discern anything at all of the buildings opposite. On their own pavement they encountered nobody.

'I like the fog,' observed Jane lamely. 'It gives an enchantment to everyday sights.'

William Harris was relentlessly silent. She supposed her remark had been foolish.

Jane's imagination seemed as blank as her surroundings. Here she was at last with the person who had excited more private speculation on her part than any other living being, and the fog bestowed on their walk an intoxicating sense of privacy, but she felt she could not offer any observations equal to the occasion. A rising desperation seemed to gather within her. The silence was insupportable.

'I was surprised to see you at the ball!' she burst out at last.

'Surprised? Why?'

'I did not think you would enjoy such an event.'

'You have formed a severe view of my character, then.'

'I only assumed – I suppose wrongly – that you would disapprove of dancing.'

He was silent for a while. 'The most touching spectacle I have ever seen', he began suddenly, 'was when I was travelling through Devon. I preach a lot in the West Country, in Somerset and Dorset and Devon. I addressed a great crowd of folk in a field above the village of Stokenpath.

'It was midsummer and I stayed there for a day or two afterwards, at the miller's. It was a most devout village and a pleasure to be among such good-hearted folk in the midst of beautiful countryside. One evening I walked the lanes and heard music. I followed it and found a barn where the fiddlers were making merry, and almost the whole village were gathered there. Old folk and babes; grandfathers dancing with their grandchildren; lovers, married couples, cousins and brothers and aunts, and all as innocent and merry as could be. It was a glimpse of Paradise.'

Jane was entranced. If only he would talk for ever. There was no difficulty now. 'Like a vision,' she murmured.

'Perhaps it was. But you can understand, I hope, the contrast between that merry gang of simple folk and the ball where I had the happiness to glimpse you the other night.'

'The contrast must, I suppose, be one of society. A public ball in Bath is an elegant affair.'

'Yes. Here, everyone's attention is fixed upon the dress and manners of others, and the object is to establish one's own sense of superiority in fashionable society and to search for every opportunity to ridicule one's fellow-men.'

'I'm sure Sir Thomas had no interest in establishing a sense of his own superiority, or wishing to ridicule anybody.'

'He was the gentleman you were dancing with when I came in?'

'Yes. He's a good man and he can't help not being poor.'

'I suppose he intends you for his son? The young man with the fair hair?'

Jane was astounded. 'I'm sure he has not the least idea in the world of it and nor have I – nor Henry.'

'You're not engaged to anyone?'

'Not at all.'

'Not even particularly fond of any young man?'

His interrogation seemed almost impertinent in its urgency and yet she felt roused by it, flattered by the intensity of his enquiries. Jane acknowledged quietly that her heart was free.

'You have an instinct that you can do great work in the world, Jane Lockhart. You are here to do something more significant than paying social calls and trimming bonnets.'

Jane felt excited at the thought of important work.

'I saw it in your face, when you first appeared before me in the congregation. You were sent.' He paused for a moment, and gazed down at her. An almost supernatural thrill crept up her back. His dark eyes seemed to drive down into her brain. She stared up, hypnotised. 'You were sent to help me, I am sure. You feel the certainty of it too. You know that unseen forces have contrived to bring you to me.'

Jane nodded helplessly. She felt as if a strange power was pouring down from him and swarming through her blood.

'We shall do great things, Jane. All your intelligence and compassion and ingenuity shall be placed on the altar of the Lord. The poor shall bless your name. You shall teach them and love them and help them to make better lives for themselves, more serious lives, more resonant lives, lives which have a radiance, no matter how humble.'

They stood for a moment transfixed, contemplating this destiny. A boy ran by in the fog and brushed William Harris's leg as he passed. This seemed to jolt them back into the actual world. William Harris looked about him. Jane was too moved by the revelation he had just pronounced to think about where she was. She could only admire her prospects, though not without considerable apprehension.

'Dear me,' murmured Harris. 'Where is the Apothecary? Which street is this?'

Jane looked about her. Despite her many walks she could not see anything she recognised. They stood beside the vague shape of a terrace of houses, indistinguishable from many in the town. The fog seemed thicker than ever and it was beginning to get dark. Jane started to shiver.

'Take my arm,' commanded William Harris. 'We shall get our bearings in a moment. Let's go this way.'

Jane's instinct was to take the other path, but she did not presume to argue. She took her companion's arm gladly and received a faint warmth from his thick black sleeve.

They walked for some time in silence. After the glowing possibilities he had described to her, Jane did not dare to introduce any insignificant topic of conversation. She longed to know more about him. He had questioned her closely about her most private feelings not only today, but on the previous occasion. Yet he had revealed nothing about himself. He remained a mystery.

A clock struck. Jane realised with horror it was five o'clock. She had been out for two hours. She must surely by now be missed by the Fortescues; she dreaded the anxiety of Sir Thomas.

'We seem to be climbing,' she said, suddenly managing to consult her own instincts once more. 'I'm sure that can't be right. The Apothecary's shop was not uphill: it was in that small street adjoining the Abbey, surely.'

They stopped and looked about them; swirling fog enveloped them so completely it was as if the everyday world had evaporated, leaving only empty bandages. Seeing nothing but blankness, their eyes rebelled at the strain. Jane began to see dazzling patterns, motes of dust, atoms, like the specks in a sunbeam. She closed her eyes to try to clear them, and shuddered.

'Confound it!' muttered William Harris. 'Confound the ginger. I must try to get you home.'

'I'm afraid I shall have been missed,' confessed Jane, with a shiver. 'And I did not obtain Sir Thomas's permission to go out.'

William Harris looked angry. 'I suppose he will blame me very much,' he remarked bitterly.

'Oh, no – he need not see you at all. If we can only find the street again I can go the last few yards alone. I can say I went out for some air and got lost by myself. There is no need for you to meet Sir Thomas, indeed I don't think I would be at all easy if you did.' Jane could not quite decide whether she wanted to protect William Harris from Sir Thomas, or Sir Thomas from William Harris, but her instinct to keep them apart was very strong.

'We'll go this way.' William Harris set off again, and downhill, but at a street corner took a left turn, when Jane's inclination would have been to suggest a right.

'We could ask somebody,' suggested Jane, her teeth chattering. The icy fog, swirling in her face, undid all the warming effects of exercise.

'There is nobody to ask.' The street was indeed deserted.

'We could knock at a door and ask where we are.'

William Harris ignored this suggestion. Jane divined, correctly, that he was mortified at having lost his way and too proud to ask anybody's help while there was a chance of regaining his bearings himself. She gave herself up to his navigation, and tried to suspend her own judgement.

'Sir Thomas will not let you out again, I'm sure,' he commented with a kind of quiet fury.

Jane could not determine whether he was angry with himself, Sir Thomas, or with her. She felt, somehow, that it was all her fault. But at least she could reassure him on one point. 'Sir Thomas is going to London tomorrow,' she said. 'He must stay there for several days on business. Nobody else cares what I do or where I go.'

'I can see you, then? You can come to our meeting?'

'Will your sister be strong enough for a meeting tomorrow?'

'Oh yes. Her headaches are always over in a day. We shall certainly have a meeting tomorrow – if we ever get home at all. I fear we shall be walking these confounded streets for all eternity.' He glared about him, enraged, at the fog. Jane thought he was not showing much Christian resignation in adversity. Not that she felt much herself – she was beginning to be really tired, and the cold air had brought an ache to her throat and a continuous tremor to her chilled limbs.

'Jane!' Henry Burton appeared through the mist. Jane blushed, though her relief at seeing Henry almost dispelled her embarrassment to be found with William Harris.

'Oh , Henry, I'm so very glad to see you – I went out, you know, to get some air, thought I might call on Mr Harris and his sister and by chance I met him at the street corner. He was on an errand to the Apothecary's, to get his poor sister some ginger for her headache. I agreed to accompany him and I don't know how . . . we got lost and we have been wandering about in this horrible fog for hours. I'm so sorry! I hope I have not caused any anxiety at home?' Her hectic confession, so candid, so artless, felt somehow as if it was all a lie.

Henry listened with an amused air, then turned to William Harris. They were of an equal height and perhaps comparable age, but one seemed composed of darkness, the other of brilliancy. 'I don't think I've had the pleasure of making your acquaintance, Sir,' said Henry pleasantly.

'Oh! I'm sorry!' cried Jane. 'I was so agitated to be lost, and so relieved to be found, I forgot myself. Pray excuse me. This is Mr William Harris; Mr Harris, this is Mr Henry Burton.'

William Harris bowed.

'It's so lucky that you found us, Henry!' Jane went on. 'Unless you are lost as well?'

'Not in the least.' Henry smiled. 'You are but fifty yards from the house. I was sent out, like an Alpine guide, to see if you could be detected. I can find my way anywhere in the dark, you know, Mr Harris. It comes, I suppose, from my having come home blind drunk on so many occasions – you must forgive me, I had forgot you are a preacher. I'm only a vile ruffian, a sailor, you know. I think I must escort Miss Jane home now, she looks quite done in.'

Henry offered Jane his arm, and she took it, though not without a tremor of betrayal towards William Harris, who stood quite dumbfounded at being boarded in this manner and having his treasure seized.

'Good-night, Mr Harris,' said Jane. 'Pray give your sister my kindest regards. I hope she will be quite better by tomorrow.'

'Indeed she will.' William Harris bowed. 'And I'm sure she will look forward to seeing you again. Good-night to you both.' He turned and walked off.

Jane quailed at the need to explain her conduct to Henry.

'Is Sir Thomas very anxious on my behalf?' she enquired timidly. 'I hope not.'

'Oh, Father has no idea you are out,' said Henry. An exquisite relief stole over her. 'He is busy in his study; he's been there all afternoon. I was the one who noticed you were gone a long time, and we saw the fog, and Mary was worried about you, so I came forth, like a knight on his charger, to rescue the fair maid from the vile dragon.'

'What vile dragon?' cried Jane in indignation.

'Oh, the fog, of course, only the fog,' Henry simpered. 'But I tell you, I don't like the look of that dark fellow. Are you sure he's one of God's messengers? He looked damned sinister to me. You're not falling under his spell, I hope?'

'Certainly not!' Jane smiled, feeling her strength return, and grateful for Henry's silly badinage.

'I hope not. For I wouldn't care to challenge a preacher to a duel. He'd have the Almighty on his side, I'm sure, and slash me to ribbons in no time. Gad, it's cold. You must be frozen stiff, poor Jane. But the fog has gathered in little pearls on your eyelashes. You look deuced pretty, you know. No wonder poor old Harris was panting over you. He's obviously quite lost his head over you and who can blame him, for who wouldn't? I am myself quite head over heels, but you don't care. You are too cruel. You'd cheerfully toast my heart, butter it and devour it without a moment's thought, eh, Jane?'

They reached his sister's house, where a servant received them, and Henry was obliged to curtail his banter. Jane walked into the drawing-room eager for the fireside and feeling equal to any indignation Mary or Eliza might express. Somehow it was Henry's silly jokes which had renewed her energies – it was the ease with which she felt able to enjoy, and dismiss, his attentions. Though she did not quite understand it, she felt she had been rescued from more than the fog, though her desire to see William Harris again on the morrow was stronger than ever.

10

The next day Sir Thomas left for London and the household
fell into indolence. The weather grew mild. The blackbird
in the neighbouring street sang ever more strongly and
Eleanor's pot of daffodils opened, bringing a burst of yellow
to the front door.

Eleanor herself began to resume her social calendar.
Friends called constantly to admire young Thomas, sometimes bringing their own children. Eleanor's husband
endured these occasions with his customary languor, only
waking up to hear his babe praised and the child's likeness
to himself remarked upon. Neither Eleanor nor George
minded what their brother and sister did. Henry and Eliza
were left very much to themselves.

The household seemed to fall into two camps. The former
was dedicated to the contemplation of infancy and its atten-
dant anxieties and delights; the latter to walks, shopping
and diversion of all kinds. Mary was the only one of the
young people to have a passion for babies, but Jane noticed
that though her sister was as gratified as ever to claim her
ten minutes with little Thomas on her knee, she did not
dedicate herself to the role of nursery maid with complete
devotion. When the dandling and cooing was done, she
seemed always eager to return to Henry's side.

As for Henry, he was an enigma. Jane could see that
Mary was becoming increasingly attached to him; indeed
Mary confessed as much. But Jane often noticed that when

Henry was whispering amusing asides to Mary his eyes seemed elsewhere, and often she received their glinting attention herself.

On the few occasions when she found herself alone in his company Jane was offered the same feverish parody of compliment and complaint with which he had always addressed her. Sometimes she was amused by it, but it could irritate. It seemed increasingly inappropriate to her that a young man offering such obvious attentions to her sister should wish to flirt with her, even in jest. She was, moreover, in no mood for jocular flirtation. Her feelings were beginning to be seriously aroused by another.

The very day Sir Thomas left for London Jane succeeded in attending the meeting at William Harris's rooms. The milder weather and a springlike softness in the air had tempted the young people out to saunter among the shops. Mary was looking for a particular lace to give a new distinction to a light gown which, if the warmer weather continued, she would soon be wearing. Eliza had very strong views on the qualities of various examples of lace and Henry was not reluctant to scrutinise Mary's lovely neck at close quarters, and comment on the effect upon her looks of different possibilities.

Jane thought she had never seen her sister looking so animated and happy. Mary had escaped from the constraints of her home much more satisfactorily in Bath than in the continual reading to which she resorted at Newington House. There were, however, dangers in the real world which books did not present. It is true that a sad book can upset a reader of feeling and Jane had in the past known Mary in tears for two or three days after finishing some particularly tragic tale. There was a tenderness in Mary's nature which made painful or disagreeable experiences particularly difficult to bear. She gave herself up, however, to her present pleasures with an abandon she had never shown before.

But Jane could not hesitate for long in contemplation of

her sister's character. She had a pressing engagement and had decided to spring it abruptly on her companions, thus avoiding the possibility of prolonged arguments or teasing by Henry. Accordingly she waited until the discussion about lace had reached an almost warlike pitch, murmured, 'I'm just going to call on Miss Harris and shall make my own way home' and walked out of the shop.

Henry looked up and exclaimed in protest, but she was gone without looking back and almost ran to the house where her imagination had already been installed for some hours. She was shown into the same room where Miss Harris had sat sewing upon her previous visit, but now it seemed crowded. There were present about six or seven people of varying ages. She sat down in the offered chair and smiled at everybody except William Harris, whose eyes she dared not meet.

'Ah. This is Miss Jane Lockhart.' His voice, however, imposed itself on her attention and at the sound of it she felt her pulse begin to race. Now she could hardly avoid looking at him, but she tried hard to prepare an expression of serenity as she turned his way. Meeting his eyes, however, she found herself quite overcome by their power, felt her cheeks burn and dreaded that the peculiar agitation that she felt in his presence must be obvious to everyone in the room.

She greeted Miss Harris and enquired after her health, and was next presented to the others: a middle-aged man, a woman of similar age, a fat young man with a heavy face and a noisy way of breathing and two very pretty young women whose presence somehow filled Jane's heart with dread. She heard their names and murmured acknowledgements and greetings, but hardly knew what she said. All her energies were devoted to a struggle to regain her composure.

'So . . .' William Harris looked around the company. He seemed more at ease when addressing a number than he had been when alone with her. His confidence and easy manner now offered a very striking contrast to the silences and abrupt transitions of their walk in the fog. 'Here we are all assembled. All of you have been chosen to help me. Some divine agency brought you to me. You felt its irresistible power.' Slowly he looked round the room, resting his eyes on each person in turn.

Jane was full of dismay. So all these people had been chosen to help him too. Somehow she had supposed her recruitment had been a more exclusive event. There had been an urgency in his manner, and an intimacy in his tone, which had stirred her heart more than the anticipation of charitable work, however heady might prove the administration of shawls, soup and kindling to the needy.

She felt she could not look at him. She contemplated instead the folds of her dress upon her knee: a sober grey wool, chosen, she now acknowledged to herself, in the hope of pleasing him. How foolish all her agitation seemed. She was not to enjoy any private importance to him. She was merely one of a company.

Well, she must resolve to find satisfaction in the work itself, and the study. She had wanted to do more charitable work. If she could help the poor, she might feel less guilty about the comforts of her own life.

'Jane Lockhart?'

She was roused from her contemplation by William Harris's summons. She could not avoid looking at him any longer and managed to retain her composure more successfully, now she knew there was no secret understanding between them.

'What are you thinking, Jane?'

His question was direct, but she had her answer. 'I was thinking of a poor charcoal burner's family who live in my father's wood and hoping that I shall be able to help them, with your assistance and advice.' She felt relieved that she had managed to answer him without blushing or stammering. Some sinew of strength was returning to her. Her molten disappointment was cooling and hardening. She had been foolish, had misinterpreted his words on their walk.

She would never permit herself that melting, helpless feeling again. He had called her to work. She would work.

'Good thoughts,' concluded William Harris, after staring at her for a moment. 'Come, let us fortify Jane's charitable inclinations by studying a text.' He read the text in his ringing public voice, carefully modulated to suit the modest proportions of the room. Then he began to discuss it.

Jane found it difficult to concentrate on the meaning of his words. She found her attention returning again and again to the quality of his voice. It soared, it dropped, it floated out on the air. It was like a landscape full of hills, lakes, glittering light and passing shadows. She had not heard anything so dramatic, so thrilling, outside the theatre. He could have been a great actor, she was sure, had he not felt called to preach.

His face was full of magnetic power. It was easier for her to observe him now that he was talking to them all generally, without making her the particular object of his attention. Despite her determination to shake off the spell he had cast over her she could not help admiring the beauty of his pale face. White linen at his throat and about his wrists contrasted vividly with the black coat, the black hair. There seemed to be no colour in him. Even his eyes were black, or rather, the darkest shade of grey she had ever seen, with the light upon them: the grey of slate, of granite, of a storm cloud in September.

His hands were long and white. Eloquent gestures emphasised his utterance, but also revealed the beauty of his fingers. There was nothing effeminate, however, in the elegance of his hands. From beneath the white purity of his cuffs, curling black hairs peered out with disturbing effect. Jane noticed that the two young women sitting opposite her were gazing at William Harris with eyes which sparkled with rapture. They were completely in his power. Jane was glad that she was fully in command of her heart once more and could hear him with quiet attention.

When the meeting had concluded, however, and she was

79

walking home again, Jane was alarmed to discover that she had scarcely any recollection of anything he had said.

'It was anxiety at the first meeting,' she told herself. 'Self-consciousness at being among strangers, and distraction at the strangeness of the exercise, for I have never studied biblical texts before in a private house in such company.' She vowed she would do better the next day and tried to compose herself to face the taunts of her hosts.

Henry, Eliza and Mary had not arrived home yet, however, so she was able to take tea with Eleanor and a friend of hers whose little boy had reached the age of destruction and was amusing himself in an energetic attempt to bite every piece of furniture. His mother seemed unable to provide any but the mildest of chiding, so Jane made herself useful in removing valuable objects from his reach and offering him a diversion by drawing monsters for him and inviting him to name them.

This experience proved so exhausting that Jane soon withdrew to her room, with renewed admiration for nursery maids and a feeling that, compared with the exertions required of a mother, the most energetic of charitable work might prove no more fatiguing than a picnic. She thought it very unlikely she would ever be a mother, concluded that she would make but a poor one and resolved instead to prepare herself for aunthood, in which happy state her eccentricities might prove more acceptable.

Supper was not a particularly exciting occasion. Eleanor had been tired by her visitor and complained to George about the wildness of the child. George mollified her in a bored voice, while forming a plan to go to play cards with a friend that evening, if his wife could be coaxed to retire early without him. Eliza had seen a young man in the street whom she had much admired, was depressed by the unlikelihood of ever seeing him again and had sunk into a torpor.

Mary had accepted a playful gift from Henry of a half-yard of coral ribbon, which she wore around her neck. She was forever touching it, or admiring its reflection in the silver tureen, and applying silently to Henry for frequent admiring glances, which he gladly supplied. Their absorption with each other, which sometimes Jane found touching, seemed now merely silly.

Jane was glad not to be under William Harris's spell any longer, but irritated by an old habit she could not quite shake off of finding her thoughts returning to him every two or three minutes. This irritation spread to a general disaffection with the occasion. She could not produce much of an appetite; the soup seemed cold, her companions boring and annoying. For a while she could not understand what made everything so dull. Then it broke upon her understanding: Sir Thomas was away.

His absence, however, provided her with daily opportunities to further her acquaintance with William Harris and his sister. She gently established a habit, which her hosts soon accepted, of going out to see them every afternoon. Most days there were several others present, and they read and studied together. Jane managed to bring her mind to the necessary state of quietness to follow the arguments which were pursued. She felt she had pressed down her former agitation with a weight of serious study. She no longer feared to look at him.

Only she could not help wishing that one day she might enjoy a private interview again with William Harris and her most persistent attempts to root out this desire proved useless. Like a rose bush in May, the more savagely she hacked it down, the more boldly it sprang up again, full of thorns and sweetness.

11

A fortnight passed in this tantalising manner, then Sir Thomas sent word that he would return in three days. Jane would have looked forward eagerly to seeing him again, but for a suspicion that he might not approve of her Evangelical excursions. The day before he was due to arrive she thought it prudent to mention to William Harris the possibility that obligations to her host might keep her at home for a day or two.

She waited behind after the end of the meeting, but seeing that the two young women, Lucy and Amy, had also stayed behind and, with shining eyes and rapt expressions, were engaging William Harris's attention, she mentioned Sir Thomas's return instead to Martha Harris, begged her to pass on her apologies to her brother and walked out.

She had scarcely reached the end of the street, however, when she heard swift footsteps behind her, turned and found William Harris himself in pursuit, her name on his lips.

'My sister told me that Sir Thomas is expected tomorrow,' he said. 'Of course you will wish to fulfil your obligations to your host.'

'Yes,' said Jane. 'I merely wanted to assure your sister – and yourself – that should I be absent for a day or two, that would be the cause.'

'I see.' He looked down at her in silence for a moment. These were the first private words they had shared since the walk in the fog a fortnight previously. Jane did not permit herself to savour the moment, however. She assumed the conversation was at an end and, removing her attention from his face, withdrew her body slightly, turning it towards her destination, hesitating for an instant only in expectation of his words of goodbye.

'Wait a moment,' he said, almost stammering in a rare fit of awkwardness. 'The afternoon is fine – would you care to walk for a quarter of an hour?'

Jane's heart leapt – she could not prevent it. Modestly she inclined her head, however, and resolved to betray no foolish emotion, but to talk serenely and enjoy in quietness this unexpected opportunity.

They turned away, therefore, from the street where Eleanor's house lay and walked instead back down Pomfret Street, passing the Harrises' house on the other side. Jane thought she saw the white flash of Martha Harris's face at the window as they passed, and that it wore an expression of disapproval, but she could have been mistaken.

William Harris had sunk into one of his deep silences. Jane was a good deal less uneasy, however, than on their previous walk. She knew there was nothing more in his penetrating gaze than a pastoral concern for a spiritual pupil. She had seen the girls, Amy and Lucy, caught in helpless admiration of him and was determined not to let herself ever fall back into the same trap. She therefore did not feel under an obligation to make any remark and instead looked about her, admiring signs of spring in the trees and enjoying the soft air on her face.

'Have our meetings fortified your sense of a calling?' he asked suddenly.

'Calling?' She could not quite understand, thinking at first of calling in the sense of a social visit.

'I told you – and you felt also – that you had been called. To God's work.'

'Oh, yes. Of course. Most helpful.' Her tone was light and self-protecting. It provoked him.

'I do not always know what you are thinking, Jane Lockhart.'

She felt the personal nature of the remark with a shock, but was roused to counter-attack. 'I don't ever know what you are thinking, Mr Harris.'

'But I've spent the last fortnight talking at length with you.'

'About Scripture. You talk very freely as a preacher. But not as a man.' She gave him a bold look.

It was a challenge he could not ignore. 'I acknowledge – I find it difficult to speak of personal matters. I have wanted to talk to you often. Every day. But I have never found the opportunity to speak in private.'

She was astonished to hear this admission that her company was particularly important to him. But perhaps he spoke like this to his other disciples. She was determined not to lose her composure and to press home her initiative. 'You've asked me many questions, Mr Harris – about my family, my home, my thoughts and fears, my strongest feelings and my most passionate convictions. But you have revealed nothing of yourself.'

They came suddenly into a square where street musicians were performing. The sound of a fiddle danced among the buildings, while in the midst of a crowd a fire-eater stood illuminated by a flaming brand.

'I have never met a woman to whom I felt I could reveal myself.' The reflection of the flame capered in all the windows of the square, as if the whole town was alight. The fire-eater held his torch aloft and gazed up at it.

She understood, then, that there was something untouched about William Harris: perhaps untouchable, too.

'Never. . .' he repeated, his voice shaking. 'Never till now.'

Jane did not dare speak, or even breathe. She could not believe where his speech could be leading.

'But you, Jane Lockhart, have touched me in a way . . . I had never expected to make such a declaration . . . it is beyond my powers, but I'm quite convinced ... the time is not right, nor the place, everything is too awkward, but I must speak now, or not at all. You are the woman to whom I can reveal myself. Marry me.' The fire-eater blew out a blast of flame: the crowd felt themselves scorched, and gasped.

Jane was thunderstruck. She could not believe what she had just heard, much less frame an answer. She had longed for ten minutes' private talk with him and found he was offering the whole of himself, for ever. She was stunned.

'I know it is customary for young women to consider their answer.' He spoke hurriedly, as if pursued. 'To keep men in suspense for days or even weeks. I tell you, I cannot endure it. Speak now. Send me away with a word if you will, and I shall leave Bath tomorrow and never inconvenience you with my addresses again.'

'No!' Jane could not help herself. Still she watched the fire-eater. She did not dare to look at William Harris, or she knew she would be lost. Every prudent instinct urged delay, but more instincts than prudent ones were engaged and had long been working within her, body and soul.

'You don't want me to go, then?'

'No.'

The fire-eater brought the flaming brand closer and closer to his face. The crowd hissed in anticipation of agony.

'Tell me you will marry me, Jane. Look at me, now!'

Jane could not withhold her gaze any longer. She turned to look up at him. His dark eyes blazed with reflected heat, shrivelling her hesitation. She felt herself caught, hypnotised, melting, liquefying in his fierce regard. 'Very well,' she said weakly. 'I will marry you, if I can.'

The fire-eater's lips approached the flame: his mouth opened; the fire was swallowed, the crowd groaned in disbelief, admiration and horror.

'If you can? What does that mean, Jane?'

'If I am permitted – allowed—'

'Of course I shall solicit the permission of your parents

and, in the first instance, apply to Sir Thomas for his agreement to visit you in his daughter's house.'

'Oh no – at least, not yet.'

'When, then?'

'Give him time – time to recover from his journey. Give me time. I must speak to him first. He must not be surprised suddenly by this.' Her instinct now was to break away. 'I must go. I must not be late.'

He nodded. She backed away, then tore herself free of his mesmerising gaze and ran back through the darkening streets. The crowd behind her broke into loud applause which sounded, for an instant, like gunfire.

She arrived to find the drawing-room full of young friends of Eliza and Henry. They were all playing at Blind Man's Buff.

'Ah, Jane!' cried Henry. 'Come on, you must join us for the more the merrier you know, in this game.'

She had met the young people before. The dark Frances was there, whom Mary feared as a rival, then there were brothers called Christopher and James Stevenson, two more young ladies whom Jane remembered vaguely as the Misses Young and the sandy-haired gentleman she had danced with at the ball, whose name she had absolutely forgotten.

She was so bewildered by what had just passed between herself and William Harris that she was very easily drawn into the game, for her secret was so momentous and so completely unmentionable that it reduced her to numbness and paralysis. Henry took her hand and drew her into the middle of the room. Eliza threw a scarf across her eyes, Henry bound it tight, seized her arms and spun her about.

She rocked wildly for a moment, then steadied herself. It was only a game, and a harmless one. Yet there was something so very unnerving about it that she heartily wished she had gone straight up to her room instead of joining the riotous company here. But there was nothing for it: she must oblige her hosts. Even now Henry was calling at her from different parts of the room, disguising his voice and darting about to perplex her.

Groping helplessly, she edged forward, struck her knee on a piece of furniture and exclaimed in pain. There was a great outburst of laughter and the noise, the calls and the rustle and thud of moving bodies, seemed rather to increase than diminish. It rocked about her ears. No doubt some foolery was being enacted by Henry. There was something horrible about being deprived of her sight. The voices seemed mocking; the drawing-room, normally so comfortable, full of danger and injury.

Jane reached out and caught somebody. The shrieks of laughter increased for an instant, then the company fell silent, watching and waiting for her guess. Warm hands closed over hers: a man's hands, a touch she seemed to know, but completely unexpected. A familiar scent reached her nostrils, the smell of somebody's skin, bringing with it a sense of calmness and safety.

'You're Sir Thomas,' she said. 'But you can't be, for he's not home yet.'

There was a general cry of triumph, a gentle hand removed her blindfold and there before her stood Sir Thomas indeed, looking very pleased to have been recognised. He must have come into the room after she had been blindfolded.

'I came back a day early.' He smiled. 'Particularly to vex you. You are looking well, my dear.' She flushed in confusion. He leaned forward and kissed her on the cheek. She was glad to experience once again his clean, manly smell. He cocked his head on one side and looked appraisingly at her, as if something new had come to his attention. 'And now tell me, my dear Jane – for you have been sorely missed – where have you been all afternoon?'

12

'Jane has taken holy orders, Father, since you have been away!' cried Henry. 'She is out every afternoon, praying for our souls, and we are very grateful for it, too, for we are all poor sinners, aren't we, Eliza?'

Sir Thomas went on smiling, but the light in his eyes dimmed a little, like a candle that has felt a sudden draught. 'You should let Jane tell me herself what she has been doing,' he rebuked his son. 'Come, Jane – let us go to the library and seek refuge from this bear garden.'

Jane followed him, her spirits sinking at every step. Here was an immediate opportunity to tell him of William Harris's offer of marriage. It was an opportunity she would willingly have postponed.

Why could not Sir Thomas have come home a day late instead of a day early? Why could not his coach have stuck in the mud somewhere in wildest Berkshire? Oh, that he had found it necessary to spend a night in an inn somewhere, and it had snowed overnight and Sir Thomas had been obliged to spend a week or two in idleness, royally entertained, of course, and fortified with as much roast goose and plum pudding as he could desire, but detained nevertheless.

But here he was, inconveniently before her, looking kind and friendly but not to be denied. Within an hour of receiving William Harris's astonishing proposal she found she must give an account of herself to her host, before she had had time to digest the remarkable events herself.

'So, Jane, how have you been amusing yourself?'

In her extraordinary state of sensitivity the question seemed barbed. It was implied that the pursuit of amusement was appropriate for her sex and age, anything more serious perhaps not. 'I have been amusing myself very much with Henry and Eliza. Amusement, in Henry's company, is unavoidable.'

He smiled, nodded and stirred the fire. 'I hope he's not been too excitable. Henry's high spirits can be irritating sometimes.'

'Oh no. It is understandable – he has been away at sea for so long, after all.'

He waited for a moment. She looked at the fire. 'And what about your soul, my dear?' Jane was silent, and started to tremble. 'Don't be afraid.' Sir Thomas smiled gently. 'There is nothing whatever to feel guilty about in a devout disposition. Good Lord! We have always been an exuberant family, not much given to contemplation and prayer, but do not think I will chide you for being differently inclined. You should rather chastise me, perhaps, for my neglect of spiritual matters.'

Jane was more grateful than she could express for this sympathetic encouragement. Sir Thomas had a way of making hard things easy. 'I confess', she murmured, 'I've been attending meetings in Pomfret Street, where Mr Harris lives with his sister.'

'Mr Harris? I don't think I've had the pleasure of meeting the gentleman.'

Jane was embarrassed. It had been wrong of her to associate so regularly with people unknown to her host. Sir Thomas stood in the office of a father to her here, in the absence of her own parents. She had taken advantage of his being away. 'I'm very sorry I could not introduce them to you,' she apologised. 'They are very good people. They think only of helping others, in practical ways as well as spiritual ones.'

'Mr Harris is the Evangelist whom you heard preach, I recall?'

'Yes. He ... he is.' Jane attempted to say more, but quailed before Sir Thomas's hard look.

'Now, Jane.' He sighed and shook his head in an affectionate manner. 'You know I can never be cross with you. I'm only a little concerned. These people are good people, you are right. But enthusiasm of their sort can sometimes lead to all sorts of excesses.'

'Excesses? I should think that their beliefs would lead to the opposite of excess.'

'There can be an excess of austerity, which is as dangerous and as damaging as an excess of self-indulgence.'

Jane smiled timidly. 'I think you will find that I still enjoy life, Sir Thomas, as you would have me do.'

'I'm heartily glad to hear it. I want you to enjoy everything. Not just what God has made, but what man has contrived too. Music, you know, and apple pie. Dancing and ear-rings, and so on.'

'Oh, I do! I promise you!'

Behind her reassurances, however, was the horrible obstacle of her engagement to William Harris – although to describe it as such, even in her private imagination, seemed curious and extraordinary. She was beginning to feel she would not manage to mention it to Sir Thomas on this occasion, and her cowardice and dread seemed to hang in her heart like lead.

Sir Thomas searched in his waistcoat pocket and brought out a small box. He looked up at her, awkward for a moment. 'I've taken the liberty of bringing you something from London – a trifle, I have similar knick-knacks for all the girls – if you don't like them, you need never wear them.' He held out a small box to her.

Jane was very surprised and touched; took it, opened it and found an exquisite pair of pearl ear-rings. 'Oh, how beautiful!' she exclaimed. 'But how kind, how exceedingly generous of you, Sir Thomas. Thank you so much. You are too good.'

He waved away her thanks, looking embarrassed. For the first time in all their acquaintance she saw him blush. 'If they are not to your taste, then give them away, my dear – or sell 'em and give the money to the poor, or what you will.'

Jane wanted to put them on immediately, but there was no looking-glass in the library and the fastenings proved difficult. Sir Thomas offered to help and came across to join her on the sofa. Soon the operation was gently accomplished and the ear-rings in place.

Sir Thomas leaned back a little to admire the effect. 'Very pretty.' He seemed satisfied. 'What dear little ears you have, Jane. I have never noticed them before.' Gently he touched them for a moment with his fingertips. 'I hope these little ears never have to convey cruel words to you,' said Sir Thomas soberly. 'May they bring you nothing but delight.'

Jane wished she could reciprocate the sentiment, but she knew that all too soon Sir Thomas's ears must be assailed with news that would prove at the very least alarming and almost certainly unwelcome. She could not bear to tell him now, though, in the happy glow of his return, with her new pearl ear-rings so lustrous in the firelight, so she confined herself to asking him what he had most enjoyed in London, and they talked about bookshops and coffee houses until it was time to prepare for supper.

Jane was sure she would get no sleep at all that night. Mary was restless too. Long after the candle was blown out Jane heard her sister's wakeful sighing. 'Are you all right, Mary?' she enquired in a whisper.

'Oh Jane! I can't sleep at all! It's Henry – I don't know what to think. He seems to pay me the greatest possible attention, he is all compliments and extravagance, talks like the most passionate lover that ever was, but never commits himself to anything like a serious declaration. It's such agony.'

'I shouldn't take it too seriously if I were you,' warned

Jane, remembering Henry's words to herself on many occasions. 'I'm afraid he might be the sort of fellow who likes to tease every girl he meets with flirtation and admiration. Don't let your head be turned by it.'

'Oh Jane! How can you be so cruel! Just because you are not in love you disapprove of my feelings for Henry. That horrid Evangelism has made you want to spoil everything.'

'Not at all!' cried Jane indignantly. 'I wish, for your sake, Henry would declare himself in a way which would set your mind at rest. I merely want to warn you against too active expectations, for I should hate above all things to see you disappointed, dear.'

'You don't think he loves me!' Mary buried her face in the pillow and shed a few bitter tears. Jane comforted her, and found some relief for herself in the act and in sharing Mary's apprehensions. It was an escape from her own continual anxiety about her engagement, which she knew she could not long conceal.

At breakfast next day Jane found a letter beside her place.

'It's a billet-doux, young Jane!' cried Henry with a mischievous grin. 'It was delivered this morning by hand, but nobody saw the messenger – mysterious! We've been in a frenzy of speculation about it – pray open it instantly, and put us out of our agony.'

Jane felt the eyes of all the company on her. She did not recognise the handwriting, but felt no impulse to open it. She would rather have cast it on the fire. It must be from William Harris or his sister – she knew nobody else in Bath who had reason to write.

'You must ignore my ruffian of a son, Jane.' Sir Thomas spoke from the end of the table. 'Pray be so kind as to open your letter after breakfast in private. And you, Sir, mend your manners, or I shall be out of temper with you.' Sir Thomas rose and walked out. Henry looked uneasy at his father's rebuke and confined himself for the next half-hour to sucking at sugar-lumps.

Jane could neither eat nor drink. Mary managed little better and it was left to George Fortescue to devour the necessary quantity of eggs, cold ham and bread and butter, which would convince the servants it had been worth setting the table.

After breakfast Jane went straight to her room and opened the letter. The script was stiff and the ink very black. It was a bleak two sentences only: 'Have you informed Sir Thomas yet? I would visit him as soon as possible. W.H.' The effect of this communication was to increase her sense of dread and she decided she could not put off speaking any longer. She walked to Sir Thomas's library, found him alone and requested an interview.

The formality of her demeanour aroused his suspicions, which had already been alerted by the arrival of the letter. He sat opposite her and looked, to Jane, more dreadfully serious than she had ever seen him. For a moment she could not speak. Her hands shook.

'Come, Jane,' he said gently. 'You know I can't be cross with you. I said so yesterday. Something is troubling you and I can't help until I know what it is.'

'While ... while you were away ...' she began quaveringly, 'I did see Mr William Harris every day ... and his sister of course ... and formed a—' Her voice quailed into silence.

'An attachment?' He seemed to pounce on the notion and sat very still, his eyes glittering in alarm.

'Yes.'

Sir Thomas grew pale. Jane struggled to find words which might reassure him – and perhaps also herself.

'Although I would not describe it as an attachment, exactly ... I was most surprised, however ... because, yesterday, Mr Harris made me an offer of marriage. Which I accepted.'

Sir Thomas gasped in amazement. 'Surely not! I've not been away above a fortnight.'

'I ... was myself astonished at the suddenness of his application.'

'But you accepted?'

'I did.' She was shaking all over.

Sir Thomas looked appalled, agitated. He sprang up and walked about the room. 'But why, Jane? Why the need for such haste?'

'I ... don't know.'

'I'm very displeased with Mr Harris. Very displeased indeed. Profiting by my absence ... but I am much more displeased with myself. I left you unguarded! Vulnerable ... helpless ... how could you know what conduct was appropriate? Eleanor has been very negligent too. And George. I cannot forgive them. But above all I can't forgive myself. We have conspired to expose you to an extraordinary danger. I – I hardly know what to say.' He paused at the far end of the room, and looked at her with such pain she could not bear it.

'I must take some blame, surely!' she cried out. 'I went there freely, I was not ... practised upon in any way. I admit I was astonished at his offer of marriage—'

'Why accept it, then?' cried Sir Thomas accusingly.

Jane felt all her resolution gone. Dear Sir Thomas, who had always been so kind, was looking at her now in anger and bewilderment. She burst into tears.

Instantly he was at her side, offering his handkerchief, pressing her hand. 'My dear, don't upset yourself. I'm only a little alarmed and surprised ... I'm at a loss, myself, I confess ... this is so altogether unexpected. But come, Jane, come.' With a great effort he seemed to compose his spirits. 'This announcement of yours is not a tragic one, after all. It must mean you are in love and that is the greatest happiness life can bring.'

He was silent for a moment, appearing to contemplate his memories. Then his attention returned to her. Jane sniffed and wiped her eyes.

'I suppose you must be very happy indeed, my dear.' His expression was distant and controlled. 'And I rejoice for you.'

'I suppose I must be happy,' faltered Jane. 'But I confess that since Mr Harris's proposal I have felt more anxiety and distress than anything else. I dreaded having to tell you, and as for my parents . . .' Her voice tailed off in perplexity.

'I must admit I am also most anxious at the thought of confronting your father.' Sir Thomas sighed. 'He will think me very negligent, I'm sure. But we must go back to Ottercombe as soon as we can arrange it. Anything else would be unforgivable.

'First, however, I must meet your Mr Harris. And believe me, my dear, if he is half the man he ought to be, I shall be your most ardent ambassador with your parents. I could not bear to see you unhappy. Indeed . . .' He got up and walked to the window, turning his back on her. '. . . any man who has shown the good taste and judgement to fall in love with you must be an excellent fellow.'

He fell silent for a while, looking out at the street. Jane wondered if she ought to say something, but did not know how to begin. She suspected that anything she ventured to say about William Harris would sound foolish.

'Tell me.' Sir Thomas had been struck by a thought. 'Mr Harris preaches a great deal, I believe, up and down the country? Where does he live exactly?'

Jane was suddenly stunned by her complete ignorance of her fiancé's life. 'I believe he does travel a lot.' Her voice had sunk to a breath. She ignored Sir Thomas's second question.

He turned from the window and looked at her with a strange, sad expression. 'And will you accompany him on his travels, do you think?'

'I – I have not thought of it yet. I suppose I shall.'

Sir Thomas looked soberly at the carpet, gave a long sigh that was almost a shudder and moved towards the door. 'Come then, Jane,' he said. 'Let us meet the gentleman.'

13

Sir Thomas declared he would call on William Harris alone, and after the necessary preparations he left the house, watched by Jane from an upstairs window. She spent the next half-hour anxiously pacing about her room, returning every minute to stare down at the street corner around which Sir Thomas must reappear.

Eliza, Mary and Henry had gone out for a walk, Eleanor was asleep, her husband out. The house was empty, which Jane felt as a relief, for she could hardly have spoken a coherent sentence to anybody, so great was her agitation. At last Sir Thomas appeared, looking perhaps a little paler than usual, though quite composed, and walking at his usual moderate pace.

As he drew near the house, he looked up at Jane's window and smiled. Relief poured into Jane's heart. He must have found Mr Harris at least tolerable, then. She had been entirely unable to imagine the slightest detail of their meeting – but then, she could scarcely remember what William Harris looked like, though it was not twenty-four hours since she had seen him.

She ran out of her room and met Sir Thomas on the stairs.

'Come into the library, Jane,' he said, not unkindly. They went in. Jane longed for reassurance, but Sir Thomas was distracted for a moment. 'The fire is gone out. Shall we go into the drawing-room?'

'No, no!' cried Jane. 'It doesn't matter – I'm not in the least cold.' She was shivering, but with apprehension.

'Well, my dear, the confidential part of our conversation can be concluded very quickly, then we can send for some tea in the drawing-room and play with young Thomas by the fire.'

Jane nodded, hardly hearing any word that was not connected to the subject of her anxiety.

'Your Mr Harris is indeed a handsome gentleman,' Sir Thomas began. 'It was interesting for me to observe the looks, and the manners, capable of captivating you. You are captivated, I take it?'

Jane could only blush and wince. Sir Thomas understood this was not a moment for teasing and perhaps did not quite have the stomach for it himself.

'And beyond his looks and bearing, his character suggests nothing, upon first acquaintance, to which your father might object. He is of course a distinguished man in his own calling, though I've not had the pleasure of hearing him preach. As to his position, his means, what he will find possible to offer you in the way of an establishment, well, that is for him to discuss with your parents. I've invited him and his sister to sup with us tonight. His sister begs to be excused, as she has a cold, but Mr Harris was glad to accept.'

'Thank you.' Jane was grateful for Sir Thomas's hospitality, but she anticipated the supper with dread as well as longing.

'I shall introduce him to my family as my guest and your friend. It would not be appropriate to make any mention of an engagement until the matter has been fully settled with your parents.'

'Of course.'

'So, my dear, if you would be good enough to go and ask for some tea in the drawing-room, I'll join you there in twenty minutes. I need a few moments to myself here first – some business to attend to—' He looked away to the papers on his desk, then dismissed her with a smile. There was something strained and preoccupied in his manner, however. His usual warmth was not extended to her.

Jane left the room feeling chilled and sought the comforts of fire and tea with eagerness. The drawing-room was empty and she waited for Sir Thomas with increasingly turbulent thoughts. The tea arrived, but still her host did not appear. She knew she had caused him some distress and difficulty, and the torture of this regret quite obliterated all pleasant thoughts.

She felt she had not said nearly enough to Sir Thomas by way of apology for her conduct and thanks for his forbearance and support, but he did not arrive to afford her the opportunity to make amends. Instead, her painful solitude was shattered by the noisy arrival of Eliza, Mary and Henry, bearing a bag of chestnuts to be roasted on the fire.

Sir Thomas kept to his library. He did, however, appear in time to receive William Harris for supper. The significance of William Harris's visit did not escape Henry's playful suspicions. He had spent much of his afternoon walk assuring Mary that her sister was in love with the preacher and Mary had laughed off his theories as wild imaginings.

When William Harris was announced and walked into the room, there was a sudden excited silence. Everybody but Jane looked at him with avid curiosity. She fixed her eyes on Sir Thomas's face. She hoped to discern there some clue as to his opinion of the man who had offered to marry her, but she saw nothing except perfect civility.

Even after all the necessary introductions had been made, Jane could not find the courage to look at their visitor. Instead she caught Henry's mischievous eye and could only look away in confusion.

'Well, Mr Harris, you are quite a traveller, I believe – on the circuit? Do you enjoy it? Or do you nurse a secret ambition for a more fixed existence in due course?' Sir Thomas floated the first mild enquiry towards his guest. It was a question of thistledown ease and airiness, but having a deeper purpose, which Jane instantly understood.

She felt a curious sense of anticipation, realising that Sir Thomas had the courage, confidence and skill to ask the questions she had never dared to frame.

'Nothing is more congenial to the human mind than variety,' said William Harris, looking round the company with a slightly more nervous and subdued air than he brought to the pulpit. He found responsive and receptive faces here, however, for everybody in the room who was seeing him for the first time was thinking what a fine-looking man he was and all but one were wondering what it could possibly be about Jane which had caught his attention.

As for Jane herself, she was beginning to think she might soon find the courage to look into his face, especially if his voice acquired its usual confident ring. Her eyes had crawled, so far, across the Turkey carpet, recognised with a shock of veneration the shine of his black boots and had dared to come to rest on his knees. She found herself quite surprised that he had knees at all and curiously intrigued by the idea. Evidently he had hitherto hovered somewhat in her imagination. This evidence of his ordinary humanity was welcome.

'Variety is not only pleasing to the eye, but healthy and wholesome to the spirit,' he went on and for an instant Jane was alarmed lest he should launch into a sermon, when mere conversation was all that was required. 'I admit I find the ever-changing vistas of the English countryside refreshing and delightful.'

'Ah, that's true! But where do you regard as home?' enquired Sir Thomas. 'I've enjoyed Bath, but I'm beginning to pine for Ottercombe. Do you pine for anywhere, Mr Harris? Where were you born?'

'I was born in Buckinghamshire. A village called Newton Longville.'

'And do you go there still?'

'Occasionally. My parents are dead, but my brother and sisters still live nearby.'

'And how many brothers and sisters have you?'

'An older brother and three sisters. My eldest sister you have met, Sir Thomas: she accompanies me on the circuit. My two younger sisters are married.'

Sir Thomas waited for further details of Mr Harris's family, but none were offered. 'Well, Sir,' he observed, 'you are free to choose an abode from whatever part of the English countryside offers most refreshment and delight. Where do you think you would choose to live?'

'The appearance of the countryside, though beautiful, could never prove a compelling enough reason for me to make my home in it.' William Harris shook his head. 'I am alas required, by reason of my calling, to think first of what is most convenient in relation to the circuit. Bath and Bristol, for the present, are the places to which I most frequently retire, but I have no fixed habitation.'

'Ah, but my question was, where you would choose to live,' repeated Sir Thomas with a gentle but persistent emphasis.

William Harris thought for a moment. 'Tahiti,' he pronounced at length.

At which Henry, who was stifling a yawn, sat bolt upright and cried out, 'But that is the other side of the earth! Beyond Cornwall, beyond America – why, it would take a lifetime to get there. And then you would be eaten by savages.'

Sir Thomas silenced his son with a gesture. 'Why . . .' He hesitated, casting a swift and most perturbed look at Jane. 'Why Tahiti?'

'The London Missionary Society has just determined the parts of the world most in need of my sort of work. Tahiti is the furthest off.'

'And do you have active plans to go there?' asked Sir Thomas, quite pale.

'Not at present. For the next two years, at least, I shall confine myself to Gloucestershire, Somerset and Devon.'

Sir Thomas was obliged to consider this a reassuring answer.

At length they went in to supper, though Jane could eat very little. She was hoping to hear more of her suitor's revelations about his family and his ideas, but in the event Sir Thomas left off his interrogation and, avoiding the contentious subjects of religion and politics and trying without success to stimulate a discussion about dogs and horses, was compelled at length to talk about the weather at far greater length than he would have chosen.

The rest of the company could not be for ever constrained. Eliza, Mary and Henry began to carve out, with Eleanor's assistance, a glittering vein of gossip at the far end of the table. Sir Thomas and William Harris were joined in their meditations upon the British climate by Jane and George Fortescue, though Jane was mortified to discover that several times in the midst of one of William Harris's observations her sister and her friends could be heard clearly in sensational speculation, at the other end of the table, about the nature of Lady Oldfield's relations with her footman.

It seemed to Jane that her friends' conversation would offend her fiancé and that his serious thoughts might appear too ponderous for them. Sir Thomas was managing somehow to steer a laborious course towards the beckoning shore of ten o'clock, a time when supper guests might feel it appropriate to tear themselves away. Jane dreaded that William Harris might find her host's family wanting in some way and that Sir Thomas was not able to perceive William Harris's exceptional qualities.

Above all, she lamented the fact that she appeared herself unable to make any contribution to the conversation beyond the most vague acquiescence. She seemed quite blank and dumb. But then, it was bound to be an uncomfortable occasion, she supposed. Eventually, at half-past nine, William Harris made his farewells, but Jane felt as completely exhausted as if it had been one o'clock in the morning. Sitting still and saying nothing had proved infinitely more tiring than dancing.

Not wishing to hear the remarks of Eliza and Eleanor, or receive the impertinent conjectures and teases of Henry, she fled immediately to her own room and walked about a while, finding some release in exercise. At this moment, surveying the evening which she had just endured, she realised that William Harris had hardly looked at her or addressed a single word to her. On the whole she was glad he had not. In fact, it struck her that this had been a considerate neglect on his part. He must have known the agitation into which she would have been thrown by having any attention paid to her. He had seemed, however, in his public behaviour as remote as possible from the awkward, ardent creature he had proved in private. She found this unnerving, but exciting too, and longed all the more urgently to be with him again alone.

First, however, there was a knock on her door. Sir Thomas appeared, though he came but a pace or two into the room. 'My dear,' he said, 'you must be tired. I won't detain you. I merely wished to confide to you my decision to take you home to Ottercombe and your parents so soon as it may be arranged. The day after tomorrow, if possible. This business is more properly theirs to consider. I confess it is beyond me. I bid you good-night.' He bowed and was gone.

14

The next day was given over to a frenzy of packing and correspondence. Letters were sent to Ottercombe to inform Jane's parents that their daughters would be returning on the morrow, and Sir Thomas's own establishment had to be alerted to prepare for their master. William Harris wrote a civil note to thank Sir Thomas for his hospitality the previous night, and Sir Thomas returned a line or two to report the departure for Ottercombe, and to suppose that Mr Harris would wish to make his own way thither and to call on the Lockharts at Newington House at the earliest opportunity.

Jane was racked with numberless torments. One of the most immediate was her regret that she had caused her sister to be snatched away from the pleasures of Bath, when she might have expected several more weeks of diversion.

'Oh, no, Jane,' Mary assured her, folding up her garments with energy, 'I am quite ready to go, for Henry is coming back with us, you know, and at Ottercombe I hope I shall see a great deal of him without having to worry about the dark Frances and those other pretty girls he danced with at the ball. Jealousy is such a torment! I wish it could be surgically removed.'

Jane was relieved, therefore, of any anxieties on her sister's account, but her chief dread was the certainty of her father's disapproval. If the tolerant and agreeable Sir

Thomas was perturbed by her engagement to William Harris, how much more pained would be Mr Lockhart's reaction. She shivered in terror all the way home in the coach, could not listen to Eliza and Mary's talk and was exceedingly disappointed that Sir Thomas was riding back separately, for she missed his friendly presence most acutely.

They arrived to find that their return could not have happened at a more inconvenient moment. Mrs Lockhart was still with her sister at Cheltenham, though her husband had sent word on receipt of Sir Thomas's letter to tell her the girls were coming home. More material to their physical comfort, the east window above the staircase had been taken out to make way for something altogether more grand. John Lockhart had not been able to resist the allure of his architect's ideas and had plunged into the works immediately, using the absence of his womenfolk as an excuse for undertaking now what might have been more suitably postponed till the summer.

March was quite turned topsy-turvy. Having come in like a lamb, it was now withdrawing with roaring winds which bowled up and down the hall, hoisting the builders' tarpaulins and bringing a most unwelcome sensation of indoors being outdoors. Jane fled, shivering, to the comfort of her own room, where Hetty had lit a fire, and looked out again at the familiar landscape.

It seemed more vast and sombre than ever after the cosy streets of Bath, and the wind, flying and crashing up the Severn estuary to the south, broke upon the face of the house with such vigour that the windows all rattled and the chimneys roared and whined like a pack of devils. The tumbling hillside seemed almost like a living thing, with the trees all bending and swaying, and small twigs thrown about by the gale.

Her own spirits were no less turbulent. Upon their arrival, Sir Thomas had requested a private interview with her father and they were closeted together in the drawing-room. Even now Sir Thomas was conveying, in terms of some disapproval she was sure, the news of William Harris's proposal. Suddenly she heard the front door slam in the wind. Sir Thomas must be gone, though the howling of the gale blotted out the sound of his chaise's wheels. She waited in quivering fear for her father's summons, and soon Hetty was at the door. Moments later she found herself before him.

'Well, Jane, you can imagine my surprise at Sir Thomas's news,' he said, though not as coldly as she had expected. He looked closely at her for a moment. 'You are looking well, my dear. Bath has given you a kind of bloom.' Jane could not have been more surprised. Here, instead of the expected rebuke, was something almost like a compliment. 'I shall be most interested to meet Mr Harris and so, I am sure, will your mother. No doubt we shall hear from him soon.'

This was all her father had to say on the subject. Jane went away extremely puzzled that Sir Thomas's anxieties had not been repeated, in a more severe form, by the father who hitherto had never seemed to do anything but find fault with her. John Lockhart was privately amazed by the turn of events, but not censorious. That William Harris had not won Sir Thomas's whole-hearted approval did not signify. It rather predisposed John Lockhart to think well of him.

He had just enjoyed a most curious interview in which Sir Thomas could not help appearing at a disadvantage. He had apologised for having been obliged to absent himself from Bath at the very time when an attachment was forming between Jane and William Harris. He blamed himself very much, and regretted the negligence of his daughter and her husband which had permitted the relationship to flourish without check.

Sir Thomas could only beg Mr Lockhart's indulgence and assure him there had been no real impropriety. Bible meetings might be thought a peculiar amusement for an attractive young lady at leisure in Bath, but they could never compromise a reputation and he understood that Miss Harris had always been present, as well as several others.

Mr Lockhart heard Sir Thomas's abject apologies and ominous conjectures with something like relish, and it was with a sort of triumph that he assured him there was no cause for alarm. Jane was at home now and whatever had been lacking in the proper supervision of her behaviour would be amended.

Thus elegantly rebuked, Sir Thomas had, it seemed to Mr Lockhart, slunk away into the stormy twilight, leaving the master of Newington House with more to admire than the gaping hole in his eastern elevation. He felt half inclined to bestow his blessing on the couple just to spite Sir Thomas.

Of course he was very curious to meet the man whom his daughter had managed to attract and not a little astonished that she had managed to attach anybody at all, for he had never thought his younger daughter handsome and had not supposed anyone else would either. The momentous nature of events drove him to a most unusual exercise. He walked down to the valley bottom and called in to see Humphrey Axton and his sister, for he wished to learn more about Evangelism in general and Mr Harris in particular.

His wife, returning the next day, was violently excited, though also somewhat perturbed at the speed with which matters had developed. Once she had recovered from her journey and spoken privately with her husband, she summoned Jane to her salon and as her daughter went in, Mrs Lockhart held out her arms. 'Give me a kiss, my dear.'

Jane embraced her mother heartily and joined her on the sofa.

Her mother took her hand and looked shrewdly into her face. 'Now, Jane, I know I often find fault with you, but I hope you understand you are very dear to me. Nothing is more important to me than my daughters' happiness. It would grieve me most cruelly to see you miserable, when I might have done or said something to prevent it.

'You're more like me than Mary is. She is a Lockhart: tall and timid. But you're a Fletcher, in temperament and looks as well. Indeed Aunt Harriet has often remarked that you greatly resemble Grandpapa.'

Mrs Lockhart paused for an instant, looking at her daughter. They were both thinking of bulldogs and feeling that a slightly less pronounced resemblance to Grandpapa might have been preferable.

'Still – we Fletchers are sociable, active people. We're affectionate and strong-willed. When I married . . .' She hesitated for a moment. '. . . I did not exactly understand my own nature. Nor did I have time to get to know Papa well enough. But never mind that. Is Mr Harris sociable?'

'He seems very much at ease in company.'

'Well, I suppose he must be – or he would not have chosen his profession. And do you feel at ease with him, Jane?'

'Not exactly, Mamma. I was surprised by his proposal. It was the last thing I was expecting.'

'He did not court you, then? He paid no attentions?'

'Not that I could recognise. He is always very serious.'

'He did not lavish you with compliments? Praise your looks and so forth?'

'Oh no. He has . . . praised my character though. He said I was the first woman to whom he could reveal himself.'

'He's not cold, is he, my dear? Haughty in his manner?'

'Not really. He's rather awkward when we're alone. He seems to be struggling with strong feelings.'

'That's good. Was his proposal . . . urgent?'

'Very much so. He said he could not bear any delay. He begged me to give him his answer at once and declared he could not even wait a few hours.'

'And where did this proposal take place? At the Fortescues' house?'

'No.' Jane blushed. 'In the street.' She expected censure,

but her mother appeared amused and reassured.

'And what are your feelings, my dear? Do you love him?'

'I think so. I respect and admire him very much. I can't stop thinking about him, and with great agitation, I confess, Mamma.'

'That's good, my dear. That's natural. Now, Papa and I have some other questions – Papa went down to the Axtons yesterday you know. He said he would join us at half-past three . . .'

Mrs Lockhart's quaint French clock struck the half hour and her husband's measured tread was heard on the stair. He knocked and entered with a reluctant and uneasy air.

'Well, Mr Lockhart,' his wife began, 'Jane has quite reassured me on every point regarding her feelings, and Mr Harris's conduct and so forth. His character suggests nothing to alarm us.'

'He's a serious gentleman, it seems,' mused her husband. 'Is that what you want, Jane? A serious man? You and Mary have always been very merry together.'

'I'd be glad of the chance of serious work,' said Jane immediately. 'I've always wanted to help the poor.'

'Yes, yes. You're different from Mary in that respect,' acknowledged her mother. 'Marriage to a clergyman might prove the very thing, I suppose. It would give you every opportunity to exercise your social conscience.'

'And quieten her wild excesses,' observed her father. 'Seriousness and composure are always preferable in ladies to loudness and hilarity.'

'Now tell us what the Axtons said,' commanded his wife.

'They are most impressed with Mr Harris. They have a common acquaintance or two and were able to reassure me as to his origins. He is a respectable man. He is the younger son of Mr Lawrence Harris who had a small estate in Buckinghamshire. Nothing significant. Modest but adequate.'

John Lockhart enjoyed the prospect of being able to patronise his son-in-law.

'An inclination towards Evangelism moreover is not confined to the lower orders. Humphrey Axton furnished me with countless examples of the gentry, and even the nobility, who have taken to it. Lord Wymondley, Sir James and Lady Newton, the Marquis of Dunstable ... It is not the same thing as Dissent, my dear. It's not to be confused with Methodism and the Baptists. The Evangelicals are still part of the Church of England, though they go their own way somewhat and preach in the fields and so on. But I'm persuaded it is an entirely elegant and even desirable conviction.'

'Well.' Mrs Lockhart sighed. 'My powers of speculation are quite exhausted. We must now meet Mr Harris, and as soon as possible. You may go, Jane.'

Jane escaped to her own room, leaving her parents to consider this sudden change in their circumstances.

Mrs Lockhart felt that so long as Mr Harris proved agreeable and respectable it would be a relief to have Jane settled. Mary would not mind. Indeed, Mary had already confessed to her mother that Henry Burton was very assiduous in his attentions and she expected a declaration at any time.

John Lockhart heard this news with alarm. It would irritate him very much to have one of his girls captured by the enemy, but his dislike of Sir Thomas was tempered by an awareness that his neighbour was a very wealthy man indeed and that his son's fortune must be considerable. He would prefer Mary to marry almost anyone else in the country of equivalent means, but he would reconcile himself to Henry Burton as a son-in-law rather than see Mary throw herself away on somebody without a fortune.

But it was Jane's destiny which intruded the more urgently on his attention. He was obliged to put Henry Burton to the back of his mind and concentrate on William Harris, who had requested an interview in a very fair hand upon good-quality paper and was therefore so far avoiding the disapproval which every hopeful suitor dreads.

Mr Harris had taken lodgings in Woolton, where he often stayed when preaching on 7the circuit. It was but a short step up Blackthorn Hill to Newington House – a trifle for a strong young man accustomed to walking. John Lockhart would have preferred Jane's suitor to arrive in his own carriage, but in truth he would have been grateful for any respectable man who would take Jane off his hands, and when William Harris arrived, the exertion of the climb up from Woolton had transformed his habitual pallor to a healthy glow and his usual good looks were elevated into something quite magnificent.

John Lockhart was astonished and his wife ravished by this example of masculine beauty. They were particularly reassured by his long white hands, which bore no unpleasant calluses or other signs of manual toil. They admired Mr Harris's flawlessly aristocratic appearance, elegant manners and mellifluous voice. Jane waited in her room while her parents were solicited by Mr Harris. There was the business of an establishment to discuss, which presented some difficulty owing to Mr Harris's itinerant habits. Although he was not a man of great property, however, there was no suggestion of real want, and he assured Mr and Mrs Lockhart that though he could never hope to offer Jane a home to equal Newington House she would never be uncomfortable.

Mrs Lockhart had always felt her daughter unequal to the demands of a great house and considered Jane might be happier in a more modest establishment. The difficulty of settling upon a place was resolved by John Lockhart's recollection that a trim Gothic lodge by the gates of his park had fallen vacant and, though rather small, might prove an acceptable home in the first instance.

Mr Harris liked the idea of his wife's being accommodated so near to her family, for it would prove convenient if he was obliged to go off on a preaching tour, leaving her behind. He was eager to ingratiate himself with the Lockharts, moreover, hoping by degrees to be able to influence the practice of Mrs Lockhart's religious beliefs, and perhaps also those of her friends and relations.

Mrs Lockhart confided the details of the agreement to Jane the moment she found her. 'And now, my dear, I'm sure Mr Harris would like to take a turn about the garden – show him the cliff walk where the ferns grow – that is a romantic prospect, to be sure. Oh! He is so very handsome! I declare, I'm quite envious of you, Jane! You've done very well, my dear, very well indeed.'

Jane ran downstairs with a thudding heart and was summoned by her father into the drawing-room. Mr Harris stood against the window which, facing west, was now ablaze with afternoon light. This threw his face into shadow – though she had not the courage, in any case, to look at him yet.

Her father was smiling at her – a most curious and unusual sight. 'I'm glad to inform you, my dear,' he pronounced, 'that Mr Harris's application for your hand has been happily accepted.'

Jane was seized by a sudden idea that good humour did not really suit her father's face and made him look almost as if he were going to sneeze. This notion, together with an acute sense of embarrassment, forced her somehow into a strange laugh, like a bark. Words, however, forsook her.

'You see, Mr Harris,' observed Mr Lockhart, shaking his head affectionately, 'Jane has never been one for fine speeches, but I think we may assume that our deliberations bring her pleasure.'

'Oh, yes, Papa!' exclaimed Jane, paralysed with self-conscious pleasure. 'I'm sorry. I was so agitated—'

'There, my dear. Take Mr Harris for a turn about the park and compose your spirits. You shall be married as soon as you like.'

Mr Lockhart favoured the idea of an early marriage. He was always eager to anticipate any agitating event, to encounter it and overcome it as soon as possible. This anxiety had led him to take his breakfast earlier and earlier, first at nine o'clock, then at eight, till at his present stage of life he broke his fast at half-past six, in order that he should not be horribly surprised and inconvenienced by the sudden arrival of breakfast later.

At least daughters only marry once, he mused, and was also comforted by the thought that he only had two of them. This reflection led him to produce the most benign smile of which he was capable. Jane escaped to put on her cloak, took Mr Harris's offered arm and led him out on to the terrace.

The wind had dropped. The air was mild and the smell of the earth was spreading from the flower-beds, where daffodils were now opening, and shoots and buds pushing up in crowds. The terrace of Newington House offered one of the finest views in the south of England and William Harris was not slow to admire it.

'Oh yes!' cried Jane. 'If I'm ever angry or upset, this landscape always has the power to compose my spirits.'

Her companion was silent for a moment. They strolled along the grassy path. 'I hope, my dear Jane, that you will not be angry or upset ever again,' he said at last.

She felt a rush of affection at this sign of tender regard and looked up joyfully into his face, but he was admiring the western prospect, where a gigantic cedar tree spread its strength.

'I'm sure I'm the happiest girl in the world,' she said, though immediately regretted her naïve enthusiasm.

'Can we go down there?' William Harris was attracted by the idea of seeing the cliff from below.

Jane conducted him down a path she had often used and they found themselves immediately in a glade, where hundreds of daffodils, protected from the north winds, were blazing beneath the beech trees. 'I love this walk,' she sighed. 'The trees – the shrubs – it is all so exuberant. Nature in all its wildness, rioting free.'

'Indeed. There are plants here I have never seen before.'

'We have a kitchen garden lower down, by the lake. Come. I'll show you the little plum tree.'

They made their way down a mazy path, and came out suddenly into a clearing with a view of the lake and the pasture beyond. The cattle were out there, and Jane and Mr Harris paused to admire the vista.

'Look at that!' exclaimed Mr Harris. 'That is indeed a ravishing prospect.'

A few seconds after he spoke the great bull suddenly mounted one of the heifers and soberly but effectively performed his duty. Mr Harris turned from the scene immediately and walked on. Jane followed, longing for him to say something. Any observations at all would be welcome. But her fiancé seemed so disconcerted by the behaviour of the cattle that he did not make any remark for quite twenty minutes.

William Harris found his tongue at last, but only to suggest that it was getting cold and it might be prudent to return to the house. They did so, and a supper was then enjoyed with every appearance of contentment by all parties. Jane kept admiring the idea of her engagement to William Harris. Only the extraordinary sight of him talking to her father and mother, and looks at once tender and satirical on Mary's part, convinced her that it was not some delirious dream of hers, but a reality of which she would soon enjoy substantial proof. 'I am going to marry him,' she whispered to herself. But still it seemed more like the ravings of a lunatic than the delightful consciousness of a rational soul.

15

A wedding at the end of April seemed possible and Mr
Harris made no difficulties about the time and place. It was
decided that the ceremony would be conducted in his
church down at Woolton. The small Saxon church at
Ottercombe was closely associated in Mr Lockhart's mind
with Sir Thomas's grand establishment which stood next to
it. By holding the ceremony in Woolton, the Lockharts
pleased Mr Harris exceedingly and retained for themselves
all the happiness of presiding.

Sir Thomas and his family would be welcome guests, of
course, but no more than that. If Jane had married in
Ottercombe Church there would have been in her father's
imagination an uneasy sense that his daughter was marrying in Sir Thomas's private chapel.

In any case, the wedding party could hardly have been
accommodated within the few square yards of old flagstones at Ottercombe. Mrs Lockhart had seized the occasion with all the determination of a sociable nature denied
its proper exercise for many years. Her husband dared not
cross her. Besides, he wished to show off his new east window to as many friends and relations as possible.

Building work was conducted with renewed speed and
milder weather arrived to end the sufferings of the family.
Mrs Lockhart, however, was almost too busy to notice
whether her house had a hole in its side or not. There were
guests to invite, hospitality to arrange, a feast to plan and

everybody's clothes to agonise over. For the first time in her life Jane felt she had made her parents really happy.

'What are you going to wear, Jane?' asked Mary eagerly. They were walking on the terrace in the sunshine with Henry and Eliza. Jane was startled. She had not given the matter any thought and confessed as much.

'Oh Jane, you're such a fool! I suppose you'd just as soon marry in breeches, and then we'd have to guess which was the bride and which the groom.'

'Wear lace!' cried Miss Eliza, whose taste was elaborate. 'Nothing is more romantic or becoming.'

'Jane is above such things.' Henry grinned. 'Don't mention romance, Eliza. It is an indecent idea. She will marry in an old calico gown and rush off straight after the ceremony to take soup to the starving.'

'But seriously, Jane, you must have some opinion,' persisted Mary. She seemed peculiarly excited by the idea of Jane's marriage, for secretly she considered it almost a dress rehearsal for her own. She was expecting a declaration from Henry any day. 'What is Mr Harris's taste? I suppose he would prefer something plain.'

'I suppose he would. Or he would never have proposed to me in the first place.' Jane's anxious joke betrayed a heart still very puzzled by the enigmas of Mr Harris's character.

'Nonsense! I'm sick of telling you you're not plain. If you were, please explain how such a very handsome man as Mr Harris has chosen you?'

'It's a mystery,' confessed Jane, trying to sound light-hearted.

'No mystery at all!' cried Henry. 'There are no two prettier girls in the south of England than Jane and Mary Lockhart.'

'What about the north?' cried Mary in alarm. 'This is hardly a compliment.'

'And what about me?' exclaimed Miss Eliza petulantly. 'I'm not pretty at all, I suppose.'

'Yes, yes, Eliza,' Henry pacified her with an elaborate

show of fatigue. 'I know I must say you're the most beautiful girl in the whole of Europe, or you'll tear my head off.'

'This is a warning to you to avoid compliments,' said Jane.

'No, Jane. I'm quite determined. You and your sister combine all the female graces one could desire. Mary is tall and fair; you are dark and comely. I only detest Mr Harris for presuming to steal one vision of loveliness from my side and replace her with a matron in a Methodist cap.'

'Shall you have to wear a cap, Jane?' asked Mary anxiously. 'I don't quite like them, you know. They make a woman look a little too much like a Chinese tea-caddy.'

'Mr Harris is not a Methodist, only an Evangelical,' argued Jane, tiring of this teasing. 'I don't care whether I wear a cap or not. What does it matter?'

'Indeed, what does it matter?' agreed Henry. 'As long as Mr Harris adores you. I think you would wear a milk-churn on your head if it inflamed his desire.'

Jane ignored this remark, and tried to take pleasure in the strengthening sunshine and glowing clouds. They were walking now through a glade leading to a ruined folly which guarded the western borders of Mr Lockhart's domain. About a hundred yards short of it they found a rustic seat carved from a fallen oak, from which a wide and airy view could be enjoyed.

The lake glittered below them in the spring sunshine; the willows glowed with strong new colour. As they watched, they saw the farmer driving some beasts from the pasture below the lake into a further field. Jane remembered Mr Harris's embarrassment on the occasion of their walk and felt disturbed by it.

'So tell us, Jane, what's he like?' Eliza could not resist any longer the promptings of her curiosity.

'Yes!' cried her brother. 'He's to be Mary's brother-in-law and our neighbour. You owe us a full description of Mr Harris's character. His looks we have admired, but what of the inner man?'

Jane felt a moment of panic. 'I confess Mr Harris's character is almost as unknown to me as it is to you,' she admitted. 'He's reserved and awkward in private. I'm expecting only to get to know him by degrees.'

'But Jane!' cried Eliza artlessly. 'You're in love with him, aren't you? How can you be in love if you don't know what he's like?'

'I only said he's reserved in private. We all know about his character from his work, his ideas, his...' Jane searched in vain for more substantial evidence.

'Well, let's begin at the beginning.' Henry's playful air was particularly irritating today. 'How old is the gentleman? When was he born? When's his birthday?'

'Good God!' cried Jane. 'I've no idea.'

'He must be about twenty-five at least,' mused Mary. 'Don't you think so, Henry? I'm sure he's a few years older than you.'

'I don't know...' Henry paused, his eyes glinting tormentingly. 'The fellow could be almost fifty, you know. These preachers lead such quiet, indoor lives. Sanctity has a way of preserving complexions. Fifty! For all we know, Mr Harris may be nearer seventy, but I'm sure Jane will love him none the less for that.'

'A man's age is nothing to me, absolutely nothing,' cried Jane, betrayed into anger not only by Henry's relentless mockery, but by a consciousness that she knew a good deal less about Mr Harris than she would like to know. 'I could be as happy with a man of sixty as twenty, so long as he was intelligent and kind. Indeed, an older man would offer many desirable qualities. I would at least be spared that foolish flirting and teasing and showing off which makes the company of many young men so tiresome.' She felt so upset by her own outburst that she got up and walked off towards the folly. The others were silenced.

Jane knew she had lost her temper with her friends because her spirits were already irritated by something else. Mr Harris had gone away to Buckinghamshire to acquaint his family with the news of his marriage. This was understandable. Jane accepted it absolutely, but she was becoming more and more uneasy as every day passed without a word from him.

It now seemed such a long time since she had seen him that she had begun to doubt whether he really existed. These thoughts plunged her at times into such a pitch of uncertainty that she began to fear for her own sanity. But she must not give in to such foolishness. Of course he had to visit his family. Indeed, Jane was hoping that some of Mr Harris's relations might find it possible to come to the wedding. So far she had only met his sister Martha and in these brief encounters Jane had become convinced that the lady's intimidating manner betrayed a deep disapproval.

She walked past the folly and turned left down a track which led to Ottercombe Valley Bottom, where she had watched kingfishers flashing to and fro with Mr Axton and his sister. Now she hardly knew where she was going, except that she craved solitude. When she arrived at the tiny road which ran along the valley bottom she found that she was in tears.

She turned to the left, thinking to make her way homewards by a circular walk which would take her up the eastern lane, past the gates of Ottercombe Park. The sun was behind her now, but its warmth could not comfort her, and after a few hundred yards she paused at an old gate which led into some of her father's fields and stared at a handsome old barn which stood a quarter of a mile away in the lee of the beechwoods.

Perhaps this barn had seen three hundred years; it might stand for another three centuries. This reflection made her own anxieties seem insignificant, but it was chilling too. Buzzards were soaring and mewing in the air above the valley, alarmed, perhaps, by her arrival so close to their nest.

A touch on her leg startled her. It was a dog. Jane recognised Sir Thomas's eager young spaniel Suzy.

Almost immediately he himself appeared around the bend in the lane. 'My dear Jane!' He looked delighted to see her, but as he drew closer he saw her tears. 'Why, what is it, my dear?'

The relief at meeting him seemed to release her passions rather than disperse them and Jane wept on his shoulder for five minutes. Then, with resort to his soft white handkerchief, she began to feel better.

'Would you like to walk for a while now?' enquired Sir Thomas, offering his arm.

'Yes, please.'

'Towards your father's house? Or towards mine? I can offer you tea and you could wash your face before going home. It would please me greatly to offer you a moment's hospitality, my dear.' Jane nodded and they set off down the road. 'Now, why the tears?' asked Sir Thomas, once he had established a sauntering pace whose gentle rhythm soothed her body.

'I was very rude to Henry.'

'I'm sure he deserved it. I've often been rude to him myself and wished I'd been ruder. Was he teasing you?'

'Yes, but not . . . in an objectionable way.'

'You shall settle the matter between you. I won't interfere. But if you wish me to say anything to him on your behalf I'll be very glad to do so.'

'Only to apologise.'

'Well, it's against every instinct. But I'll try.' A faint smile seemed possible after this reassurance. 'And what was he teasing you about?'

'My marriage – to Mr Harris.'

'Ah.' Sir Thomas's voice dropped into a minor key. 'And what exactly about Mr Harris?'

'The trouble is . . .' Jane hesitated. In some ways Sir Thomas was the very worst person to receive any confidences. If she betrayed disquiet at her approaching marriage he would repeat the guilt and regret he had expressed before. Sir Thomas was uneasy at having

119

neglected her at the time when she was forming her attachment to Mr Harris.

'I'm very happy,' she began cautiously. 'Only I wish Mr Harris did not have to be away now, in Buckinghamshire. I shan't see him until a day or two before the ceremony. He has not written. I suppose he's too busy. I wish I knew what he's feeling, that's all. I'm afraid he may regret—'

'Nonsense!' cried Sir Thomas with a sudden surge of determination. 'I'll tell you what he's feeling, child. I'm an old fellow that was married once, and very happily, as I'm sure you will be. I know what Mr Harris's thoughts are very well, even if he's too reserved, or too busy, to share them with you.'

'What, then?'

'He thinks of you night and day. His first thought when he wakes in the morning is of your lovely eyes, those intelligent hazel eyes, with their shadowy understanding, their fierce wit. He longs to hear your voice. He wakes early and hears the dawn chorus, but all the blackbirds in Buckinghamshire can't replace your delightful growl, my dear.

'Your deep voice is like a river and he wishes his windows might open on to its music all his life. And his happiness is that in two or three weeks he will take this little hand in his. He will open his heart to you, he will share every idea with you, he will search the heavens for a special star and name it after you.

'Even now he is talking to his friends and family about you. He can't pronounce your name without a physical thrill of joy. He longs to be in your presence again, he lies awake at night in an agony of yearning. He wonders whose company you are in at this very moment and curses in his heart the villain lucky enough to be walking in this enchanted valley, with you on his arm.'

Jane was so stirred by this extraordinary speech that all her doubts and fears quite vanished. She felt she was floating in sunlight. She could not speak, however, and it seemed Sir Thomas could not either. The last ten minutes of their walk passed in silence, but Jane thought that if such feelings of tenderness and exaltation as she felt at this moment were awaiting her in her marriage to Mr Harris, the future must be anticipated not with anxiety but rapture.

16

Soon they arrived at Ottercombe Park. Henry and Eliza were evidently still at Newington House. The peaceful atmosphere at Ottercombe was deepened by the striking of a pretty French clock.

'My dear,' said Sir Thomas quietly, 'you must forgive me for an instant. There is a dressing-room for you to use – Alice will show you where – and afterwards if you go into the drawing-room they will bring you some tea and I shall be with you directly.'

After she had washed her face Jane ventured into the splendid drawing-room, its long windows looking out on to a wide sweep of grass studded with jonquils and fritillaries, and beyond the immediate prospect the trees of Sir Thomas's deer park were beginning to show their varying hues of green.

The room was exquisite, with a pair of sofas and many beautiful old chairs all upholstered in a fine and restrained gold brocade. Firelight flickered on the polished mahogany, on etched glass, on the crystal of the chandeliers. A quaint old spinet stood in the furthest corner, a bunch of jonquils upon it scenting the air, and Jane noticed a small portrait of a beautiful woman hung on the wall above the instrument. She supposed it must be Lady Burton and the corner was become now something of a shrine.

She took a seat by the fire and received the tea from a most civil and refined maid, whose manners would not have disgraced a countess. Jane felt the same pleasure stealing over her as she had experienced on the day of Julia's wedding, although then all had been public, grand, festive, and now the atmosphere was intimate, domestic and subdued. Looking at the portrait of the wife Sir Thomas had lost, Jane thought that his grief must be quite frightful, although she had never been especially aware of it. In general his manner had always been easy and tranquil, though he spoke of love with great feeling.

Jane felt a serenity settling over her. She heard Sir Thomas come quietly into the room and turned to him with gladness. He sat beside her, took her hand and kissed it, then looked most attentively into her face. 'I think you're feeling a little better now, Jane.'

'Oh yes! In every way. I can't thank you enough. You rescued me.'

'I'm feeling a little better, too. You rescued me also, my dear.'

Jane was puzzled by his words, but felt it would be indelicate to ask more.

They talked for a while quietly about the things in the room which Jane admired; about the ball and about the health and prospects of Eliza. Sir Thomas hoped Jane's parents were not too much disturbed by her sudden engagement and approaching marriage.

'Why, not at all,' said Jane. 'It's curious, but I feel they are more pleased with me now than they have ever been.'

'Of course they are, my dear,' said Sir Thomas. 'It's natural for you to feel some apprehension as you approach the married state, but be sure, when you are used to each other, it will bring you nothing but delight – as it has brought pleasure to your family and friends. You're to live in the lodge, Henry tells me.'

'Yes. Mr Harris does not have an establishment and he travels very much.'

'You will accompany him?'

'Oh yes – at least, I hope so. But I'm sure I shall be very often at the lodge too.'

'I like the thought of you there,' mused Sir Thomas. 'It will be easy for us to call. We will always be passing your gate. You will find our constant attendance very trying, I'm sure.' He smiled and she felt encouraged.

'Nothing will give me greater pleasure than to receive you there as often as possible,' she assured him. He acknowledged the invitation with a smile. There was, however, a subdued air about him since they had arrived back at Ottercombe Park. He seemed preoccupied and Jane soon felt it was time to go home.

Sir Thomas accompanied her to her father's gates. Some workmen were repairing the small lodge. There was the sound of hammering.

'So, here's your little nest, my dear,' said Sir Thomas. 'Here's the place where you will be so happy.'

'Oh! Shall I, Sir Thomas?' Jane felt, for an instant, a fluttering echo of her previous misgivings. He took her hand and at his touch she felt reassured.

'Of course you will.' He smiled. 'And if, at any time, there are any difficulties, of any sort whatever, things perhaps you might feel reluctant to acquaint your parents with, you must come straight down to me. It is but a five-minute walk. Promise me, Jane.' There was something solemn in his manner, which touched her.

'I promise.'

'Only one thing could break my heart now,' he went on, though in a quiet, undramatic tone, as one might talk of the weather. 'If I heard that you had been in any sort of trouble, struggling, alone, and not come to me for help.'

'I promise I never will.'

'Good. And now, if you are quite sure you are happy, I will bid you good-day.'

Jane assured him that she was, and he bowed and walked off down the lane, without looking back. She turned towards her father's house with renewed confidence and hopeful energy, met Henry and Eliza going home, exchanged apologies and became good friends again, and spent the rest of the day discussing her wedding dress with her sister and mother, with every appearance of happy anticipation.

Five days before the wedding William Harris returned to Gloucestershire and called at Newington House to assure Mr and Mrs Lockhart of his family's delight at the proposed marriage. They were honoured to be contemplating an alliance with a family of such distinction as the Lockharts, but alas! family commitments and indifferent health would prevent any of them making the long journey from Buckinghamshire to attend the wedding, and he was obliged to present their apologies and deep regrets. His sister, Martha, would of course be present.

John Lockhart heard this speech with disappointment. He would have preferred a number of Harrises at the ceremony to augment the scale of admiration for his terrace and peacocks, his maze, his lake and, above all, his east window, which was triumphantly in place, its coloured glass glowing like a tapestry and casting red and gold patterns of light upon the floor of the landing, like a Turkey carpet.

However, there was always the possibility that Mr Harris's relatives might have proved less handsome, and even more devout, than Mr Harris. The thought of a roomful of gloomy religious folk in their customary dark clothes was not attractive. They would certainly not have contributed to the elegance of the occasion. Perhaps on the whole it was for the best. He received Mr Harris's apologies with a cordial regret.

Mrs Lockhart assured her future son-in-law that everything was in hand, all arrangements made, and received for her pains the most elegant of acknowledgements. Mr Harris had a trick of speaking which made the most formal of utterances seem to spring straight from the heart. Mrs

Lockhart found his magnetic eyes upon her, and heard his eloquent thanks, with some agitation. No wonder he had bewitched poor Jane. She hoped that her daughter might find in this handsome fellow a passion and commitment which her own marriage had lacked.

The conversation concluded, Mr Harris rose to go, but was instantly implored by Mrs Lockhart to enjoy a few minutes' private conversation with his betrothed, 'for you must have a very great deal to say to each other, I'm sure.' Jane had been sitting all this time in the window, staring at a piece of embroidery, her heart beating violently.

Mrs Lockhart bundled her husband out of the room with the embarrassing theatricality which mothers find impossible to resist on such occasions. Mr Harris had no choice but to approach the young woman he had asked to marry him and make some remark. She put down her work. Her hand shook. Despite the confidence of Mrs Lockhart's assumption that they had a very great deal to say to each other, neither found it possible to speak.

At last she raised her eyes and found his face full of anxiety. All the confidence with which he had addressed her parents was entirely gone and Jane saw in an instant, to her astonishment, that she must put him at ease. 'I hope your journey was not too arduous,' she said, rather flustered, aware that the subject of Mr Harris's journey had been rehearsed at length with her parents and had not proved particularly diverting the first time. He shook his head, as if her remark had not been worth saying. Indeed she thought so herself.

'I've missed you very much,' she burst out, surprised at herself, but feeling the agonising silence required a directness and authenticity of emotion she could very readily supply. 'It was so strange being here while all the preparations were made, and not being able to see you and talk to you about it.'

'I have thought about the wedding a great deal.' His voice was husky. It had lost its customary ring.

'Do sit down, please.' Jane became aware it was an advantage to be addressing him in her own house. He was less intimidating, though his silence and awkwardness disorientated her more than his public eloquence. He sat nearby, but at a respectful distance. 'I hope you have no apprehensions about it.'

He looked very apprehensive indeed. It was odd to be offering reassurances to an older and more experienced man, but Jane had seen her mother's constant domestic initiatives and had inherited something of her confident spirit when she was out of her father's eye.

'Please believe me, Mr Harris, when I say that I desire nothing more than to make you happy. I feel more deeply honoured by your proposal than I can express and if the modesty of our lodging is acceptable to you, be sure you will want nothing for your comfort or contentment that it is possible for me to provide.'

She admired the length and composure of this speech of hers, though aware it was much more formal a form of address than she would ever have expected to use to a fiancé. Having enjoyed effortless understanding recently with Sir Thomas, she had not thought it would be more difficult to talk to the man she must love most in the world.

'Thank you,' he muttered and, looking at his knees for a moment, brushed away a speck of dust. 'These admirable sentiments I of course reciprocate. Indeed, it was my duty to have spoken first. I am not used to intimate conversations with ladies. You must forgive me.' He looked up and it seemed his face was almost fearful.

'Oh, don't worry at all about that!' cried Jane, wishing she could find the reassurances which would encourage him to discard his severe manner and offer the informal and affectionate words for which she longed. 'Everything will be easy once we are married. We'll get to know each other by degrees; it will be a joyful journey of discovery. We have made everyone so happy.' She remembered Sir Thomas's words and was fortified by them.

'When you asked me to be your wife, you said I was the first woman you had met to whom you felt you could reveal yourself. That is the seed from which our happiness will grow.' He nodded, and fixed his tremendous eyes upon her. She felt her words must ebb away and sat and looked at him in a stillness. It seemed extraordinary to her that in less than a week she would be able to touch him. She could not imagine it at all.

They were married with appropriate ceremony and made a very handsome couple, and a rainbow appeared as the wedding party gathered on the terrace to admire the view, which everyone said was propitious. Jane believed them. She was sure this was the happiest day of her life and that she was the most fortunate woman in the world.

17

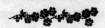

Mr and Mrs William Harris took possession of their modest lodge before nightfall. There would be no wedding journey. Mr Harris wished to resume his preaching in the open air immediately, as the season required. Indeed, his first sermon as a married man was to be the next morning, in the fields below Woolton. Jane longed to hear him preach again.

But first there was the curious business of being alone together. They walked through their small parlour and into the scullery, Mr Harris stooping slightly to avoid the beams, and admired the snug hearth, the range newly blacked, the kettle shining, everything trim and neat. It was so small as to be almost a doll's house. This pleased Jane, though she was aware that her husband seemed rather too tall for his abode.

'I hope you will be comfortable here, William,' she began timidly. She had been asked to use his Christian name, but it seemed like an impertinence.

'Oh, certainly. My wants are few.'

'Mamma says they will look for something more spacious for us in due course – but to me it seems perfectly charming.'

'Indeed.'

'And Hetty's niece, Kitty, will come up from Woolton every day to wait on us.'

'I am perfectly content with your arrangements.'

There was an uncomfortable pause. Mr Harris was looking out of the low window which gave a view across the park.

Jane snatched at an excuse to escape the confinement of the tiny cottage. 'I want to see the garden,' she said. 'It's still light, and I remember Mamma said she had asked the gardener to dig it for us.' She opened the back door and surveyed the small triangle of newly turned earth. It could not be more than forty feet across at its widest, but it delighted her. Here she could sow beans and parsnips, and grow lettuce and herbs, and roses, lilies and pinks, just as cottagers always did.

'I'll train a sweet woodbine to climb up about the eaves,' she cried eagerly to Mr Harris, who was stooping out into the last of the daylight. The sun was sinking beyond the imposing silhouette of Newington House, some half a mile away across the park. Jane admired the reflection of the red light on her husband's profile. She felt a deep tenderness and attraction, and longed to touch him, but lacked the confidence.

'It will soon be dark,' he remarked. 'Go in, my dear, and light the lamps.'

'Aren't you coming too, William?'

'In a moment.' His tone was almost impatient. Jane understood, too late, that he wished to visit the privy, and fled indoors without any more words, her face burning.

She lit the lamp awkwardly, with shaking hands: found, with much fumbling, how to set the kettle to boil and had just succeeded in making a pot of tea, when her husband came back indoors.

'They lit a fire for us. Wasn't that kind?' she said, for the sake of filling the silence. 'And I've made a pot of tea. There's a can of milk in the scullery and sugar, and this is my grandmother's china. It was Mamma's wedding present to us; it's very pretty, I think, don't you?'

Mr Harris looked at the china teacups, but made no remark.

'I'm sorry, I am prattling,' Jane burst out. 'I will not always be so irritating, only I feel a little agitated, William, as you may understand.'

'Sit down,' he said. 'Drink your tea and then go to bed. It has been an arduous day for you. For both of us. I will follow soon.' He walked over to the window and stared out into the night.

'Don't you want some?'

'I never drink at night. I'll have something in the morning.'

'I'm sorry – I'm not yet familiar with your habits.'

'Have your tea, since you have gone to the trouble of making it.'

Jane found she hardly wanted any now, but drank a cup, scalding herself in her haste. 'It was so kind of Mamma to give us this china,' she said, unable to restrain a desire to speak. 'I've always admired it. But I think Sir Thomas's looking-glass was the handsomest thing we were given.'

Sir Thomas had presented the happy pair with a delicate oval looking-glass. It stood beside the sofa, wrapped in thick paper for protection until it found its place on a wall.

'I'll ask somebody to put it up for us. Where do you think it should hang, William?'

She dreaded that he might be indifferent. But he stirred, came towards her and sat down beside the fire. 'I'll put the glass up myself,' he said, looking into the fire. 'You have your domestic duties and it's proper that I should have mine.'

'Oh, thank you! You are very kind. But where will you find a hammer? I suppose one of our men could lend you one.'

'I have a hammer, Jane.'

'Do you indeed? You surprise me. Where is it?'

'In my chest, which is in the outhouse. I have a saw too, and nails. I am not unprepared for physical toil. Indeed, I welcome it.'

'Oh, so do I! What shall we plant in the garden?'

'A few cabbages, I suppose. I don't mind at all. You may plant what you like in it.'

'Oh, may I? I should like a little apple tree.'

'Let there be no serpent there, however.'

She understood this was a joke and smiled gratefully, feeling relieved. They had enjoyed something like a conversation. She finished her tea in calmer spirits.

'Now go to bed, Jane. I will be up directly.'

Trembling, she climbed the steep, groaning stair and set down her candle. It was tactful of him to come up afterwards. There was no dressing-room. She began to feel the awkwardness of the tiny lodge. There was another bedroom, but no real opportunity to claim a small private space for modesty's sake.

Swiftly she undressed, her hands shaking so, she could barely manage her buttons and laces. She had never needed Hetty's assistance so much and now, at her hour of greatest need, she was alone. At last, however, she was in bed, wearing a light lawn night-dress especially made for the occasion. Assuming the candle-light would be helpful to him, she did not extinguish it, but lay in the flickering light, looking at the strange low ceiling above her head and trying to compose the intense agitation of her heart.

No young woman who had grown up next to a farm, and played with a farmer's children, could be wholly ignorant of the curious ways in which the animal kingdom express their affections and propagate their kind. Jane was not entirely unprepared in this regard, though her mother had told her nothing. Indeed she had always had as healthy a curiosity on the subject as any young person. She could hardly believe, however, that the moment had arrived when she was to experience for herself a husband's caresses.

She heard his step on the stair. For a moment she had a sudden instinctive fear that he might avoid her company and go into the other room, where a small bed stood. But he came into her chamber. She tried to welcome him with a timid smile, but it was not convincing and besides, he did not look at her, only blew out the candle and got undressed in the dark. Then he drew back the covers and got in beside her.

Jane lay still, hardly daring to breathe, in an agony of anticipation, yet longing to be able at last to kiss that face which had so captivated her, to wind her warm, eager arms about her husband's neck. There was a pause, a silence, a sigh, then she was seized, and in such a brutal manner she almost cried out in alarm and fear.

Understanding she must submit, Jane suffered what differed very little from a violent assault. There were no kisses, no caresses, only a fierce exercise of power. She was in great pain, but did not utter a word, only longing for it to be over.

His duty completed, her husband turned his back on her. She heard his breathing quieten and eventually deepen into sleep. She dared not move in case he woke, but felt as far from slumber as she had ever been, so frightful and shocking had been her first experience as a wife. Only when the glimmers of dawn began to peep about the eaves did Jane at last drop into exhausted slumber; and when she awoke she found her husband had gone.

There was no sound of him downstairs. Swiftly she rose, washed and dressed, and went down to find a sulky fire dawdling in the range. She struggled to revive it, but the wood was too damp, so her tea was barely warm. Still, it did not signify. The farmer's boy had left a can of milk on the back doorstep and that was all the breakfast she required.

She wondered where her husband had gone, but was relieved in some measure to find herself alone. Her thoughts would not have been easy to share, nor her pain to dissimulate. As her eyes played about the tiny room, she caught sight of Sir Thomas's looking-glass and was moved to unpack it. The frame was gilded and delicately carved. Two small cherubs crowned it, their arms wreathed about each other.

The glass cast trembling shafts of light across the room. Jane tried the effect of it above the fireplace, but the glass was too tall to fit in the space. Beside the door it would be in danger of getting knocked as people passed by. She wondered if it might be better upstairs and found a place beside the washstand where it seemed to look well. Turning it to see what arrangements had been made on its back for fixing, she found a tiny label stuck there with a message: 'May the face you see in this glass always be happy.' She recognised Sir Thomas's small, stiff handwriting and was touched. Turning the glass again, she looked at herself in it. This was the face of a married woman. A curl was out of place on the crown of her head – she had not properly attended to her appearance this morning. Smoothing it down, she looked into her own eyes. The reflection seemed another being. She would not have been surprised if it had spoken to her.

A door closed below and footsteps sounded on the stair. Her heart leapt with embarrassment. Her husband entered and his tall figure seemed to fill the tiny attic.

'I have been for a walk, to prepare my sermon,' he said briskly. She had the feeling he had prepared this speech also. 'Be so good as to make a cup of tea for me. We must leave for Woolton in half an hour. I will hang the looking-glass for you.'

She handed it to him, hesitating for an instant in the hope of a kind look. Though she had experienced her matrimonial duties with dismay, she longed to find the words and actions which would express her love without offence and provoke from him something beyond civility. He was looking into the glass, however. He seemed to avoid her eyes. Perhaps he was also struggling. She went downstairs.

He came down and fetched his hammer, and Jane busied herself about the tea-table, preparing some bread and butter. There was a pot of jam made from the fruit of her own plum tree. Hammering came from above; then stillness. Jane waited. The kettle started to sing above the fire.

She felt a sudden curious affection for the sound and was astonished to feel tears start into her eyes: tears of gratitude, it seemed, for the kettle's company.

'I have hung the glass in the other room up there,' observed William Harris, descending. 'It can serve as a kind of dressing-room.' He smoothed his hair, brushed his shoulders and drew down his cuffs.

'The tea is almost ready.' Jane hastened with the last preparations. 'I thought you might like some bread and jam – it's made with fruit from my own little tree, down near the lake. I picked it myself last year. Do try some.'

William Harris ate and drank swiftly, without sitting down. He looked out of the window as if he wished to be already on the road. 'Put on your bonnet, Jane,' he said. 'We must not be late. There may be a good crowd gathered as it is the start of the new season.'

Jane felt some excitement at the idea of going down to watch him preach in the fields and was grateful that he had used her name. It seemed almost like an endearment.

She ran to fetch her cloak and bonnet, which were upstairs, and went into the dressing-room to admire her husband's work with the looking-glass. But he had hung it too high. No doubt it suited his tall person exactly, but Sir Thomas's intentions in the gift were, alas, utterly thwarted. Jane was far from seeing her own happy face reflected. She could not see herself at all.

18

A great crowd was assembled in the fields below Woolton. The morning air sparkled and as they drew near, Mr Harris offered Jane his arm. 'Come, my dear,' he said, looking down on her with a smile, 'I must show you off to my congregation.'

The more they ventured into the crowd, the more contented he seemed to become, receiving congratulations on all sides with every appearance of pleasure. Jane was increasingly happy, for everyone seemed to smile and wish her well, and her husband often stroked her hand while assuring his friends of his great delight in being a married man.

Passing on through the congregation, they arrived at the place from which Mr Harris was to preach. It was the highest part of the meadow and a large box had been set up there to serve as a kind of pulpit. Miss Harris was waiting and received Jane with a kiss, though Jane felt that of all the salutations she had been offered that morning Miss Harris's was the most forced.

'May I present Mr Colin Watts,' said Miss Harris, indicating a fair young man standing by, who offered his hand and congratulated Jane in the accents of Bristol, and with an energetic and heartfelt air. His figure was slight and his eyes large, doe-like and imaginative. 'Mr Watts travels with us on the circuit,' Miss Harris informed her.

Colin Watts returned Jane's gaze with a smile which

seemed both enigmatic and alluring. Then he turned and raised his eyes, for William Harris was about to speak.

Jane was much surprised to hear her husband refer to her immediately. She had not expected to be mentioned at all in his formal address, but he informed his congregation of his great delight that they were present to celebrate the first morning of his married life.

'This is my wife Jane.' He looked down and by a graceful gesture indicated that he wished her to climb a little higher up the knoll to be more visible. This she did, though very much embarrassed. There was pleasure and pride, however, in her burning face and she saw, once she dared to hazard a glance at the sea of faces turned up towards her, that every one seemed to regard her with admiration and joy.

She found it difficult at first to attend to her husband's sermon. She was standing too close to look up at him without discomfort. It seemed more appropriate to gaze out over his congregation. Their attention was so absolutely fixed upon him that she realised scarcely anybody marked her and she began to be more at ease, noticing several local people she recognised. He was speaking, as befitted the fine morning, of the coming of summer, how eagerly it was anticipated by man and beast, how the warm rays of the sun felt like the caress of a gigantic hand and how the Almighty, whose hand it was indeed, would in time reveal himself in all his glory like ten thousand summers.

Jane felt moved and excited by her husband's words and she could see that his audience did too. He asked, now, in tones peculiarly intimate, which yet could be heard at the other end of the field, how each of them would long for such a sight and yet how deeply they would be ashamed if they had said or done things to displease their Maker, who felt for every one of them the kindness of a dear father.

William Harris spoke about fathers in a way which encouraged every member of the company whose father had died to reflect upon their best memories, and everyone whose father yet lived to resolve to love him better. Jane thought of her own father with some tenderness and realised it was easier to think of him thus, now she was out of his house. It was many months, now, since he had found fault with her appearance. Indeed, on her wedding day he had complimented her on her looks. Perhaps now she was married, some anxiety about her welfare would pass from him, and she would enjoy a greater intimacy and affection than she had yet experienced.

But still she could not help envying Eliza Burton her easy manners with her father. She lolled upon Sir Thomas's shoulder and caressed his head with the perfect freedom of an eager puppy, or a very young child, and these were liberties, Jane was sure, which would never be possible with her own father. She found herself wondering where the Burtons were this morning and what they were doing, and became sharply aware that in marrying she had removed herself from the effortless access to the friends of her maiden years and placed herself at the mercy of her husband's acquaintance.

The sermon ended, with most of the congregation in tears. The sun flashing on so many wet cheeks presented a curious spectacle. Jane did not feel the least inclination to weep and hoped nobody would blame her. In the sudden silence at the end of her husband's sermon she heard a lark singing high above in the brilliant heavens. A moment later, the congregation, denied the discipline and leadership of an organ, broke into a ragged hymn and the skylark was obliterated.

They had dinner at the house of one of the congregation, with Miss Harris, Mr Watts and some others. Jane was grateful for roast beef, for she felt exceedingly hungry, and ate heartily and listened to the conversation with curiosity.

She heard her husband reveal that he planned to set out and travel into Somerset and Devon the following week. 'Our people in the west will be eager to make your acquaintance, my dear,' he said, casting one of his rare smiles down the table to her.

'I'm looking forward to it greatly,' she replied. 'Both to meeting them and seeing the country, for I have travelled very little.'

She also looked forward to some private hours with her husband, away from the familiar scenes of Ottercombe, where she felt he seemed at a disadvantage in being a stranger. This journey would be something of a honeymoon, despite his duties. He had spoken feelingly about the beauties of the landscape. She would share these sights now.

She made her preparations, therefore, with some eagerness and packed only what was necessary, hoping by her thriftiness to impress her husband. But he did not notice she had only packed two bonnets, nor the neatness with which she had contrived the business. It did not disappoint her particularly. She was rather enjoying the practice of neatness and thrift for itself, which she had never attempted as a girl. Besides, William was understandably preoccupied with books and thoughts, for a new season of sermons required many hours of study and meditation.

Her parents bade her farewell with a curious sense of suspended anxiety. They would have preferred her to stay in the neighbourhood, although a conventional honeymoon would have required her departure in any case. Their son-in-law's calling exacted a kind of respect which made them uneasy, although they took pride in his reputation and admired his looks exceedingly. On this occasion he was more silent than usual, no doubt preoccupied by the responsibilities facing him, but Jane's mother, ever an eager talker, had always been used to furnish her husband's silences and was not in the least put out.

'Well, all this travelling will be a great adventure for Jane,' she remarked, 'and I must say, you were always the one who loved gadding about, my dear. You will be out of doors a lot. Take care you always wear your bonnet or you will come back quite brown.'

'Jane is always brown in the summer, Mamma!' cried Mary, who was in excellent spirits, having received an invitation to supper at Ottercombe Park that evening. 'The sun only has to touch her face for five seconds as she passes an open window and the damage is done. She is instantly transformed into an Indian princess.'

'Please keep us informed of your progress,' said her father, who was finding some difficulty in addressing his daughter in tones suitable to her new status. 'And perhaps you will let me know of any fine houses you are fortunate enough to see.'

'Oh, I will indeed, Papa!'

'Never mind the houses, Jane – you must write to us about the people you meet. They may not be persons of the highest quality, but no doubt you will observe many diverting characters.'

'I'm sure I shall, Mamma.'

Jane was only a little sad that the intricacies of her husband's route would make it very difficult for her family to write to her in return, though her mother promised to send letters to wait for her at certain places such as Taunton, which Jane might have the opportunity of collecting in due course.

'Do make my farewells to Sir Thomas, and Henry and Eliza,' she whispered, embracing her sister at the moment of departure.

'Oh, I shall! And you, dear Jane, I so envy you! You will be having such a happy time!' Mary was imagining herself setting out upon the adventure of married life, though not with Mr Harris.

'My dear Sir,' said John Lockhart, taking his son-in-law's hand, 'I wish you Godspeed.' He congratulated himself afterwards for having found, in the nick of time, exactly the right salutation. It was crisp, benevolent and godly, and John Lockhart felt he had acquitted himself with honour in this most exacting interview and could now withdraw without guilt into the contemplation of his next architectural plan for an obelisk at the eastern end of the glade.

Jane saw much to admire in the first days of travel, though she was disappointed to find that she was often separated from William. She found herself instead in a crowded post-chaise with Miss Harris, while her husband and Mr Watts made their way separately on horseback. Jane would have liked to ride, but the weather was uncertain, and when she proposed it, in a private moment, her husband appeared quite offended by the idea. He implied it would be an intrusion on his solitude, so necessary for the composition of his sermons.

'But Mr Watts rides with you. Is that not an intrusion?'

'Certainly not. Mr Watts serves me as a kind of assistant. He has unusual spiritual capacities and insights. He is, moreover, capable of riding in silence for a whole day if that is what I require.'

Jane was aware that her uneasiness in his company often caused her to prattle in a way which she found most irritating herself. How much more irritating it must be to a man of contemplative habits.

'Besides,' he went on, 'if you were to ride with us, apart from the additional inconvenience to you of violent rain or hot sunshine, you would condemn my sister to solitary travel in the chaise. I'm sure she would feel the loss of your society very much.'

Jane did not speak. She felt herself justly rebuked, although she could not help thinking that if Miss Harris found their time together as onerous as it seemed to Jane, she would very willingly exchange it for a lively solitude.

This conversation had taken place in the dark, in an old carved four-poster bed, in an inn on the road south of Bristol. Having completed his instructions, William Harris turned his back on his wife and went to sleep. Jane had found that matrimonial duties were not often required and was relieved, though she could not help feeling that some expression of affection ought to be possible and felt frustrated that she had not yet discovered how to arrive at the happiness which everybody assured her she must be feeling.

She was most contented in the public meetings, where she was presented as a bride with greater enthusiasm and radiance than her husband ever managed to display in private. The warmth of his smiles on these occasions were rare moments of delight for her, and she longed for him to conquer his reserve and smile so when they were alone together.

But privacy was very seldom possible. When they were not separated by travel, they were accommodated as a party of four, either in the public glare of an inn, or the somehow more painfully close scrutiny of a private house, for members of Mr Harris's congregation considered it an honour to offer hospitality to their preacher and his entourage. Many times Jane felt the friendly attention of a host or hostess and her spirits were raised, but the necessity of always moving on meant that new friends had to be abandoned almost before they were made.

Her letters home spoke with admiration of the landscape. She particularly recorded, for her father's benefit, the façades of a couple of great houses she had glimpsed. For her mother's sake she described the most engaging of her hostesses, and for Mary's the curiosities of fashion in Somerset, but a perceptive reader would have felt something lacking in her letters home, which she herself sensed and struggled to repair with the addition of a few sentences about her great happiness and her enjoyment of the married state. Luckily, she knew her parents would not discern anything to distress them and she had reason to believe Mary would be too pleasantly distracted by her own contact with the Burtons to notice anything amiss.

And in any case, there was not really anything amiss. Only she wished she could feel, in her husband's regard, some pleasure in the closeness between them, which she had so eagerly anticipated. He was always polite, but she felt that as a reproach. There was something about his authority, and the rapture with which he was received everywhere, which worked its way into her understanding and made her feel that any want of spirits was entirely her own fault.

After six weeks' travelling they turned back towards Gloucestershire and Jane felt relieved. She had not realised how weary she had become. The long journeys, the broken nights in strange rooms, the necessity of talking all the time to strangers, the impossibility of intimacy with her husband and his sister, had all worn down her spirits. She had begun to envy women whose husbands were not burdened with admiring congregations. Their very exhilaration at his arrival had begun to fatigue her.

Occasionally she received a smile from Colin Watts that suggested he understood her, at a deeper level than she could guess, and that he sympathised with her. But she hardly ever had the opportunity of speaking to him alone and therefore never managed to discover whether his smiles really did offer insight and understanding, or were simply a chivalrous manoeuvre or a nervous habit of self-defence.

At length she saw the hills of Ottercombe. From the opposite hillside she observed her father's house, standing solitary upon its tremendous cliff; and to the right of it, and set slightly lower down among shadowy woods, Sir Thomas's mansion, gleaming gold in its sheltering park. She had been permitted to ride for these last few miles, as it was midsummer and the weather exceptionally fine. She reined in her horse for an instant and looked across at the house where she had spent her childhood. 'It looks lonely,' she murmured, half to herself, but her husband was at her side and his hearing was acute.

'It looks very handsome indeed, and I hope you're aware of your great good fortune in having been born and brought up in such a place.'

'Oh yes,' cried Jane instantly. 'I'm very aware of my

great good fortune.' Some silent tears coursed down her cheeks as they resumed their journey. It was but two miles, now, to their own abode.

'Why are you crying?' asked William suddenly, almost with alarm.

'Only that I shall be so glad to see Mamma again, and Mary. And Papa.'

'Ah. Of course.' He looked relieved. She was glad to have been able to reassure him, though she hardly noticed, now, that he had offered her no comfort. She had become accustomed already to his curious self-absorption and had begun to endure as patiently as possible what she sensed she would never be able to change.

19

The lodge to which they returned was trim and neat, but there was no fire and the pantry was unprovisioned. Jane's letter informing her parents of their likely day of return had evidently not arrived. In the garden, however, Jane was delighted to see rows of young peas, sown by her father's gardener. She was determined to attend to her young plants, if her husband's work would now permit her some time at home.

William Harris spent no more than twenty minutes at the lodge, studying a few letters which awaited him there. Then he begged Jane to excuse him, for he needed to go down to Woolton on business. He supposed she would in any case be happier to be reunited with her parents and sister in private; he sent them his apologies and greetings and hoped to be able to call on them that evening.

Jane hastened across the park with lively anticipation. It would be a relief from the contemplation of her own difficulties to be able to see her dear Mamma and Mary again. She had been away from home for almost two months and had not received word from Newington House for four weeks. Her only uncertainty was in an awkwardness she would feel if asked for her opinion of married life. At least she was in health and she hoped her family would discern nothing in her spirits to alarm them.

In the event, any anxieties about her own case were immediately forgotten. She found her mother at her desk and Jane saw instantly, beyond Mrs Lockhart's surprise and pleasure at her daughter's unexpected arrival, something disturbing in her look.

'Oh Jane, my dear, I'm so glad to see you again. We did not expect you so soon – I must ask Hetty to send Kitty to wait on you at the lodge. And we shall see about some provisions. But oh! We have been in such a state! I was just writing to Aunt Harriet ... we have been so ... I did not know where you were and I wanted so very much to—'

'Is something wrong, Mamma?'

'Mary—'

'What, ill?'

'She has had a very great shock, my dear. Well, a disappointment. She has not eaten for quite ten days – just lies in her bed and weeps. I've been quite distracted, but your father will do nothing. I should be with her now, but she fell asleep half an hour ago, so I tiptoed out to write to your aunt. Perhaps you should go to Mary – but then, we ought not to awake her quite yet, I think – or perhaps ...'

Her mother's evident distraction thoroughly alarmed Jane. 'Tell me, Mamma,' she cried, 'what is this shock, this disappointment which has so disturbed her?'

'Henry Burton', Mrs Lockhart pronounced the name with bitterness, 'left for London, with his sister, without a word, without so much as a hint, despite all his attentions to poor Mary, which have been quite fervent – I never saw any young man so full of compliment and admiration. Everyone who saw them together thought so. Mary expected a declaration at any moment, poor girl. And I'm sure I don't blame her – I considered them as good as engaged.

'But no! Mr Henry Burton is not content to be merely engaged, I'm afraid. Too mundane a destiny for him, it seems. Nothing but breaking hearts will satisfy that young man. I'm sure Mary was not the first and I dare say many other girls will be made desperate before he is done.'

Jane was silenced. Though horrified at her mother's

words, she was not altogether surprised. 'He may come back, however, quite soon, Mamma. Mary's happiness may not be quite lost – only delayed.'

'No, no, Jane. He is gone. He is to join his ship again without coming back to Ottercombe at all. In a couple of years, perhaps, he may condescend to reappear. Though if poor Mary is here to see him it will be a miracle.'

Here Mrs Lockhart gave way to tears which had been threatening to arrive for some time. Jane comforted her as best she could, assuring her that the first violence of the shock would turn in time to acceptance. Mary would recover health and spirits, her sister was sure.

'Oh! She will certainly be glad to see you, my dear. It was such a misfortune that you were away when it happened. Mary has always been very much influenced by you, though you are the younger. Go and see her, Jane. Yes! I'm sure that is by far the best thing; she won't mind being woken by you – she has been asking for you for days.

'See if you can get her to eat something. I will not be by – she does not like to see me so distraught.'

Her mother wiped her eyes and turned back to her letter to report the sudden and very welcome return of Jane. Mary's prostration, and Jane's marriage, had changed the way Mrs Lockhart had been used to think of her daughters. Jane had been gauche: but as a married woman, especially the wife of a clergyman, she had acquired considerable authority.

Now Mrs Lockhart had somebody in the household who could support and assist her. Hitherto, she had been frustrated in her attempts to console her daughter by her husband's impenetrable reserve. Ordinary social intercourse he was prepared to endure, but at the first hint of emotional difficulty he withdrew.

Mrs Lockhart longed for her husband to express their outrage to Sir Thomas. She felt that Henry Burton's behaviour had disgraced his name and, at the very least, Sir Thomas ought to register his own disapproval and regret.

These thoughts she confided to her sister in an unsteady hand, for Mrs Lockhart was never more hectic in her handwriting than when she had an injury to rehearse.

Half a minute later Jane was in her sister's room. Mary awoke and, with many tears and embracings, confirmed her mother's account of Henry's behaviour. 'Oh Jane!' she sobbed. 'I can't sleep at night, or eat, or even get out of bed. I'm ashamed to be so completely useless and to upset Mamma, but he had led me to hope – even to expect – he said such things . . .'

Jane could easily imagine how her sister's impressionable nature had been imposed upon. She had herself watched the process begin and had experienced Henry's insinuating manners at first hand.

After many words and tears, Mary lay back on her pillows with a shuddering sigh. 'Poor Jane.' She managed a pale and fleeting smile. 'I've not even asked how you are – and your husband. Oh! You must have been so happy together.' The loss of her own prospects of happiness with Henry, which she had permitted herself to imagine in considerable detail, now rose up again to haunt her and her face began to crumple.

Jane was seized with a sudden urge. 'You must not think that marriage brings happiness, Mary,' she said briskly. The unexpected sharpness of her tone caught her sister's attention and distracted her momentarily from the contemplation of her own sorrows. 'You might have been spared something even more painful by Henry's departure, whatever you may feel now.'

'What do you mean?'

'I have to confess that Mr Harris's behaviour perplexes me exceedingly at times.'

'Oh! How?'

'I won't tell you anything more till you have had something to eat.' Jane could see that her sister was thoroughly intrigued, despite her weakness. 'No one should be exposed to the extraordinary tale of my marriage without sustenance.'

It seemed odd to be making a tease out of her unhappiness, but if it would distract Mary from her sorrows, Jane was prepared to disguise her anxiety with a satirical smile. Refusing absolutely to say any more on the subject, Jane was able to inform her mother five minutes later that Mary thought she might manage a little toast and tea.

'Oh Jane! You're so clever! I always said you were so clever, my dear!'

'Now, Mamma, after I have seen Mary eat a little I'm going to Ottercombe Park to see Sir Thomas.'

Her mother was thunderstruck. 'But my dear, I'm afraid ... but then, why not? You must know Sir Thomas quite well, having spent so much time with his family in Bath. Yes, do go, Jane. Well done! That's a good idea.

'Ah! If only you had been a boy. Your father is worse than useless. You have all my father's spirit, as well as his looks. If you were a man, you could tell Sir Thomas what we think of his precious Henry.'

'Don't worry, Mamma. I shall tell Sir Thomas everything. You may depend upon it.'

Half an hour later Jane left for Ottercombe Park, waved off by a mother who had never admired her so much as at this moment. 'It is that Mr Harris,' she told herself approvingly. 'The love of a good man has done wonders for our Jane.'

20

Jane had not passed through the gates of Ottercombe Park for almost three months: since the occasion, indeed, when she had quarrelled with Henry and met Sir Thomas in the valley bottom. She was most struck by the transformation which midsummer had brought to the land. The season of blossom was past, but every tree now enjoyed the splendour of full leaf, without any of the ragged dustiness which might disfigure them later in the summer.

Ottercombe Park was sheltered by a magnificent cedar, which looked well in any season. Beeches stood behind the house, marking an informal boundary between Sir Thomas's domain and the grounds of the rectory. The great trees seemed to glow in the thick afternoon light. It was a hot, still day. The blinds of Ottercombe Park were drawn against the westering sun, the whole estate seemed sunk in a torpor and Jane began to be afraid that Sir Thomas was not at home.

She had no very clear idea of what she would say to Sir Thomas. Jane was very far from being the truculent ambassador of her mother's wishes, though she sympathised deeply with her sister and was dismayed by her decline. But she did not see what, with propriety, Sir Thomas could make Henry do. If Henry had had any serious intentions towards Mary he would certainly have spoken. However, she longed to share her thoughts with Sir Thomas. She suspected he had not heard of the despair into which Mary had been thrown by his son's departure and guessed he would rather be informed than continue in ignorance.

She rang. The footman appeared. Jane identified herself and was invited to wait in the drawing-room. The footman assured her Sir Thomas was at home, but had intended to go outdoors and was probably somewhere in the grounds. Would Mrs Harris like some tea while she waited?

'I'll go and look for him myself,' declared Jane. 'I should like some air. Please do not trouble on my account. I was not expected. I was merely on a walk and thought to look in. In any case, I should like to see the garden.' And with this assurance she left the house.

Jane had never explored the grounds of Ottercombe Park. She found, on the southern side of the house, a series of shallow terraces, where a quaint knot garden slumbered in the heat, sheltered by a mighty yew hedge. The place seemed full of retreats, of cunning alcoves secreted among the trees, of mazes, paths and intricacies. Jane realised that though she had spent so much of the previous two months out of doors, she had been travelling so relentlessly that she had scarcely ever had the opportunity to enjoy a garden.

Despite her anxieties about Mary, she could not help being very much pleased to find herself beneath Sir Thomas's arbours. His rose-beds sent out their exhalations upon her skin and his warm grass, bruised by her feet, had been cut short enough to make her progress easy, but not so severely as to exclude the daisies.

Still there was no sign of Sir Thomas. She had half expected to find him enjoying the prospect of his park from a retired gazebo, or throwing sticks for his spaniel Suzy. Jane passed beyond the outmost ring of rose-beds and came upon a strange little building. It was completely round, with a single door and no windows. The walls were about seven feet high, the whole structure some forty feet across.

She thought she heard the sound of water within. Perhaps it was a well. Curious, she pushed through the half-open door and found herself standing at the side of a circular bath or pool, about six or eight yards wide. In the midst of the water stood Sir Thomas, naked to the breast.

He looked astonished to see her and she, as surprised to find him here, was also speechless with embarrassment to have intruded on his privacy in this way.

'I'm sorry,' she stumbled, 'I had no idea ... I did not know this was a bathing pool—'

'Stay, Jane. Jane!' he commanded. Though amazed by her arrival, he was not in the least uneasy. Green and glittering water veiled his body in modesty and he was too glad to see her to care what sort of figure he made. 'My dear,' he went on, as she hesitated, 'please don't go. You must excuse my deshabille, but for the Ancient Romans, you know, the baths were a place of social resort – then why not for us?

'Are you well? When did you return? We were disappointed to hear no word from you on your tour, but I can see you are in health. And how did you find your parents and your sister? Bless me, it is more than a fortnight since I saw Mary. We have been talking of you very much.'

Jane was reluctant to deliver her message, for he looked somehow very agreeable there, smiling at her, with the water's reflection dancing upon his neck. But she still felt the embarrassment of her intrusion and only Mary's plight could excuse it. 'I'm afraid Mary is not well at all,' she said.

Sir Thomas looked immediately concerned. 'But she was in excellent health and spirits here a fortnight ago – a day or two before Henry and Eliza left for London.'

'It was precisely their leaving, I think, which upset her. Henry had been paying Mary the most marked attention since he first joined our party in Bath. Perhaps she was wrong to feel a significance in it which he did not intend. But the plain truth is that his leaving without indicating that she meant anything at all in particular to him – that has given her the greatest possible distress.'

At last, Sir Thomas understood. He looked both perplexed and dismayed, and began to shiver slightly, as if the water had grown suddenly cold. 'Has she made herself ill by it?'

'She has been in bed for ten days and, Mamma said, has eaten nothing. Though I did persuade her to a piece of toast before I left just now.'

'Good God! Poor child. I'm most disturbed by what you say, Jane. As to what Henry intended, he is a young man whose delight is to be delightful, without any regard for the consequences. Be so kind as to return to the house. I'll come to the drawing-room directly, and we will decide how best we may persuade your poor sister back into spirits.' He dashed some water in his face, as if to shake off the disagreeable news which Jane had brought.

'I'm really very sorry, Sir Thomas, to have spoilt your afternoon.'

'My dear Jane! Nothing could matter less. The issue is rather whether my thoughtless son has spoilt your sister's summer, or – God forbid! – worse. I'm extremely glad that you have come to me.'

Jane noticed that the hairs on his chest were brown, though those upon his head had been bleached a little by the sun. She had never seen her husband's nakedness, though she had felt the curious roughness of the male body from time to time, in the dark.

'And you must tell me how you are enjoying married life.' He seemed to sense her thoughts. She blushed. 'But there will be time for us to admire that idea later. Go now and wait for me.'

Jane departed. Though she had brought Sir Thomas anxiety, and regretted disturbing his seclusion, she felt better for having seen him and having been able to resume the effortless understanding she had always enjoyed with him, in spite of her marriage and his nakedness.

'Now, Jane, how are we to help poor Mary?'

Sir Thomas had wasted no time in making himself

presentable. Tea had been brought and proved very refreshing to Jane, who had walked for some time in the heat and had been glad at last to return to the shade and seclusion of the drawing-room.

'I don't know.' Jane considered the problem. 'I suppose there is nothing very much anybody can do – I only wanted to inform you of the case, as soon as I discovered it myself. For the relief of my own feelings, I suppose, I wished to discuss it with you.'

Sir Thomas sat across the room in his usual chair and as he considered the sad case of the elder Miss Lockhart his eyes played speculatively over the face of the younger. Travel, and being so much out of doors, had given her face a healthy glow, but the perturbation she felt at her sister's condition showed all too clearly in her restless eyes.

'My dear,' resumed Sir Thomas after a moment's thought, 'I'm grateful that you wish to share your anxieties with me – but I suppose you don't want me to force Henry to marry the poor girl?'

'Oh no – of course not. Where there can be no natural inclination to marry, no happiness can result.'

'Of course you are now a married woman and can bear witness yourself to the bliss which follows if the parties have followed the inclinations of their hearts.' Sir Thomas's remark was half teasing, half questioning, and Jane felt herself caught out by it and blushed. Though Sir Thomas had shown every concern about Mary, Jane wished he would confine his remarks to her sister's state. She did not welcome his enquiries about her own situation. His perceptions were too acute.

'Did you not think Henry attracted to Mary?' she enquired.

'They spent a lot of time together and enjoyed teasing each other. But that is the way with high-spirited young people.'

'Mary is not generally high-spirited. She was more animated with Henry than I have ever seen her – and I

154

could only attribute it to her exhilaration at being so much admired. You must have seen it.'

'What I saw, Jane – especially when Henry first arrived – was that he was equally attentive to you both and, if anything, you were the sister he particularly favoured. I noticed it especially at the ball. But of course you became increasingly drawn to your religious inclinations.'

'I must confess that Henry's attentions were not welcome to me, though I liked him very much.'

'This often happens. The woman who attracts a fellow most acutely is disdainful and he finds consolation in the company of her sister.'

'Henry's attentions to me were never seriously meant. They were always playful – indeed they seemed to me intended as a kind of satire upon the whole business of courtship itself.' She spoke sharply. Sir Thomas sighed. Jane felt she had imposed on him for too long and her company was becoming irksome. After all his kindnesses she dreaded giving offence.

'I must not detain you longer, Sir Thomas.' She began to rise, but Sir Thomas stopped her with a look.

'Now, Jane! Nothing has pleased me so much, these past two months as your sudden arrival in my bathhouse today. I am only embarrassed that your difficulties have been caused by my own son.

'To be frank, it is not the first time a young lady has been deceived in him. I told him on that occasion that he must be more circumspect in his behaviour, or he would find himself committed to an engagement he had not anticipated, nor perhaps whole-heartedly welcomed. He assured me then that he had no intention of marrying before the age of thirty. Till that time the Navy must claim his whole attention.'

'Thirty! But that must be—'

'Seven years. I guess that is not news which will delight Miss Mary.'

Jane thought for a moment. 'But perhaps it may. Perhaps

this is the very news to give her heart. I don't think she is capable, in her present state of weakness, of learning to do without the idea of him altogether. But if she could entertain the fact that a few more years must pass before he is likely to commit himself to anybody, she might reconcile herself to a long wait. She might find that after all, to die for love is not absolutely necessary.' Her own relief at the idea found release in this small spark of wit and she saw Sir Thomas liked it very much.

'Well, let us hope you are right. And if there is anything I can do . . .'

Jane hesitated. 'You have always helped me to feel better when I was in difficulties, Sir Thomas.'

He gave a graceful shrug and a smile. 'Then I've done so without the least exertion, my dear.'

'I only wondered . . . if perhaps you could do the same for Mary.'

'The same for Mary?'

'I mean, comfort her, as you have comforted me. She will perhaps gain some relief from talking to you about Henry – as you are his father.'

'But of course. So soon as Eliza gets back from London, we will have some parties. Some entertainments.'

'And when does Eliza return?'

'In a week or so.'

'Could we not plan something before then? Just you and I? Forgive me for imposing on you, but you have such a gift for making people feel better.'

Sir Thomas looked at her for some time in silence and with frank affection. She felt lucky to have such a friend: one who, no matter how he was provoked, never appeared displeased with her. 'We shall restore poor Mary to spirits,' he said at last, summoning his energy with a sigh. 'Bring her to dinner here tomorrow night. I'll send my carriage for you, as she must be weak. But ah—' His expression altered. 'Your handsome husband. I would of course be delighted to entertain him too.'

Jane felt a curious pang at the thought of her handsome husband. For a moment she had quite forgotten she had such a thing. She got up. 'I'm sorry,' she faltered. 'I have forgot the time. Perhaps he is—'

'Waiting for you and alarmed. Most likely.' Sir Thomas also rose. 'Shall I accompany you?' He seemed only half inclined.

Jane found she would rather make the short walk by herself and insisted she would not dream of intruding further on his time. Sir Thomas acquiesced, though an air of uneasiness had crept upon them. He did not kiss her hand, only shook it in a curiously formal manner and stood back as he bade her farewell, as if from a fierce fire.

Jane almost ran home, fearing that her husband would be waiting for her and dreading somehow that she might have displeased him by her absence. As she climbed the hill, a hot wind sprang up from the south, tossing the trees about and fretting at her skirts. She reached the lodge quite out of breath and, irritated by her own weakness, opened the door and stepped inside. She saw her husband's boots in the hall and knew he was at home.

Somehow the handle slipped from her grasp. The wind snatched at the door, which slammed shut with a bang that shook the whole house, like the sound of a great gun going off. Upstairs, there was another crash and, though smaller, it was accompanied by a splintering, tinkling sound which froze Jane's heart.

'Jane!' She heard her husband's voice ring out angrily in the room above. 'What are you thinking of? You've smashed Sir Thomas's pretty little looking-glass quite to pieces.'

Jane's horror at the accident was deepened by a conviction which entered her at that moment like a fatal splinter: that she had not displeased her husband by her absence, but by her return.

21

Jane visited her sister next morning and delivered the cheerful news that Henry Burton was to remain a bachelor for seven years. Mary was imaginative enough to find some comfort in this idea and, since she was beginning to be irritated by her own grieving, took a hearty breakfast, got up and dressed. She announced, moreover, that she would be quite well enough to go to supper at Ottercombe Park that evening.

Jane returned to the lodge for the day. Her husband was not downstairs, though she saw signs that he was at home. Somebody had lit a fire. She dared not call his name and an instinct led her instead into her garden, which enjoyed in the mornings some dappled shade. Here she began to pull the choking weeds from among the rows of tender young carrots. The exercise refreshed and soothed her more than she had expected, and her dread of seeing her husband had been subdued to a kind of faint uneasiness, when she heard his step on the path and his shadow fell across the earth.

'I would like some tea and the servant is not here.'

Jane got up, hastily brushing the earth off her hands and, since she had neglected to put on a pinafore, she marked her fine muslin gown with dirty streaks.

Her husband saw it and sighed. 'How you do defile and break things, Jane,' he said. 'To work in the garden you ought to be dressed like a farm girl, not a lady.'

Jane passed him and went into the house, her eyes

smarting with his rebuke. He followed her into the scullery and watched as she filled the kettle from the heavy stone pitcher. Her hands felt weak. She wished he would wait in the parlour. She did not like him to see her shaking.

They went into the parlour and she heard her husband exclaim with annoyance, 'Look here! You have let the fire go out.' He seized the poker and stabbed at the embers.

Tears sprang from Jane's eyes. She was not used to thinking if the fire had gone out or not. A servant had always attended to such matters. 'I can't think where Kitty is,' she murmured. 'I'm very sorry, William.'

'In Kitty's absence, there is no shame in looking after ourselves. Honest toil is more of an adornment to a female soul than lounging on a sofa.'

'I wasn't lounging on a sofa! I was—'

'I know perfectly well what you were doing.' He reset the fire as he spoke. His white fingers seemed quick at the work. 'Don't just stand there, set the table. I want some bread and butter, and a mutton-chop. If you can't see to it, get somebody who can. We are all in disorder here, the most elementary things neglected. A man needs food before anything.'

Jane ran to the scullery, found some potatoes and peeled them with such trembling haste that she cut her thumb and worked in her own blood. She had not dared to say anything in her own defence, though she felt his rebuke was undeserved. She was disinclined to apologise. Though she longed for his good opinion, she would never beg for it. Silence was her only comfort now.

She returned to find the fire beginning to blaze up. Her husband stood at the window with his back to her, blotting out the light. Jane struggled to command her nerves, for she felt she must say something, despite a persistent instinct to hold her tongue. 'I'm sorry you were not properly looked after.' Her voice broke slightly. 'We had never discussed ... domestic arrangements as perhaps we ought. On our journey we were always entertained by others. When I was a girl at home the servants made us comfortable. Kitty should be here. I do not know ... anything,' she ended weakly, regretting her attempt to claim his understanding.

He turned and looked at her with contempt. 'Are you saying you are too grand to be bothered with simple tasks?'

Jane could only gasp at what seemed like a deliberate mistaking of her meaning. She felt an emotion spring into her breast which must find expression. 'Oh why do you hate me so much?' she cried. 'What have I done?'

He blanched and, with a look of horror, walked out of the house.

Jane heard a frightful roaring in her ears and had to sit down for some moments before her heart slowed to its habitual pace. Now she did not know what to do. Her foolish cry had made worse what might have been amended by a quiet, civil remark. Should she prepare some food for him? When would he return?

She went back to the scullery and put the potatoes in water. Her thumb, still bleeding, cast a few drops of blood into the pan, which bloomed into small red clouds. Jane set it to boil, refusing to change it. She found some cruel meaning in the idea. Then she struggled with a mutton-chop, the kettle, milk and tea, assembled at last some kind of meal and placed it in the warming oven.

Now she did not know what to do. Inactivity seemed abhorrent. Yet she was too distracted by anxiety to settle to anything for long. She cleared up the debris in the scullery and swept the floor. Still he did not come. She dusted the parlour and polished the candlesticks. Her husband did not return.

She began to wonder keenly if he had gone down to Woolton, or had set out for one of his long walks, or if perhaps he was loitering somewhere near the house. She hesitated to look out of the windows on the ground floor, in case he was immediately outside. There would be something horrible in suddenly confronting him like that, through the glass. Instead, she went upstairs. The windows on the first floor were so very small – almost like defensive slits in a castle wall – she could look out without fear of being seen.

Nothing was visible from her own bedroom, though Jane felt reproached by the bedclothes which she, always the later riser, had left in disorder. She made the bed with unnatural care, trying to smooth from the pillows the creases left by their sleeping heads. The bed seemed a curious object. Could it be possible that she spent so many hours, every night, so close to William Harris that their bodies warmed each other in sleep? Jane stared at this enigmatic piece of furniture like one hypnotised.

Shaking herself from her reverie, she decided to go down to her garden again. At the top of the stairs, however, she hesitated. Something in the other room caught her eye. She went in and was surprised to find a small writing desk installed, with many books and papers arranged neatly. William had established here a kind of study.

A sheet of paper lay upon the desk, half-covered with his small, intricate handwriting. She picked it up, eager to find her husband's thoughts committed to paper, longing to read the private expressions of ideas and feelings which she was never granted in his company. But it seemed to be part of a religious or political treatise and her perusal of it was interrupted by the sound of his footsteps on the path below.

Hastily she put the paper down and saw, with dismay, that her still-bleeding thumb had left a smudge of blood upon the margin. Her fastidious husband could not fail to see that she had trespassed on his private papers. Haunted by her helpless accumulation of offences, she went downstairs.

He was standing by the fire. Her heart lurched at the thought that she might have let it go out again. She had no idea how long she had spent upstairs, or how many hours had passed since he went out. He took the poker, stirred the fire and threw on another log. The flames leapt up again: she felt redeemed.

'I'm very sorry, William,' she said at once, looking at the floor, 'that I spoke as I did. My only care is to learn how to look after you.'

His silence forced her, in the end, to raise her eyes. She found his face very white, but not unkind. His hand moved out awkwardly towards her. She almost flinched, in anticipation of a blow. But he placed his palm on the top of her head. Her scalp prickled strangely at his touch. He said nothing, but she understood she was forgiven.

He moved away and sat at the table. Hastily she placed the meal before him, praying she would not spill anything.

He noticed her injury. 'What have you done to your thumb?'

'I cut myself, peeling the potatoes.' She admitted with reluctance this new manifestation of her clumsiness and expected a rebuke. Instead he rose, examined the cut and, finding the necessary materials in a small box upon the mantelpiece, washed and dressed it himself with care and precision.

She sat receiving these attentions with an astonished awe. It was the first time her husband had touched her with gentleness when they were alone. It was almost unbearably delightful and it was only with the most severe control that Jane avoided bursting into tears of relief.

When he returned to his dinner, it was cold. Jane offered to place it in the oven again to warm, but he waved her away. 'It is of no significance. Sit still. It does not suit you to bustle about. No doubt your injury upset you.'

She nodded, dumb with gratitude for his attempts at understanding.

Jane sat beside him at the table, but could only take a little tea. He stared into the fire as he ate; she looked across at the back window, which gave a glimpse of the garden. She saw her newly weeded young carrots, their feathery leaves moving quietly in the breeze.

One more thing must be said, however. She could not dispel from her consciousness the blot of blood on the margin of his work upstairs. She dreaded his discovery of it and felt she must forestall his displeasure. 'I noticed you have made a study for yourself upstairs, William,' she said, trying to sound quiet and civil, though her heart was racing with apprehension. 'It is a very good use for that room, I find.'

'I must have somewhere to retire to work,' he replied, with something a little defensive in his tone.

'Of course. You are writing something, I think? A piece of paper had fallen on the floor. I picked it up and marked it with my blood. I'm sorry.'

'Those are only preliminary notes.' He swept her concerns aside and she celebrated quietly the success of her small lie. 'I am at work on a pamphlet at present, which will take me a week or two. Until it is finished we must remain here. But I expect you will be glad to see your family again? Your parents looked well when I called last night.

'Oh, by the by, how is your sister this morning?'

'Much better. She is coming with us to supper with Sir Thomas tonight.'

'Ah yes. I had forgot that engagement. I cannot be doing with too many engagements, Jane. I hope you will not commit me to many more social occasions in the next fortnight. I am here to work.'

'Of course.' Jane felt strengthened by the sense that they were managing to have a conversation almost without any anxiety on her part, or reproach on his. 'I shall guard your privacy most jealously. And I shall ensure that Kitty resumes her duties – or if she can't, I shall recruit another servant.'

'Do so.'

'What is the subject of your pamphlet, William?'

He looked at her for a while, finishing the last of his dinner and considering what her intellect might be capable of embracing. 'Some thoughts on authority, in particular the authority of kings. I tell you this in confidence, Jane. You would not do well to mention it to your father, or indeed to anybody. It will be enough for them to know it is some religious matter.'

'But—' Jane faltered. 'Surely . . . the authority of kings is not a religious matter – is it?'

He looked irritated. 'To some extent it is. But that is what I wish you to say to anybody who asks. Some religious matter.'

'I understand. But . . . what do you think about kings, William? What is your opinion on the subject?'

Jane was genuinely curious and not a little apprehensive. Only six years previously, the French had executed their king and the land fallen into a bloody disorder. Jane had grown up with the idea of King George presiding over England as naturally as the stars and clouds. But in recent years King George had been afflicted with a most disturbing attack of insanity – though now he was, it was hoped, restored to his original lucidity.

'Does it not seem absurd to you', William Harris's voice modulated slightly into the tone he used for public address, the tone in which he always seemed so much more fluent and at ease, 'that a man should have charge of a nation, not because he has been chosen to rule over them by his particular gifts and capacities, but by an accident of birth?'

'Well . . . I suppose it does.'

'What could be a clearer illustration of this absurdity, than the case of our own King, who was recently so disordered in his senses as to be unable to govern himself decently in public – let alone govern a kingdom?'

Jane could only nod, and stare.

'Would it not seem to you an altogether more rational constitution for a country to be governed by an assembly of godly men, elected to that office by their fellows?'

'Why, yes. But . . . how could one . . . remove the King without treason?'

'That, my dear Jane, is the subject of my meditations. As you can divine, it is no insignificant matter. It will require attention of the most exacting kind.'

'I understand.'

'Nothing is so abhorrent to me as the arbitrary exercise of absolute authority.' He wiped his mouth and stood up. 'Nothing does worse violence to the lives of the common people than the certainty that a king's authority may be exercised over them at any time, destroying any aspiration to true liberty, which may console them in their poverty.

'Now I will return to my work. Please see that I am not disturbed until it is time to go to Sir Thomas's for supper. Set this house to rights, get us a decent, quiet maid and let us have no more distractions and hysterics here from this day forth.'

He went upstairs, entered his study and shut the door. Jane contemplated a new anxiety: that her husband was engaged in studies which might be regarded as dangerously subversive. She was so shocked by this thought, which afflicted a sensibility already harrowed by her private difficulties, that she did not notice that she herself was submitting to an authority more absolute than anything she had ever suffered from her father, for all his remoteness and severity.

22

Jane felt drowsy later in the afternoon, exhausted by her anxieties. She tiptoed up the stairs, lay down on her bed and fell into a deep sleep, from which she was roused with alarm by a loud rap at the door below. Dazed, and hunting for her slippers, she heard her husband go downstairs and some hasty conversation outside.

'Go to Newington House for Miss Lockhart first – we will be ready when you return,' she heard her husband say. The door closed, Jane heard a coach and horses move off and realised with horror that she had slept far beyond the time when they should have been dressing to go out to supper, and here was Sir Thomas's carriage already arrived to collect them.

In an agony of haste, she pulled off her dress and was seizing another from the linen press when her husband burst in, boiling with indignation. He seemed to recoil for a moment at the sight of her in her shift. He did not look at her with pleasure: rather with distaste. 'You fool, Jane!' he cried. 'I told you to inform me when it was time to prepare. Now we have but five minutes.' He strode into the next room, where he had made a habit of keeping his clothes. She heard him tear off his shirt.

'I'm sorry, William, but I was so tired I fell asleep and, I don't know why, but somehow I couldn't—'

'Oh, do not make it worse with your wretched explanations!'

Silently weeping, she put on her clean gown and her evening slippers made of soft kid. Her tears, however, gave way to resentment when she realised that as William had been awake for the whole afternoon he might easily have noticed the lateness of the hour himself and waked her in good time. She washed her face and brushed her hair, and was ready some time before her husband. She heard prolonged rustling in the next room and some angry words, half swallowed, half intended for her ears.

'And you have broken the damned looking-glass as well – I shall have to use your old one.'

He came into the room and bent down before the old glass Jane had always used as a child. His appearance was already immaculate and magnificent, but Jane watched in some surprise at the manoeuvres he felt obliged to execute before he regarded himself as fit to present in public. His hair was brushed again, although already in order; his cuffs pulled down, his shoulders dusted with a handkerchief; the handkerchief then artfully positioned on his person, so that its mere austere edge might be admired.

Finally, he astonished Jane by brushing his eyebrows, smoothing his cheeks and showing his teeth like a chimpanzee she had seen once in a travelling menagerie from Bristol. She turned her face away, for in her state of heightened anxiety she had to suppress an hysterical laugh at the sight. Suddenly she saw upon her shelf the small box containing the ear-rings Sir Thomas had given her in Bath and, seizing them both in grateful memory of his generosity and to distract herself from the thought of her husband's toilette, she put them on.

They turned to face each other.

For an instant there was uncertainty in his face. 'Do I look presentable?' he asked.

'Very fine indeed.'

Jane did not dare ask the reciprocal question. She feared she would be informed in any case.

'It is fortunate that you are not the sort of woman to

spend hours at your dressing,' he observed. 'But those earrings I do not like. They give you a coquettish air.'

'They were a present from Sir Thomas when I was in Bath,' Jane flashed with anger. 'I shall wear them to please him, since I cannot please you. And I could never aspire to a coquettish air – I don't know how you can accuse me of such a thing, since you have just spent twice the time that I have in contemplation of your looks.'

'You damned impudent minx!' he cried, his eyes flaring. Jane was shaking all over and felt the strangest inclination to hit him, for all that he was her husband, a minister of the church and twice her size.

They were denied the opportunity for further endearments by the arrival of Sir Thomas's coach, and Mary, very agitated and pretty, within.

'Oh Jane, do I look all right? Mamma says I have got very thin. But you two are such a handsome pair! I so envy you, going out together for the evening so happily. I am quite the gooseberry! Ha, ha!'

Luckily the happy pair were spared the necessity of any remark, for Mary's torrential excitement was more than equal to the task of filling the few minutes it took to arrive at Ottercombe Park.

Everybody's anxieties seemed to subside at the sight of Sir Thomas. The leisurely grace of his welcome stole over Jane's heart like the return of serene sunlight after a violent storm. He was all courtesy and attention: he complimented both young ladies on their looks, particularly distinguishing Mary with his praise, which Jane observed with gratitude. He congratulated Mr Harris on his evident health and enquired as to the success of his tour, and Jane's husband, finding company as usual a more congenial environment than intimacy, was able to reply with eloquence and at length.

They were only four at supper and Sir Thomas had ordered a menu which tempted the delicacy of Mary's reviving appetite. Trout, fresh from the stream in the valley bottom, had been poached in a little white wine, and new potatoes from Sir Thomas's kitchen garden which were but an hour out of the earth, and peas so tender they had barely needed cooking, were served warm with a few leaves of lettuce and the butter in which they had been simmered. Fresh herbs brought to the table a delicious smell of summer.

Jane saw Mary eat heartily and was glad. Sir Thomas was as attentive to Mary as any doting father could have been to his own child. He was forever offering her dainty morsels and delightful compliments, and Mary smiled a great deal; her cheeks began to glow and Jane's uneasiness about her sister's health abated. At one moment she caught her host's eye and tried to express with an eloquent look the intensity of her gratitude. She received in return a brief glance of great tenderness, which proved such a contrast to the way she had been addressed all day she was almost moved to tears by it.

Her husband was also enjoying his dinner. Poor William! she thought ruefully. Her own efforts at cookery had been grotesque. That he had managed to eat the horrid mutton-chop at all was heroic. It would have been more appropriate to mend a shoe with it, prop open a door, or stop a draughty hole in the wainscot. The absurdity of these thoughts almost toppled her again into that hysteria which had dogged her all day.

Quietness of spirit was denied her. She felt torn between tears and a threatening kind of uncontrollable laughter, which, if it seized her, she knew would almost suffocate her. This would disgrace her absolutely in company. She dreaded it. Only by attending to Sir Thomas, she felt, could she obtain some composure. She turned her gaze to him, therefore, and he felt it.

'Jane, some more potatoes? You have hardly touched a thing all evening. Here is the daintiest little fellow, no bigger than a songbird's egg, and it is his ambition to enter your pretty little mouth.'

As he spoke, Sir Thomas lost his composure for an instant and a blush fled across his cheek. Only Jane saw it. He rose instantly and, turning his back on the company, went to the side-table. 'I am hunting, here, for some delicacy to tempt Jane – what do we have, Antony?'

The footman looked surprised that Sir Thomas had got up.

'Have we any asparagus?'

'Asparagus? Why no, Sir – I don't believe it was requested. But I can certainly—'

'No, no!' cried Jane. 'Please, Sir Thomas, I have had a banquet, truly. My appetite is very moderate you know.' She knew that Sir Thomas had often seen her eat heartily in Bath, but she felt her stomach a little disordered this evening, by the distress of the day.

Sir Thomas hesitated for a moment, then sat down again and applied himself to the easier task of amusing Mary. Jane was left with a sense that something strange had happened, but she could not say what. She was only grateful that her husband seemed at ease and looked at her, when it was necessary, without rancour. She was also increasingly distracted, as the meal progressed, by difficulties of digestion, and was glad when the party left the table and strolled out on to the terrace to admire the evening.

Sir Thomas's gardens and park looked majestic in their pools of deepening shadow, and when they turned to admire the façade of the house they found all the dressed stone etched in golden light and the windows ablaze with the reflected sunset.

'Why, that is Eliza's room, I believe!' cried Mary, pointing to the window on the most southerly corner. 'And the one next door is Henry's, I'm sure.'

'You're right,' said Sir Thomas. 'While Henry is away, I mean to repair the decoration there. A young man soon wears the wallpaper out, hurtling to and fro. Perhaps you will be kind enough to assist me with your advice, Mary?'

Mary very readily agreed to this excuse to loiter, in some happy hour in the near future, among the books and possessions of the man who had made her so wretched.

Jane was surprised at Mary's familiarity with the geography of the house, until she recalled that while she and William had been travelling in Somerset and Devon her sister had enjoyed many happy hours at Ottercombe Park in the company of Henry and Eliza and their father. She felt, at this recollection, a strange pang of envy, for while she had been exposed to fatigues and anxieties, Mary had enjoyed diversion, comfort and repose.

Sternly banishing the absurdity of this jealousy, she contemplated for a moment the strange spectacle of Mary taking Mr Harris's arm, strolling about the terrace and talking with the greatest animation about Henry: his looks, his accomplishments, his ambitions. William Harris had met Henry often enough to encourage her happy reflections with civil assent. Jane was struck by Mary's perfect ease with her brother-in-law. She talked to him as if he were as transparent and well-meaning as she was herself, without the least trace of apprehension, seeming not to notice his severity.

Jane was pleased to see her sister so animated, but a moment later her anxieties on Mary's behalf were succeeded by increased uneasiness on her own account. She felt suddenly quite ill and walked quickly to the furthest edge of the terrace, went down some steps and found a little wrought-iron seat shielded by close-clipped yew, where she sat down and struggled to regain her composure.

Sir Thomas was instantly beside her and most concerned. He saw, without needing to ask, that she was ill. Her pallor, and a sudden sweat which had broken out on her brow, told the story.

'It is nothing – please, Sir Thomas, don't say anything – I shall be better in a moment . . .' She reached imploringly to stop him calling for help and found comfort in the support of his strong hand.

171

'Don't ... tell my husband ... he will be angry ... bear with me ... forgive me ...'

'Jane, Jane!' Sir Thomas whispered, a look of outrage and astonishment in his eye. He found his handkerchief and gently wiped her face.

'Don't be alarmed – I am better now.' She sat up determined to be well, and breathed as evenly as she could. 'It was a qualm, merely – I am a little disordered in my stomach, that is all. I have felt not quite well all day – it is nothing. Please say nothing to my husband.' She shook off Sir Thomas's kind hand, to reassure him and insist upon her independent vigour.

Sir Thomas leaned back in perplexity, staring at her in the greatest possible frustration and concern. They could hear Mary behind the hedge, still chattering happily to Mr Harris about Henry.

'Mr Harris is very kind always,' murmured Jane hurriedly, 'only I do not wish to distress him.' Her eyes pleaded with Sir Thomas to accept the lie. He could only, for her sake, offer the slightest inclination of his head. But she knew he had glimpsed the painful possibilities which she so dearly wished could stay for ever unsuspected, by him above all men.

23

Jane succeeded in sustaining her composure for the rest of the evening, but was glad enough to exchange the elegance of Ottercombe Park for her own small dwelling. Only the presence of William Harris at her side distracted her. She hoped not to disturb her husband by her own restlessness at night, but growing worse and worse, she was at last so ill that he offered to retire to the other bedroom until morning, which she gladly accepted.

He did not help her, for there was nothing of the nurse-maid in his nature, but her prostration seemed to disarm rather than irritate him. He did not look angry any more, rather he contemplated her with the curiosity one might bestow upon a strange fish washed up half alive on the shore. Her illness took away her dread of his temper. She could only attend to herself.

In the morning Mr Harris walked across to Newington House and Mr Lockhart's physician was summoned to the lodge. Very little examination was necessary for the doctor to establish that Jane was expecting a child, which would arrive early the following year. Mr Harris received the congratulations of everybody with appropriate pleasure; Jane could only lie and stare at the wall in disbelief and terror.

Her mother was soon at her side. Jane heard her skirts whisper on the floor. 'My dear Jane!' she cried, taking her daughter in her arms. 'This is the most delightful news! We are so overjoyed. Papa has put away the plans for his obelisk to look for a better house for you, for this', she glanced about her at the low ceiling and shuddered, 'is nothing really but a doll's house, my dear, a little cage for two lovebirds; but now you are to be a family, we must do better, I declare. Well! How are you feeling, my sweet?'

'Not so bad, Mamma. Now I know what is wrong, I think I understand what I may expect. But please don't think of moving me from this lodge. I like it here.' Jane felt so deeply exhausted, the thought of moving into the next room was too much for her.

'Well, we shall see. Dear me! It so very hot up here, however. I walked across the park and I am quite fagged out. I should like some tea. Where is Kitty?' Mrs Lockhart looked about her.

'Kitty has not been here since we arrived home. It has been hard, Mamma – I'm such a hopeless housekeeper.'

'What? My daughter keep house? I won't hear of such a thing. Kitty should be here. I shall speak to Hetty directly I get home. This is disgraceful behaviour.'

Mrs Lockhart seized at the offence with gusto. To pursue a wrong offered her more immediate gratification than the contemplation of a grandchild: she rose to see about it and, having delivered Jane her father's salutations, she left the room.

A fear of embarrassment, and a distaste for illness, had kept her father away. He never knew how to speak to his daughters even when they were in normal health and spirits. At the thought of Jane in her present condition his soul recoiled – though he had promised his wife he would visit the lodge as soon as their daughter was well enough to permit a dignified discourse.

Sir Thomas, however, cared little for such ideas. His only fear was for Jane's health and he arrived at the lodge gates just as Mrs Lockhart was leaving. Jane heard his voice below her window and sat up to listen more clearly.

'My dear Mrs Lockhart! Good day to you, Madam – and how is your daughter? She was not well at my house last night.'

'Oh, Sir Thomas, Jane is not so bad at all, she's expecting a child, that is all – we are all so delighted.'

'A child!' There was a pause. 'May I congratulate you, Mr Harris. My warmest good wishes upon this happy occasion.'

Jane understood by this remark that her husband was also present and she heard him murmur an acknowledgement.

'But, dear me, we are in such a pickle!' Mrs Lockhart went on, coming to a more inviting subject. 'Poor Jane has been struggling without a servant since she came home, for Kitty is nowhere to be seen, wretched creature. She is my Hetty's niece, you know, Sir Thomas – her sister Alice's child – and a more honest and obliging character than Hetty you could not find.

'But I'm afraid that Kitty takes after her father's family. Poor Alice! What that woman has suffered only the Lord knows and one only hopes He will reward her in the end, Mr Harris. Drink, et cetera. And Kitty has always been very fine, putting on airs when she was only thirteen, I recall. There is no excuse for this neglect. I shall go home and put it in hand immediately.'

'Perhaps I might help,' Sir Thomas suggested briskly, as if to detain her. 'My parlourmaid's sister is just returned from London, a neat and orderly young woman with excellent references. I was unable to offer her a position, as my own staff is complete, but I know she is in Woolton at present and looking for employment. Her name is Bessie Stevens. Shall I send her to you, Mrs Lockhart?'

'Oh, Sir Thomas, pray do – I'm sure we are very much obliged, for that Kitty would be little use even if one could depend upon her being here, for she is fat and clumsy, and very stupid, too.

'I shall still summon her, however, and tell her what I think of her for letting my poor daughter down – poor dear Jane! And at a time when she is feeling so ill.'

'May I . . . see her?' enquired Sir Thomas. Jane was glad to hear this request.

'I think she may be asleep,' Jane heard her husband say. 'She was very restless and ill all night.'

'Perhaps I should not disturb her, then.'

'Oh, no, Sir Thomas, do go up. She will be delighted to see you, I'm sure. I left her just now, and she was quite awake and in very good spirits.'

'Perhaps if Mr Harris would be good enough to go up and ask . . . ?'

Jane had been on the point of crying out aloud that she wanted to see Sir Thomas. Now her husband came quickly upstairs. 'You don't want to see Sir Thomas, I suppose,' he whispered. 'All the world and his wife will have the impertinence to come bursting through our doors now.'

'Oh, no, William! I want to see Sir Thomas very much. He has always been exceedingly kind to me, and to Mary; and remember he is our neighbour, and a man of great influence and judgement.' To contrive a visit from Sir Thomas, she would have described him as an Eskimo, or Indian Prince, but she sensed what would appeal most acutely to her husband's mind. 'If only he could hear you preach, William,' she murmured, 'think how splendid it would be. A gentleman of such an estate and establishment . . . so many souls in his employment. He is such a good-hearted man, I never met anyone so generous and kind. Let him in.'

She had exhausted her catalogue of Sir Thomas's virtues, but it was enough. William Harris had already begun to feel that Sir Thomas brought with him an entire congregation of maids and men, and he went down and begged him to step up.

Sir Thomas gladly agreed to sit with Jane while Mr Harris escorted his mother-in-law back across the park. Mr Harris was hoping to make some discreet enquiries as to the state of her soul, but Mrs Lockhart was determined to rehearse her poor opinion of Hetty and her family, and Jane spared a moment to smile at their fading voices. She knew that her husband would have to submit to her mother's conversational energies.

But now she heard Sir Thomas's footsteps on the stair and he stepped into the room. His face was full of concern. 'My dear Jane. How are you?'

'I'm well, thank you, Sir Thomas.' She reached out her hands; he came forward and kissed them, and sat close by on a chair. 'Now that I understand my condition,' Jane went on, 'I can easily bear the discomfort. And indeed, at this moment I feel perfectly well. I'm only sorry that last night I spoilt our evening by my indisposition.'

'Not at all, not at all.' Sir Thomas frowned. 'I was only concerned for you. Very concerned, Jane. I don't think I have ever seen you ill and I shall not be properly easy in my mind until you are safely delivered.'

This was the first time anybody had expressed the fear that Jane herself felt. 'I'm sure it will all be all right,' she faltered. His look was as uncertain as her voice. 'Though I am anxious, I admit.' She abandoned her attempt at polite reassurance.

'You must be properly taken care of,' he murmured, looking as if he would like to perform the office himself. 'You must be cherished, indeed.'

He produced suddenly a small box from his pocket, a little larger than the one which had held the earrings. Jane opened it and was enchanted to find a small bird's nest, containing several tiny strawberries arranged like eggs. She cried out in pleasure at the sight.

'I wanted to bring you something ... to tempt you. But you must put them by until you feel equal to them.'

'How is it they are so small?'

'They are Alpine strawberries. I brought some plants back from Switzerland when I was a young man. They grow in my dell. They are best in the shade.'

'But I adore this! How you have arranged them here, like eggs in a bird's nest!'

'And brought them to you like a bird to its chick. Shall I feed you?'

'Oh, yes, please!' Jane opened her mouth. Sir Thomas

177

carried a strawberry to her lips, then another. She ate with relish and without any kind of discomfort.

'And this is the last,' said Sir Thomas playfully. 'Come, my little fledgling, open your beak.'

'Oh, no, you must have this one!' insisted Jane and, snatching the fruit from him, brought it to his lips. Playfully, for a moment, he refused to open his mouth; her fingers tried at first by force, at length by gentle coaxing, to find a way in. At last Sir Thomas accepted the strawberry and for an instant sucked one of her fingertips. At that moment Jane saw the light that was dancing in his eyes turn to a fierce blaze.

It was gone in an instant. He released her hand, and sat back and smiled at her with a more cautious air. 'Now, my dear, I know of a good servant, Bessie Stevens, who is looking for a position. I've told your mother, and if you like her, take her. I shall feel easier once you are being properly looked after.'

Jane thanked Sir Thomas and assured him she would soon be well.

'As to that ...' Sir Thomas consulted his memory. 'I believe the case varies. Charlotte was only a little disordered when her pregnancies were first confirmed. A slight fatigue for a few weeks and a disinclination to food, but she soon found her spirits and energy again, and for the last six months she was usually very well. Except with Eliza.' He was quiet for a moment and smoothed the counterpane with an abstracted air.

'You must miss her very much,' said Jane quietly.

He nodded, but said nothing for a moment. 'We must submit to the stroke of Fate.' His voice had sunk almost to a breath, but he recovered. 'Luckily I have many distractions. Wild girls all. My Eliza is a wilful creature. And you, my favourite, with child by this handsome fellow. I'd like to knock him down, but he's too damned tall.' Sir Thomas's tone was odd. He was trying to tease, but it was awkward.

'And you are to mend poor Mary's broken heart,' she reminded him.

'Ah! That. I had forgot. I'm most obliged to be reminded of my duties. Yes. I had hoped you would assist me in that task. But here you are, lounging about, useless. Lazy hussy!'

They managed to laugh, and Jane assured him she would help him mend Mary's heart, and reconcile her to a long wait for Henry, as soon as she could get up again.

Jane began to feel hungry and Sir Thomas, having no more strawberries, went downstairs and returned having found some bread and butter, which she ate with astonishing appetite.

'I'm glad to see this,' he said heartily. 'I like to see my livestock flourishing, you know.'

Jane laughed. 'I could not think of eating till you came with your strawberries.'

'My dear! I would willingly return to Switzerland on my hands and knees if necessary to ensure you a supply. But I trust that will not be necessary. There is quite a crowd of them down in the dell. You will not lack strawberries, I promise you.'

'Tell me about Switzerland.'

Sir Thomas told her of his travel to the Alps, and to Italy and France, and she listened with enchantment to his descriptions of the mountains, the cowbells, the frescoes and the gondolas.

'But ah!' concluded Sir Thomas. 'I was twenty then. I wish I were twenty now!'

'I expect you fell in love with an Italian beauty,' suggested Jane slyly, trying to imagine Sir Thomas at twenty and deciding he must have been not substantially different from Sir Thomas at forty.

'Not in the least,' cried Sir Thomas. 'I was but a green youth. I knew nothing of the delights of love. I admired everybody, but kept my heart securely locked.'

'That showed good sense,' said Jane. 'For I think young

people often throw their hearts away, without regard for the pain which . . .' She could not finish her sentence.

He gave her a sharp look. 'Oh my dear,' he said quietly, 'believe me, the pangs of young love are as nothing compared with what is suffered in that line by us old ones. Do not expect amendment. It gets worse.'

Mr Harris, at this moment, arrived back at the lodge and the conversation was terminated.

24

Jane slept. She awoke in the middle of the afternoon feeling refreshed and ventured downstairs. The garden was a great temptation, but she had not walked up and down the rows for more than two minutes before the dreadful fatigue began again to steal over her, and she was glad enough to claim a seat in the parlour and admire the progress of her plants through the window.

She was able to take tea with her husband. The meal was prepared by Hetty, who had been sent across from Newington House as a temporary measure to repair the damage done by her niece's neglect. Jane was relieved to find she could eat dry toast without any discomfort whatever, and her husband condescended to take a little bread and butter, and to admire her plum jam. He seemed more comfortable with a servant present and looked at Jane without any of the irritation which had marred their recent days.

At half-past four Mary arrived and, after enduring her hectic chatter for a minute or two, William Harris went up to his study.

'I am going to discuss colours with Sir Thomas, for Henry's room, you know,' confided Mary, after the first ecstasies had been expressed over Jane's condition. 'We are to plan how Henry's room might be made new. I think blue – because of the sea, and also his eyes, of course.'

'I am not sure I would like a room to match my eyes.'

Jane smiled. 'Nobody would be able to see anything in the dark.'

'Ah, but Henry's eyes are so light and clear,' cried Mary. 'Sometimes they seem to be blue and sometimes green. What do you think, Jane?'

Jane declined to offer an opinion, reminded Mary that Sir Thomas would be waiting for her and watched her sister depart with some envy. She had sent Sir Thomas her good wishes, but was not at all confident of Mary's ability to deliver them. Shades of blue were, she had to admit, a much more fascinating study.

She was stopped, in the midst of a sigh, by a knock on the door. Hetty ushered in a small young woman with a pretty pink face, large, imaginative eyes and a rapid tongue. She advanced towards Jane with an expression of eager goodwill.

'Good afternoon, Mrs Harris. I am Bessie Stevens. Sir Thomas said you might be kind enough to consider me for a position and being at present without a situation I would be most grateful to be considered. I have but lately come home from London, where I worked for six years for a family in Primrose Hill; and indeed the hill was delightful.

'But I was so homesick for the air here and then my sister Jenny – who's in Sir Thomas's employment you know, she's his parlourmaid – wrote saying mother was ill – mother lives down in Woolton, my father was a weaver, we always paid our bills, Madam, not that that is to the purpose . . . Oh, dear! I've lost my drift . . . ah yes – to conclude, I'm come home, and my last employer has given references, and I beg you will forgive my tongue, I've always been called a rattle, but it is worst when I'm agitated, as I am now, as you will understand.'

At last the girl subsided. Hetty, turning to Jane for further orders, expressed with a slight roll of the eyes her contempt for this person who had come to claim her niece's place, but Jane, who had been diverted as well as a little astonished by Bessie's speech, merely asked Hetty to make some more tea and Hetty withdrew to the scullery.

'I'm but a poor housekeeper, Bessie, and it is now made worse by my condition.'

The girl nodded eagerly. 'Yes, Madam, I've already been informed thereof by your mother whom I had the honour of attending just now.'

'My husband's a clergymen. He's studying above.' Bessie cast a venerating glance at the ceiling. 'He must have quiet.'

'Oh, yes, Madam,' Bessie whispered. 'Indeed I can be quiet, as quiet as a mouse, well quieter; we did have a mouse in the attics at Primrose Hill who kept us awake all night.'

'Yes. Good. Quietness, then, and cookery. Can you cook?'

Bessie's eyes lit up. 'I love nothing better, Madam! And I see you have a kitchen garden. Ah! I spy rosemary.' She looked out of the window. 'And here we are of course sheep country. I don't think you need be anxious on that score. If you study my references you will find Mrs Edgemoor was quite satisfied with my cookery. Indeed, it was as a cook that I was employed by her, as she kept a large establishment.

'But previously, Madam, I was employed as a general servant in Islington and to be candid I preferred it, for I do love variety. Polishing and scrubbing are my delight. I love to make things clean and bright. Ah! That is a rhyme. I beg your pardon. I'm agitated.'

'Compose yourself.' Jane smiled, reading the references which Bessie had handed to her. Here was expressed not only satisfaction, but affection, and though this was Jane's first experience as an employer she suspected Bessie's references were unusually complimentary. 'Well, Bessie, I'm more than happy to offer you this place.'

Bessie's face burst into a radiant smile and she uttered a small involuntary squeak, covering her mouth with her hand like a child. 'Oh Madam, I'm sorry, thank you.'

'Now, as to where you will live . . . There's no room here. There are but two bedrooms and my husband uses the other as his study.'

'Oh, Madam, don't be anxious on that account – I've a friend who lives in the cottage at the far end of the wood, one of Sir Thomas's tenants, Annie Dearlove, and she will gladly offer me a room. It won't take me five minutes to walk here in the morning. What time shall I come? You'll want the fire going by six, I should think – it gets light so early these days.' Bessie's delight in anticipation of her chores was as reassuring as it was mysterious to Jane, who felt a deep comfort in the girl's arrival.

Hetty entered with the tea and Jane asked her to step upstairs and summon Mr Harris down, for she supposed he would want to meet Bessie Stevens to cast an approving eye over her appearance, which was indeed very neat and modest. But Hetty returned to report that Mr Harris wished not to be disturbed and that he would be obliged if his wife would make all the necessary domestic arrangements herself.

Jane was glad to be given this freedom and bade a cheerful goodbye to Bessie, who promised to be at work by six o'clock the next morning. At this thought Jane sat back in her chair with profound relief.

Hetty now appeared with a brow creased with jealousy and resentment. 'Our Kitty has been ill, Miss Jane,' she remarked. 'Else she should have been here to help you most willingly I'm sure.'

'Give Kitty my best wishes for a speedy recovery,' said Jane, feeling that her moment of repose had been rather too short. 'I'm sorry I'm too ill myself to manage without immediate assistance. It was all decided while I was asleep, between Mamma and Sir Thomas.'

Hetty shrugged and looked sour. 'Well, our Kitty would have done her utmost to serve you, Miss Jane, and what's more, she knows how to hold her tongue.'

Jane was irritated by the persistence of this grievance, but as Hetty had known her since she was a child, she found it difficult to assert her authority. 'No doubt I shall have a larger establishment in due course and I'll remember Kitty then. Have you prepared some supper? I know Mamma wanted you back at seven.'

'There is a fricassee prepared, Madam, though I can't claim to London cookery.'

Thanked and discharged, Hetty departed with a slam of the door. Jane sighed. Beyond the weakness caused by her condition, she was beginning to feel the fatigues of domestic administration and thought ruefully of the days, not so long ago, when she had been a carefree girl.

After supper Jane retired early. Her husband spent two more hours in his study. It was ten o'clock before he came into the bedroom. Jane, who had been dozing, awoke in fear, but was reassured by his unusual expression. Repose and satisfaction were apparent in his face and in the movements of his body. He sat down on the bed and took her hand.

Jane's heart leapt in delight. Perhaps some invisible barrier had been removed: perhaps now the intimacy she had longed for would make their private hours a pleasure. She smiled, longing but fearing to give words to the love she still felt for William Harris, despite everything.

'So, I am to be a father,' he said, with almost half a smile. 'The thought is very curious in its novelty, but it's what I have wished for. You must be very well taken care of, my dear.'

'Oh, I'm sure I shall be, William. Bessie Stevens impressed me greatly and she comes with excellent references. I'm sure we shall both be comfortable now.'

'As to myself, I shall have to resume my work on the circuit in two weeks or so.' He released her hand, and instead began to stroke his own hair, as if in thought. His eyes had wandered from her face to the pillow beside her: his pillow. 'But I leave you in very good hands and I shall write often.'

Jane was hurt by the necessity for him to depart alone for what might be months, but she was far too ill to consider going with him. She sighed.

His eyes returned to her face. 'You might prefer, while I'm away, to go back to live with your mother in greater comfort.'

'No!' cried Jane. Though she had been most unhappy at times in this small lodge she found she loved it and would rather stay. 'I'll be quite comfortable with Bessie. I'll wait for you here. I may be a lot better by the time you return. Sir Thomas says that Lady Char—'

'And till I have to go off again,' he interrupted, getting up, 'it will be easier for us both if I sleep in the other room.' Jane felt this withdrawal with some pain. So there was to be less intimacy, not more. This was the reason for the repose and satisfaction of his manner. He had found an excuse to abandon her.

She banished this treacherous thought the instant it leapt into her mind, but it left a kind of mental bruise which she could not erase from her memory for many weeks afterwards. 'Oh yes, William.' She managed to keep her voice steady. She must accept his departure gracefully. She must avoid those displays of hysteria which had made her days so difficult recently. 'I should be sorry to keep you awake by my restlessness. You must have the refreshment of a good night's sleep while you are working on your paper.'

He nodded, made a slight bow, and withdrew, shutting the door behind him. She heard him also shut the door to the little room opposite. Was it so necessary to shut both doors between them? What if she became really ill in the night and required his assistance? Could he hear if she called? Did he want to hear?

She turned over and lay on her side. The candle still burned. She stared into its flame, remembering what he had said on the day he had proposed to her, watching the fire-eater in Bath. 'You are the only woman to whom I feel I can reveal myself.' But he had never revealed himself to her at all. He had withdrawn, now, to another room, with evident relief. Jane felt she had seen and heard all of her husband that he would ever be prepared to share – with her, at least.

These were terrible wounds, but she was too tired to

weep. She must not permit herself to regret the haste of her marriage, nor the resentment which arose whenever she considered how much older and more experienced William Harris was. It would be easy to think she had been preyed upon, that his proposal had been an unscrupulous act – except that it always seemed to her that her husband did not want her. What, then, had been the point of his proposal? This was the enigma which she was left to ponder alone.

She blew out the candle and stretched out in the bed. There was more room now he was gone. Ever since her marriage she had dreaded disturbing his sleep. She had lain still and narrow, as one in a coffin. Now she could sprawl at will. She began to feel that solitude might offer some comforts. All the same, she would a thousand times sooner have felt a husband's arms around her and the attic of the little lodge seemed a very lonely place, as owls hooted outside under the moon.

25

William Harris completed his paper and departed for the circuit. Letters arrived from him with great regularity, but Jane searched in vain through them for any expression of affection beyond the civility of customary form. There was not even much that was personal in them. He described his travels, and his congregations, as if he was not there himself but watching from far off.

She almost began to resent the arrival of the letters, brought to her with eagerness by Bessie. She felt he was offering her the outward signs of devotion, without any private substance. Of course it was marvellous that he was saving so many souls – that his progress through the West Country provoked such ecstasies – but after scanning the letters and finding as usual nothing except sermons and transfigurations, Jane would drop each to the floor for the sunbeams to pass across. It was left to Bessie to pick them up, smooth them and place them in a drawer.

Bessie had moved into the lodge when Mr Harris had left for his tour, and she brought Jane more comfort and diversion than anybody. The sensitive girl could tell whether Jane required to be amused by an anecdote, or soothed by a silence. Now she had the ordering of the household, Bessie's conversation had grown more subdued. Though she still enjoyed an opportunity for digression, she usually knew when chatter would be unwelcome.

Jane's mother and sister often called, but soon tired her

with their busy confidences. The one visitor Jane longed to see scarcely ever came. Sir Thomas was much occupied with business. He called once or twice with Mary or Eliza and frequently sent small gifts of strawberries, or other fruits as the season progressed, but he did not appear often in person. Jane listened to Mary's accounts of parties and walks at Ottercombe with the greatest envy and was obliged more than once to avoid tears of self-pity by thinking of those whose lives were infinitely more pitiable than her own.

Bessie had a tender heart. She was also blessed with a great curiosity and soon discovered the sad case of the charcoal burner's family, Mr Lockhart's poorest tenants who lived in the wood. 'Those poor people, Madam!' she cried one morning, bringing Jane some tea. 'The Smiths. That unfortunate woman struggling with the palsy, and their oldest girl must bear the whole duties of the house. I pity them.'

Jane had intended more than once to help the family, but had been distracted by her own affairs. 'What can we do to help them, Bessie?' she cried.

'Well, they are your father's tenants,' observed Bessie. 'You could perhaps suggest ... although that tumbledown old cottage will always be damp and cold, even if money were spent on it. But the cottage next to Mrs Dearlove's at the other end of the wood falls vacant at Michaelmas. Old Jasper Fielding is going to live with his daughter at Hawksley and that cottage of his is neat and dry, it's twice as good as that old hovel – excuse me for saying so, Miss.'

'No, no; my father has neglected his duties in that respect, you are quite right.'

Jane knew her father was more inclined to improve the magnificence of his own accommodation than amend the squalor of his tenants'.

'Old Jasper's cottage is another of Sir Thomas's,' Bessie went on. 'I wonder if he has decided yet who is to have it after Jasper? Sir Thomas thinks the world of you, Madam – a word from you at the right moment could secure it for the Smiths, I am sure.'

Jane resolved to speak to Sir Thomas on the subject as soon as she had the opportunity of seeing him again. At present, however, he was away on business for a few days, so she was obliged to attend to other things.

One of her greatest pleasures, as she began to grow stronger, was to inspect her garden. At first she only peeped through the window; then, as the heat of August gave way to the mildness of September, Bessie placed a chair for her outside the back door and she was able to admire the late sunshine and gather a few last peas and beans. The gardener had kept the little patch free from weeds throughout the summer.

In time, some of her old energy returned. Towards the end of September William Harris was due to come home and she found she longed for him in a peculiarly piercing way. This time, refreshed by absence, he might come to her arms and bring her release at last from the yearning which seemed to gnaw at her mind and body.

'I wonder if William will come home this week,' she mused one morning, as Bessie tended the fire and stirred the porridge.

'You said he was delayed for some days in Bristol, Madam.'

'Yes. But I don't know for how long. Perhaps somebody down in Woolton will know. He has many friends down there, in the church. One of them may have received some message.'

'Would you like me to ask about?' Bessie's eyes brightened. Such an expedition was a delightful opportunity for one so sociably inclined.

'Would you like to go down and see your mother this afternoon?' asked Jane. 'You may leave me without any anxiety. I'm quite a different creature nowadays.'

'Bless me, yes, you are, Madam.' Bessie beamed, glad to admire in Jane's face the effects of an improving appetite and her own skilful cookery. 'I would indeed like to visit Mother and I'll find out what I can.'

Bessie returned that evening to report that Mr Harris was not expected yet, but his friend and assistant Mr Watts had returned early from the tour and had excited the neighbourhood the previous evening by a meeting at Mrs Gurton's house. It was said Mr Watts could communicate with the dead and at last night's meeting he had appeared, while in a kind of trance, to deliver messages to those present. He had convinced them, by several authentic and secret details, that these communications had come from their dear ones in the next world.

'Folks say he spoke to Mrs Arkwright in the very voice and tone of old Sam Arkwright, who died last March – and the extraordinary thing is, Madam, Mr Watts never met old Sam in his life, nor Mrs Arkwright neither. Mother says she won't go to see it, though she would dearly love to hear my father's voice, for she says she would be so disappointed if there was nothing: no message for her at all.'

'Ask Mr Watts to come up here, if he will,' said Jane, giving way to a sudden impulse. 'I don't wish him to deliver any messages from the dead but I suppose he has been travelling with my husband for the past few weeks and will be able to give me a good account of William's health and spirits, and what keeps him in Bristol and when I'm likely to see him again.'

Bessie conveyed the message the following day and Colin Watts presented himself at Jane's door that evening, just as the sun was setting and the rooks were gathering with their evening noise at the opposite end of the park, where the great trees had been thrown by the setting sun into looming shapes of absolute blackness.

Mr Watts seemed taller than she remembered, but perhaps it was the effect of the low ceiling. He looked about him, on entering, with undisguised curiosity.

'Would you care for a glass of port, Mr Watts? Do sit down.'

He accepted both invitations and was soon established in the chair opposite, and found the fire quite welcome, for the

191

evenings had begun to be chilly. Bessie retired to a corner of the room, where by her own candle she busied herself with hemming a blanket. Such large stitching could be done at night, though the light was not good enough for finer work.

'So – I wondered how the tour went and how William was, and hearing you had returned, I thought you might be able to give me an account of him.'

'Indeed.' Colin Watts spoke with a halting air and glanced at her with shy hesitation. She examined the angles of his face, which was delicate and pointed, but curiously irregular. Slanting cheekbones, and a lack of symmetry, made it seem as if he was smiling on one side and grieving on the other. His eyes, however, were large and expressive. In them she saw thoughts which formed and passed across his brain, but were not articulated. It was evident he was cautious and prudent in his speech.

'I left ... your husband three days ago in Bristol. He wished to ... attend some meetings – about the missions. He was in good health, I think.'

'And has he been well all the time?'

'Oh yes. He's almost never ill. At least I've not seen him so.'

'How long have you known him?' She seized the opportunity to find out more about the man she had married, for she felt almost anybody must know him better than she did.

'Oh, about – some years. Certainly. Five, I should say.'

'And where did you meet?'

'In ... at a church, in Bristol.' He seemed uneasy.

Jane paused. She wondered if he might feel too much interrogated. 'He's an odd character, I think, my husband.'

'We are all odd, perhaps. I know I am.' Colin Watts permitted himself a sudden grin. He glanced at her as if in apology.

'Well, you are odder than most, from what I hear.' Jane had not meant to touch on the subject of Mr Watts's trances, but his reserve on the subject of her husband's character was so impenetrable she abandoned her researches in that area and found herself more intrigued by Mr Watts himself.

'What do you hear?' He cocked his head slightly. The angle was almost impertinent, or perhaps flirtatious.

'I hear you carry messages.'

His eyes grew dark and reflective. 'It is a gift. Some do not approve.'

'How is it achieved?'

'I must listen. But first I must prepare myself.'

'And can you do so anywhere?'

'Not anywhere. I must have quietness and sympathetic souls about me.'

'Could you do it here?'

Mr Watts hesitated. He looked about the room, a degree of indecision very evident in his face. 'I'm not sure—' He glanced at Bessie.

'You need not fear my servant. Bessie and I are most sympathetic to you, Mr Watts. No one will ever hear of it, I assure you.'

'Particularly your husband?' He looked directly at her, with a face so apprehensive she was shocked.

'Does my husband not approve?'

'He has seen it, but he does not . . . like the work.'

'Why not?'

Colin Watts shrugged, but Jane felt he knew the reason well, only would not divulge it.

'Well, Mr Watts, be sure that if you hear any messages here tonight, neither Bessie nor I will say a word to anyone. Will we, Bessie?'

'Oh, never, Madam.' Bessie paused in her work with an uneasy but avid air.

'Very well.' Colin Watts put aside his glass, stretched his body, loosened his cravat and undid the first two buttons of his shirt. 'Permit me . . . ?'

'Of course. What else do you require?'

'Oh nothing but silence, and patience for a while. And I would rather only the far candle burned.'

Jane hastily extinguished the nearer candle. Only the firelight played now on Colin Watts's face. The far candle, where Bessie sat, was almost spent.

Jane watched in awe as his head inclined downwards. Very slowly, it seemed, he dropped into a kind of sleep. The fire hissed and seethed. The clock on the mantelpiece seemed to tick more loudly than before. The wind stirred some trees outdoors, a door banged, a dog barked far away in the wood – the charcoal burner's dog, perhaps.

Suddenly Colin Watts's head jerked upright. His face seemed to shudder and be drawn up, twitching, towards the ceiling, like a puppet who feels the irresistible pull of a string. His face grew contorted and his breathing deepened till it came with rasping force, a sound so unpleasant that Jane longed for him to stop. Yet she was transfixed with fear and expectation, so that when at last he spoke, her whole body leapt in shock.

'Little puss!' he cried, in a growl completely different from his usual light voice. 'Little puss! Little puss!'

Jane was as puzzled as she was disconcerted. His features grew more and more contorted.

'Little puss! Let us give it a saucer of tea!'

There was a sudden rustle behind Jane and Bessie flew out of her chair to Mr Watts's side and knelt beside him, tears pouring down her cheeks.

His hand began to shake. It dropped upon the girl's head and stroked her.

Bessie was seized with a violent shuddering. 'Oh, Pa!' she whispered. 'Oh, Pa! Is it you?'

'Yes, little puss: yes, yes, little puss. Tell your mother not to fret, not to fret little puss, and keep you warm, and see to the door, where my old cloak hangs, and tell your mother sell it, sell it. Sell it, little puss.'

'Sell what?' Bessie was bewildered, but Mr Watts's head fell forward upon his chest. The visitation was gone.

Bessie recollected herself and drew back a little till her back touched her mistress's knees. She was still shaking.

Jane placed a soothing hand on the girl's shoulder till she was quiet. Mr Watts's breathing grew more shallow. He seemed suspended for minutes between breaths, then came a deep sigh. Gradually Jane saw his face was unfolding again, so slowly one could barely see it move, like a flower that feels the sun.

His very features seemed to alter. The grotesque expression of the previous manifestation had given way to something beautiful, exalted. His features seemed to float in some dimension beyond the mortal world. Jane hardly dared to breathe.

'Yes.' He spoke suddenly in a light and musical voice. 'I am here. I have a message for you, Jane Lockhart.'

'Who are you?' Jane asked breathlessly.

'A friend,' came the reply. It was a woman's voice. 'He loves you, though he cannot show it.' Mr Watts spoke rapidly and with authority, very unlike the previous rambling and mumbling.

The blood rushed to Jane's cheeks and the hairs seemed to stand up on her head. So he loved her! The suspicion fled through her mind that Colin Watts was perfectly conscious and this message a charade to reassure her, but it went so acutely to the heart of her distress that she was for a moment utterly silenced by it.

The stillness seemed frozen for an instant. Nobody stirred or spoke, then quite unexpectedly the door burst open and William Harris stepped into his house. He stared in astonishment at the tableau before him: Mr Watts in an ecstasy and his wife embracing her servant, who was kneeling on the floor, her face streaked with tears.

'Oh, William!' cried Jane, scrambling astonished to her feet. Bessie lunged up also, floundering in her panic, and Colin Watts, roused from his fit by the sudden interruption, awoke and blinked, amazed, at the company, as if he had only just arrived himself. When he saw William Harris standing at the door he uttered a strange sound, like a choke, but seemed unable to move or speak.

'How dare you!' cried William Harris. 'After everything I said?'

'Oh, William!' cried Jane. 'I'm so sorry—'

'How dare you?' William Harris stepped forward now, his indignation gathering and deepening. His glare swept the company. 'Knowing what I think about such shows, deploring it as I do – how dare you come here, above all places, where I have explicitly forbidden you to come, while my back is turned, you insinuating, treacherous fiend ... you ... you devil!'

Jane understood with surprise that she was not the object of her husband's fury. He was addressing Colin Watts.

26

Colin Watts fled into the night; Bessie escaped to the scullery. Jane prepared to face her husband's anger alone. For some moments he said nothing, looking about the room.

'I asked him to come,' said Jane. 'I only wanted him to tell me how you were. I knew he would have seen you recently.'

'Then why could he not simply satisfy your curiosity and have done with it?' William Harris gnawed at his sense of injury. 'Oh, no. He must indulge in his wretched posturing, his superstitious mimicry, to impress you.'

'I thought he was your friend.' Jane was bewildered. 'When we were travelling together in May he always rode with you. You praised him. You said he was your assistant. I should never have asked him to come if I had known you disliked him.'

'I had not found him out, then,' remarked William grimly. 'It was on this last tour that I discovered his true nature. He is a man devoured by envy. He resents my eloquence and turns to his absurd fits and trances to impress females. He works upon their passions. Hysterics are what he likes to provoke. Then he feels he can manipulate you.'

'He never manipulated me,' insisted Jane. 'I was nothing like hysterical. I was perfectly calm throughout.' This was not completely true. Colin Watts had caused her heart to pound and the hairs to stand up on the back of her neck. But these were symptoms best denied at present.

'Your maid – what's her name – was clearly hysterical. When I come home after months away I don't expect to find the servant crouching on the floor like a dog and my wife's arms around her, both hypnotised by a mountebank.'

'I was not hypnotised, William! I observed Mr Watts's fit with interest, I admit. It would not be human to ignore it. Even you have been present at his trances.'

'I wanted merely to satisfy myself that he was a dangerous charlatan. And I'm especially angry because I have told him explicitly to keep away from this house.'

'Why?'

'To protect you! He is an evil influence. His messages could disturb a delicate sensibility and even unhinge a woman of a nervous inclination.'

Jane did not know whether to be flattered or insulted by this speech. 'I hope I'm rational enough to consider any message he might deliver merely as a mystery, a curiosity to ponder in a quiet moment, and not to be distracted from the main business of life.'

'What message did he give you?'

She hesitated and blushed. She could not answer him immediately and took refuge in an oblique reply. 'I said nothing to him about you, William, except to ask about your health. I have never spoken about you otherwise.'

'Ah, so the message concerned me?' He pounced, his eyes flaring.

'It was only ... "He loves you, though he cannot show it."'

'That is not a message about me.' Her husband's indignation was coldly expressed. 'Nobody who had ever seen us together could doubt the warmth of my affection for you. No, it is himself he is forcing upon your attention with this insinuating invitation, this seductive mystery.'

'Oh, nonsense, William! I'm sure there was no intention of the kind. I've hardly ever spoken to the man.'

'That would not stop him. He wants to fascinate you to

198

spite me. He hates me, Jane. He would destroy my happiness if he could.' William Harris spoke with a fierce passion. 'Fear him, avoid him, if you love me.'

'But of course I love you, William!' She could not prevent herself from a declaration at last. 'That is why I invited him here. Because I love you, and have missed you. I've longed for you, indeed, these months you have been away.'

He looked at her with some alarm, and instantly became awkward. 'Yes,' he said flatly. 'I've missed you too, of course. And this business has prevented me from a proper greeting. How are you, my dear? I hope you're well.' He reached out a hand and touched her shoulder stiffly, almost like an officer inspecting some detail of an infantryman on parade.

The extraordinary emptiness of his greeting, following so soon upon his fury about Colin Watts, presented Jane with an unavoidable conclusion. Her husband had not missed her, had never longed for her and, finding himself now alone with her, was pretty much at a loss.

She assumed that, for some reason of his own, Colin Watts had wished to reassure her. She had often felt he understood her deeply in some instinctive way. But there could be no truth in the message. What her husband did not show, he could not feel. She kissed him on the cheek, for form's sake, and sat down again.

'It's not your fault.' He seemed to consider her own case more sympathetically for a moment. 'I left you vulnerable. And that servant is clearly—'

'Hush, William!' Jane knew that every word in the parlour could be heard with perfect clarity in the scullery.

'Send her home now. It's late.'

'But this is her home, William. She's been sleeping here since you went away.'

'Ah. Yes. Of course. But she had a friend at the end of the wood, a Mrs . . . Dangerfield—'

'Not Dangerfield, William. Dearlove. Annie Dearlove.'

'Well, she can take lodgings there again, I assume.'

'Perhaps. But not now – without notice. It may not be

convenient. We can't just send her out into the night.'

'Perhaps not.' He poked the fire and stared into it. 'I suppose I'll have to trespass on your hospitality for this one night, my dear.'

'No trespass in the world,' said Jane quietly, but avoiding any suggestion of pleasurable anticipation. Indeed she felt none, now. The fierce yearning she had had for her absent husband had cooled, since his arrival, into ashes.

Demurely they went to bed, she first, he later, undressing as he always used to in the dark. Lastly Bessie, having put the parlour to rights and dealt with the fire, came up to the neighbouring room.

William Harris could not conceal his irritation at the sound of her moving about in there. 'I must have my own room tomorrow,' he murmured. 'In your condition you require seclusion also.'

Jane did not like to be told what she required by someone who had shown so little curiosity about her needs that he had never thought to ask. She said nothing, however, dreading an argument beyond anything. As the night wore on she began to despair of ever sleeping and, though she could not tell whether her husband was asleep or not, she did not dare whisper an enquiry. His return had reminded her that silence, with him, was often preferable to speech.

The next day Bessie was accommodated once again at Mrs Dearlove's, but she continued to come in every day and to help Jane not only in every practical way, but by her sympathetic presence. William Harris's poor opinion of the girl as an hysteric was not much amended, despite all her excellent accomplishments. However, he seemed disposed to tolerate her for the present.

Another period of study was to occupy the winter months for William Harris. He lived almost twenty hours of every day in the small room beneath the eaves, only coming out every morning to walk for two hours. He spared an hour for dinner and an hour for supper. Jane lived a parallel life a few yards away. The same floorboards resounded beneath their feet, the same plaster felt their clothes brush past, air which had been expelled from his lungs entered secretly into hers, yet she felt as remote from him as if he had been at the furthest ends of the earth.

He asked her every day how she fared and she replied with cheerfulness, for as the autumn progressed she felt more energetic, despite her increasing heaviness. She never presumed to go with him on his walks, but often she would declare her intention of taking some exercise and make a circuit of the park. Her husband did not like these excursions of hers and expressed his disapproval as a concern for her health and safety, but she felt it was her freedom he feared.

Jane had convinced herself that her only course was to live quietly from day to day, and keep herself in health, until she was delivered. Then, she supposed, the pattern of her life would be greatly changed, though whether for better or worse she could hardly guess.

The presence of William Harris at the lodge deterred casual visitors, though Mary still called on her sister from time to time and seemed triumphantly recovered from her disappointment over Henry. She scarcely ever mentioned him now, and when she did, it was only with amused affection. Jane felt Sir Thomas had done his work very well and was grateful also to Eliza, who had become so close a friend to Mary as to need her company at Ottercombe almost every day.

When William Harris was required to interrupt his habitual study and go down to Woolton, his sister always came up to sit with Jane. This was a measure, Jane was told, imposed for her safety and comfort, but endured by her as intrusion and espionage. Miss Harris had lodgings in the town and had made friends there, but her conversation was never either animated or diverting. They spent their evenings together reading and Jane felt in her sister-in-law's scrutiny a persistent disapproval and jealousy, though Miss Harris was always polite. Jane was restless in her company and would much rather have been left alone.

As autumn deepened into winter, and Christmas approached, Jane felt an increasing agitation of mood very difficult to dispel. It was not wholly her apprehensions about childbirth. Rather it seemed a persistence of that fierce longing she had felt while her husband was away. Now it appeared undirected. Perhaps it was a symptom of her condition. She walked round and round the park, the garden, or the parlour, expressing in her ceaseless exercise a heart crying out for something beyond the blank custom of her daily life.

One day towards Christmas Mary called, on her way home from Ottercombe Park, and found Jane lying on her bed, as she had begun to feel tired in the afternoons.

'We're having a great party at Ottercombe on Christmas Eve, Jane,' she whispered – for Mr Harris was working in the adjoining room. 'You must come – Sir Thomas particularly instructed me to bring you, if Mr Harris will allow it; and I'm sure he must, for it is Christmas after all and you haven't been out all autumn, as far as I remember – have you?'

'Not much.'

'Sir Thomas said you have been sorely missed.'

'I would love to come.'

'Will Mr Harris permit it? He's invited too, of course, but between you and me, Jane, I think we would prefer it if he stayed at home, for though he is so handsome, he is so severe in his manner it is rather like trying to talk to a portrait of Cardinal Richelieu. Don't be offended, he's your husband and of course you won't feel his strangeness as we do. But if he would rather stay at home with his books, let him.'

Jane smiled. 'I know what you mean. I'd rather come on my own and I'll do what I can to contrive it, tell Sir Thomas.'

'Excellent! Well, I must go now, Jane, or I'll be late for

supper and Mamma will thrash me soundly with her cat o'nine tails.' Mary got up and walked to the door. 'Oh! I almost forgot. Sir Thomas sent you some sweetmeats, in his handkerchief.' She tossed a soft white parcel through the air and Jane caught it.

Mary went home and Jane undid her parcel with sudden eagerness. It was a long time since Sir Thomas had sent her a little treat. She folded back the corners of the handkerchief and three exquisite sweetmeats were revealed, made of sugared almonds, icing and marzipan. Jane ate them with relish, for she had developed a keen appetite once the first few months of her pregnancy were past. She was very grateful to Sir Thomas for his kind thought and lifted his handkerchief to wipe the crumbs from her lips.

Holding it for a moment against her face, she suddenly felt upon it the faintest exhalation of Sir Thomas himself. This handkerchief had been close to his skin at some time and the scent of him came as a curious shock. Breathing it in, she recalled all the times when she had been close to Sir Thomas: quiet talks on the sofa, walks in Bath and dancing with him at the ball. She had never before been able to enjoy the scent of his skin without his physical presence: his reassuring warmth, his quick understanding, his sympathetic eyes. She felt a piercing sense of loss.

'Jane?' Her husband opened the door and looked in. 'I want my supper and I suppose you're hungry too. I'm going out tonight, so let's go down early. I have alerted Bessie – she knows – and I think I hear Martha arriving now.'

Jane felt that faint lowering of spirits which always accompanied Miss Harris's arrival. It would be easy to think of her as a kind of jailor, but Jane knew that if she indulged such ideas it could only make her more unhappy. She had acquired a kind of equilibrium which she needed to survive this passage of time and she knew she must preserve it.

She was accordingly very polite to Miss Harris and made many enquiries about her health, her reading, her friends, et cetera, but they had scarcely had time to do justice to Bessie's lamb cutlets when a sudden rainstorm of great ferocity broke upon the house. Bessie herself ran home under a borrowed cloak, but the weather offered Mr Harris no choice but to cancel his excursion, nor did it permit his sister any thought of returning to Woolton that night.

'You must sleep in my study, Martha, if you can tolerate the disorder. Papers are scattered everywhere, I'm afraid.'

'I shall be glad to read over any parts of the work that are completed.' Miss Harris smiled at her brother with a peculiar purity of devotion which Jane had begun to find very irritating. 'Have you read any of it yet, Jane?'

'Oh no, Martha. I'm afraid William has such a poor opinion of my understanding he's never shown me anything he's written.'

Her husband looked at her with astonishment and anger. 'You're free at any time to read what I have written and always have been. I would welcome your comments.'

'Don't be cross, William.' Jane had now to deflect his defensive anger with a parade of flirtatiousness. 'I'm not clever enough to understand your work. Luckily Martha is and you must depend on her for sound advice, as you always have done since long before you ever met me.'

William Harris looked suspicious at this speech, as if he detected something subversive in it, but Jane's smile was so artless he was able to put away his misgivings and turn his attention once more to his sister.

Clean linen was put on the visitor's bed. William Harris and his sister performed this office together, insisting that Jane must be spared the exertion. She had begun in any case to be tired and hastened to her own bed with a feeling of anxiety, for she knew her husband would be joining her and she had not been burdened with his company at night since the first evening he had come home at the end of September. Almost three months had passed since then.

Jane lay and thought about that night, and Colin Watts's trance and his mysterious message. Unhappily, Mr Harris had not said or done anything since his return to dispel her sad conviction that he did not love her, despite the encouragement of supernatural opinion. She heard him enter in the dark, undress and get into bed. Immediately he turned his back on her, pulled the bedclothes over his shoulders and gave a great sigh, as if enduring some necessary ordeal.

Though Jane was quite used to her husband's coldness, this renewed evidence of his indifference was particularly wounding now. She felt tears come and, reaching under her pillow, found Sir Thomas's handkerchief and buried her face in it. Her husband heard no sob and felt no shudder. He was soon asleep, for he had worked for half the previous night, but it was more than two hours before Jane found rest at last.

She dreamed she was running across the park with her husband and his sister beside her. It was as if they were running a race. As she ran, she looked to the left and saw William Harris's face alongside. On the right, his sister reached out her hands and clutched at Jane to stop her. Jane knew she must escape and, with a violent concentration of the will, she rose into the air.

Astonished to find she could fly, and triumphant to see her husband and his sister below, looking up in frustration, Jane turned away from them and gave herself up to the luxurious sensation of flying. Her limbs beat rhythmically; the warm breeze licked her skin and caressed her hair. It was like swimming in the air. She became aware she was not flying alone. Sir Thomas was with her, smiling and offering his hand. Together they ascended through the clouds, flying more closely together, and it was with a mounting rapture that Jane felt his arms close round her. As they broke through the last wisps of vapour, the sun burst upon their heads and Jane felt a convulsion of joy which made her cry out, and she awoke.

'What is it, Jane?'

For a moment she thought Sir Thomas had spoken. She

was sure he was in the room. She could smell him. The exquisite sensations were still echoing through her body.

Quickly, however, she recognised that her husband was beside her, that she had woken him up and that the scent of Sir Thomas came from the handkerchief, which she clutched on her breast. 'I'm sorry, William.' She trembled. 'A nightmare. I thought . . . I thought there was someone in the room.'

'Compose yourself,' he said. 'You are safe. There is only me.'

27

Her husband was soon asleep, but Jane could not find rest. The dream had gone, but the feelings it had aroused persisted with violent power. A hundred recollections flooded into her heart. She recalled standing with Sir Thomas at a window in Bath, looking down on the street and feeling peculiarly happy. As she now re-examined the whole course of their acquaintance she believed she could detect, in his words and actions, a partiality for her company which she had enjoyed without valuing it properly at the time.

But from the day she had confessed her engagement, Sir Thomas's manner had become more restrained, only briefly regaining his old playfulness when he brought her the strawberries. She had been too preoccupied by the anxieties of her marriage to lament Sir Thomas's withdrawal, though she had noticed it. He had hardly been to see her during the whole autumn. She acknowledged this neglect, now, with distress.

Jane pressed the handkerchief to her face. The dream had been a revelation, unfolding to her in an instant what, in due course, she would certainly have discovered more slowly. The arrival of William Harris had hypnotised her and, while she was paralysed by his glamour, Mr Harris had seized her. For what purpose he had wanted to marry was a mystery. But Jane began to feel that if she had never met William Harris, she might in time have found that she was in love with Sir Thomas.

Her husband awoke and got up. It was still dark. He dressed quietly. Jane lay still, her face hidden in the crook of her arm, pretending to be asleep. He left the room and went downstairs. Soon afterwards, Jane heard his sister go down. Their voices sounded indistinctly in the room below. Jane was glad she could not hear their words. She did not want to be distracted from her own reflections.

After an hour or so, Jane got up and dressed. She was determined to see Sir Thomas today. Her condition made every physical act laborious, but her fingers were quick and her heart determined. She had no intention beyond seeing him. Though she knew he sensed the unhappiness of her marriage she would not mention it. Sir Thomas must not be disconcerted by this visit.

She wished merely to revive her former intimacy with him and Eliza, as her nearest neighbours and dearest friends. What she might feel privately at the sight of him she did not dare to conjecture. Her face in the looking-glass seemed different. Her eyes danced with expectation.

Miss Harris went home in the late morning. William was distracted, at dinner, by thoughts of his work. Jane surprised him by announcing that she was walking down to Ottercombe Park that afternoon.

'What! In this weather?'

'The rain has stopped, William. There's only a light wind and that will refresh me.'

'You can't go alone in your condition.'

'Bessie will escort me. She's made all the preparations for supper already, so there will be no inconvenience to you. I'm sure you would not wish to interrupt your work to come with me?'

Jane made this innocent enquiry with a secret prayer. Her husband hesitated. He had long wished for the opportunity to talk to Sir Thomas about religious matters.

'And Eliza wishes very much to consult me about some little gowns she is sewing for the baby.' Jane invented, with some recklessness, a skill and pleasure in needlework entirely absent from Miss Eliza Burton's character. 'She's very excited about our child.' Jane went on, knowing that at the mention of his paternity her husband would grow uneasy, 'Mary says Eliza is always speculating about whether it will have your nose or mine.'

Mr Harris was defeated by these indecencies. 'Very well. But it's a shame you can't find time for useful charitable work instead of giving yourself up to vanities.'

'Oh, it is also a charitable mission,' answered Jane, amazed at how smoothly her brain provided her with lies and excuses. 'For I've been meaning for some weeks to ask Sir Thomas if my father's tenants, the Smiths, who live in the wood, you know, could have old Jasper Fielding's cottage when he leaves at Candlemas.'

'Very well,' said William Harris. 'Get Bessie to bank up the fire before you go, and leave a kettle on the hob.' He sighed and went upstairs heavily, like a man who has a great deal to bear.

Jane, however, felt herself grow lighter and lighter, despite her physical weight. She put on her bonnet and scarf, wrapped her cloak about her and, taking Bessie's arm, walked down the lane towards Ottercombe. Though but three o'clock, it was already growing dark. The last scraps of the departed storm tossed the leaves about. Jane could hardly hide her exhilaration at the thought of seeing Sir Thomas.

Bessie was a shrewd and perceptive soul and could feel, through her mistress's arm, an unusual vigour 'You should have come down to see Sir Thomas and Miss Eliza before, Madam,' she said. 'It would have done you good.'

'Yes, Bessie. I should.'

There was a truculence in this reply which alerted Bessie. The girl had formed her own opinion of Mr Harris's fitness to be Jane's husband and had to bite her lip a hundred times a day. 'If Mr Harris had had any consid—'

'Don't!' cried Jane suddenly. 'Don't mention Mr Harris,

Bessie. See how we float down the lane! Getting to Ottercombe is easy. It's almost like flying.'

'Aye,' agreed Bessie. 'But getting back afterwards will be another matter.'

At the house they parted. Bessie went round to the kitchens to look for her sister. Jane passed the drawing-room windows, glanced in and saw, in the indistinct fire-light, the back of the sofa and what looked like the top of Sir Thomas's head, with Eliza sprawling with her usual ease, a few of her curls visible on his shoulder. Jane felt a flash of anticipation. Her need now to see Sir Thomas was so desperate that when she found the front door open she rushed straight through without alerting the servants or waiting for any announcement. The drawing-room door was ajar. She walked in.

Jane saw Sir Thomas now at last, but he looked up with astonishment and alarm, rather than pleasure. It was not Eliza with him on the sofa; it was Jane's own sister, Mary, who leapt up and threw herself into Jane's arms.

'Oh! Jane! I'm so glad to see you! We're so inexpressibly happy! I'm engaged to Sir Thomas! We're to be married at the end of February and then I shall be Lady Burton; what do you think of that?'

Jane was unable to speak.

Behind Mary, Sir Thomas had also got up, but Jane could not look at him. She felt she could best survive this extra-ordinary shock by holding on to her sister and looking into her radiant face.

'Why, Jane, you've gone quite white! Sit down, dear!' Mary bounced down beside her, laughing at her sister's amazement. 'Look, Sir Thomas, poor Jane's quite speech-less! I know it's a surprise. Get your breath back, Jane, and we'll tell you the whole wonderful story.'

'Not yet.' Sir Thomas hovered at a distance. 'I'll get some brandy. I had not thought Jane would hear of it like this.' Jane could not look at him.

Mary jumped up and wound Sir Thomas's arm about

herself. 'Look, aren't we a handsome couple, though?' she exclaimed. 'Not as handsome as you and William, of course, but every bit as happy, I'm sure. You must congratulate us, Jane; don't just sit there gaping, you make me feel I've confessed to some appalling crime. I haven't murdered Sir Thomas, dearest – merely accepted him.'

Jane found her voice at last. 'I do congratulate you, Mary, I congratulate you both. I wish you every happiness. I'm only so very surprised, it's made me feel quite weak.'

'I'll get the brandy,' said Sir Thomas and went out.

Mary seized the few moments' seclusion to confide to her sister, in a hectic whisper, some details of her courtship. 'Oh, Jane! Don't disapprove! Please be happy for me! You may consider Sir Thomas is too old and ugly for a husband, but he's quite a dear, once you get to know him as I have done. I've become so fond of him these past few months, he's been so very kind! Oh, Jane! If only you could know him as I've come to know him, you would not disapprove at all.'

'I do not . . . disapprove.'

'Oh, good! For you must be friends, you know. Sir Thomas will be your brother-in-law. Isn't that delightful? We never had a brother. And you'll find him a dear. He indulges me in every little whim, Jane. Look at this pearl necklace he gave me.' Mary lifted her head to show it off. 'He says I have the sweetest neck – don't you, Sir Thomas?'

Sir Thomas had returned with the brandy. He offered it to Jane, but his hand shook and a few drops fell on her skirt. 'I'm sorry,' he said hastily. 'I'm clumsy.' He took out a handkerchief and, kneeling beside her, attempted to remove the stain.

'Don't trouble yourself,' said Jane quietly. He was close enough, now, for the scent of his skin to remind her unbearably of her dream. She wished he would go further off. 'Please – it's of no significance. It's only my old cloak.' She took a sip of brandy, felt its restoring heat and dared at last to look into his face.

He was still kneeling beside her, concerned and anxious.

211

But the expression in his eyes was dark and turbulent. 'You must forgive us', he said warily, 'for not acquainting you with this more gently.'

'Oh, no,' cried Jane. 'You must forgive me for coming in, unexpected and unannounced.'

They both took refuge in politeness.

Sir Thomas stood up awkwardly, and considered for a moment what to do. 'We were about to take some tea,' he said, looking vague and lost.

'Oh, yes, Sir Thomas, let's have some. I'm sure Jane would like it and perhaps we can have some of Hannah's marzipan cakes, for I know Jane's very hungry these days.'

Sir Thomas gave orders for the tea. Mary smiled at her sister and squeezed her hand. Jane felt she would be unable to eat anything, but that some tea might help her to maintain her composure and find the strength for the walk home.

'We were not expecting the pleasure of your company now.' Sir Thomas attended to the fire and lit some candles. 'I thought you'd be keeping close to home until after your confinement.' It was the subtlest enquiry as to her sudden arrival.

She found she must account for it. 'I've been meaning to ask you about Jasper Fielding's cottage for some time,' she said faintly. 'I was hoping you would call to see us at the lodge.'

'I do not like to disturb your husband's study.' Sir Thomas gave her a look she did not quite like. There was something aggressive in it. 'But what about the cottage?'

'Our ... my father's tenants, the Smiths, live in the greatest discomfort in the wood. Indeed, I'm ashamed that my father has not done more to improve their cottage. But I wondered if you might consider them for Jasper's house? I understand he will move out at Candlemas.'

'He will move out by the end of this week.' Sir Thomas seemed glad to speak of something other than his happy engagement. 'But unfortunately I've already offered the tenancy to another party. I'm very sorry not to be able to oblige you, Jane.'

This disappointment was stinging. Jane was dismayed for the Smiths' sake, but also felt it as a particular injury. It was the first time Sir Thomas had denied her anything.

Tea arrived. Jane's task was to endure the next half hour without losing her composure and Sir Thomas was also unusually quiet. Mary, however, would have found it hard to contain the ebullience of her spirits even if other talkative souls had been present. As it was, she profited by the silence of her companions in the fullest possible rehearsal of her happiness.

The opportunity came to leave and Jane was glad to go. She embraced her sister with a return of her old affection. It was not Mary's fault that she was to enjoy what Jane most ardently craved. Jane knew she had denied herself any possibility of such happiness by her own actions. She had married William Harris. Her sister would marry Sir Thomas and Jane would have to bear it.

'Kiss Sir Thomas now, Jane, like a sister!' cried Mary. 'Come, dearest, kiss Jane, if you can get near her – you're grown so very big, Jane.'

Jane prepared to receive what she supposed would be a civil kiss on the cheek, but to her surprise Sir Thomas took her suddenly in his arms and embraced her with evident passion for several seconds. 'Dear Jane!' he said in a kind of gasp. His mouth touched her ear; he kissed her cheek with vigorous feeling. She felt almost faint and, releasing herself from his arms, reached out once more to Mary.

Jane saw tears in Sir Thomas's eyes as she left. She could not guess at his feelings, nor did she dare to examine her own heart. Bessie was waiting and, seeing that her mistress was too upset to speak, devoted all her energies to helping her back up the hill, which had never seemed so steep.

Nor had her own bed ever seemed so sweet. She almost fell on it.

Her husband, observing her return, could not resist an

213

observation. 'I told you it would be too much for you. It was a foolish errand and very wilful of you to persist in it. You would do well not to go out again till you are delivered. It shows a cruel disregard for our child.'

28

Next day Jane was too disturbed in spirits to eat anything
and too distracted to sit still for more than a few moments.
At last, even her husband noticed it. 'Jane,' he said at
dinner, laying down his fork, 'you're exceedingly restless
today. What's the matter?'

'I can't get comfortable.' She had been walking about the
room, but stopped.

'Well, I suppose it's to be expected. But please try to sit
still until I've finished my dinner.' Jane sat down and
looked out of the window across the park. 'You might consider again my suggestion that you move to your father's
house until your confinement is past,' her husband went on.
'You would be more comfortable there, I'm sure.'

'And I would disturb you less.'

As Bessie was present, William Harris confined himself
to a warning look. 'I'm only thinking of your requirements.'

Jane had sometimes thought of Newington House with
longing. To escape from her husband's stern presence, and
to be fussed over by Mamma among the dear familiar
things of childhood, had seemed an inviting prospect. Now,
however, it would expose her to Mary's rapturous contemplation of Sir Thomas. Jane did not think she could bear it.
She wondered how long it would be before she could spend
half an hour without thinking of him, and with such agony.

Suddenly the small gate opened and Sir Thomas himself
walked up the path.

Jane leapt to her feet in alarm. 'It's Sir Thomas—'

'Open the door, Bessie.' William Harris rose from his dinner with an irritated sigh. Jane turned away from her husband to hide her face, but he was not observing her.

'Good afternoon, Mr Harris.' Sir Thomas sounded confident and at ease. 'I must apologise for disturbing you, but Mrs Harris called to see me yesterday with a request about the housing of some tenants and I've had some further thoughts on the matter which I'd like to propose to her.'

William Harris stood aside and Sir Thomas stepped in. Jane felt her agitation must be obvious to everybody.

'Ah, my dear Jane. I hope I find you well?'

'Very well, thank you, Sir Thomas.'

Sir Thomas looked about him, saw instantly that Mr Harris was but half-way through his dinner, and hesitated.

'I'll come out and walk with you in the park,' said Jane. She would rather not talk to him with her husband by.

'No, Jane, you overtaxed yourself yesterday,' said Mr Harris firmly. 'Sir Thomas will not mind me finishing my dinner; he's a man of the world, he knows we must all eat.'

'Oh certainly, certainly.' Sir Thomas took a chair, and smiled genially at Mr Harris.

'Bring Sir Thomas a glass of wine, Bessie,' said Mr Harris. Bessie obeyed.

'I'm very much obliged,' said Sir Thomas. 'Now, Jane, as to the Smiths—' His manner was brisk and kind. Jane did not like his brisk kindness. It seemed meant for someone else. But perhaps in Mr Harris's company she was someone else. 'Although Jasper's cottage is not a possibility I've had another thought. The gamekeeper's old cottage down in the valley bottom is empty.' Sir Thomas had built for his gamekeeper a trim new bothy convenient for the pheasant pens. 'I believe the old place could be made comfortable with very little trouble, and if you think Mr Smith and his family could benefit perhaps we should discuss it with them. And with your father, of course. I'm going to pay a call on him directly. Shall I mention the matter?'

'Oh – if you please. Yes.' Jane was still too affected by his unexpected arrival to reply very coherently.

'Please be so kind as to give my regards to Mr Lockhart,' said William Harris. 'I've been too deeply engaged in my work to call on him recently. He must find me a negligent son-in-law.'

'And do you find him an intimidating father-in-law?' enquired Sir Thomas. He seemed much more in command of himself today; especially when he addressed Mr Harris. 'I confess I'm much in awe of him now, and though he's given his consent, I feel obliged to ingratiate myself with a series of respectful attendances, which he must find most trying, poor fellow.'

William Harris frowned. 'His consent . . . ? I don't understand you, Sir Thomas.'

'Jane has not told you? I'm to marry her sister Mary.' Sir Thomas glanced quickly at Jane. He flushed and faltered. The blush spread to Jane's cheeks like an infection. She had found it impossible to inform her husband of Sir Thomas's marriage. To speak of it would provoke emotions which would be most painfully apparent and inappropriate. She could only, now, look into the fire and try to smile.

'What?' William Harris was astounded. 'Why did you not tell me this, Jane?'

'I wasn't sure—' Jane stammered at last. 'I thought perhaps Mary would like the engagement kept secret.'

'As to that, I think poor Mary would broadcast the glad tidings to the four corners of the globe if she could.' Sir Thomas smiled uneasily. 'No,' he went on, striving for a teasing air, 'I fear Jane does not approve of the match. She does not think me good enough for her sister, and she's right. I shall make but a poor bridegroom, I fear. Jane is wondering how such a fine girl as her sister can bear to throw herself away upon such a vile old toad as myself.'

William Harris looked rather shocked at this fierce exercise in self-mockery. Sir Thomas now fixed his eyes boldly on Jane, who began to feel that only her own wit could rescue her from this most painful situation.

'You're right, Sir Thomas!' she cried, rousing herself. 'You are not nearly good enough for a Miss Lockhart. I would not have you for a prince's ransom.'

Sir Thomas admired her courage and she found strength in it.

'Jane!' murmured her husband, dismayed at her impertinence.

'Oh, don't mind our jokes, Mr Harris,' cried Sir Thomas. 'Jane and I are old friends. I've only ever received insults from her and Jane's insults are very much to my taste. Now I'm in training to be her brother-in-law, I'm hoping for even more deadly abuse.'

William Harris looked puzzled, but was distracted from the challenges of irony by the arrival of one of Bessie's egg custards.

'Well, I suppose I must totter across the park to pay my respects to my father-in-law.' Sir Thomas sighed, rising. 'Before I crumble quite into dust.'

'I'll see you to the gate,' said Jane.

'Thank you, my dear. I'll do my best not to expire on your flower-beds.' Sir Thomas laughed and said goodbye to Mr Harris in hearty terms, anticipating with pleasure their future as brothers-in-law. There was a feverish quality to this jocularity, but it helped Jane out of the house and down the few yards to the gate.

'My flower-beds are in no danger. Everything's quite dead now,' murmured Jane, looking at the blackened stalks.

'Ah, but they will spring into life again. Miraculous nature,' observed Sir Thomas. He passed through the gate and as he closed it, his public geniality fell away. He leaned on the gate for a moment in grave reflection. 'Will you come to our little supper party on Friday?' he asked quietly.

'No!' She leapt to answer almost before his question was completed. 'I think it's best if I keep indoors now.'

There was a moment's silence. A robin sang loudly in a

thicket nearby. They could hear Mr Harris asking Bessie for some more custard.

'I would like a private interview with you, Jane.' He was looking at the gate and picking at a splinter. 'I must give an account of myself.'

'Your engagement?'

'Yes. I want you to know how it came about.'

Jane's heart leapt. 'That is your private concern, Sir Thomas. It's no business of mine.'

He looked alarmed and wounded. 'Don't talk so, Jane,' he urged in a low voice. 'I beg you, grant me a private interview. Your husband walks in the mornings. I could come then. Let me see you then.'

'No.' Jane was trembling. 'I'm not quite strong enough at present.'

Sir Thomas's expression was most troubled.

'Jane!' William Harris's voice sounded from the house. 'You will catch cold!'

'Only one more thing.' Sir Thomas caught her hand and held it close to his heart. 'Why did you come to see me last night – so unexpectedly?'

Jane felt his pulse throb against her wrist. 'I felt a desire – for your conversation.'

'But you will not grant me a conversation now?'

'Not now.'

She began to move away. He clung to her hand and kissed it fiercely, then released her.

'Forgive me,' murmured Jane and turned to go into the house.

'Why did you say "Forgive me" to Sir Thomas, just now?' enquired her husband as she passed his chair.

'He wished us to go to the supper party at Ottercombe on Christmas Eve. But I don't feel strong enough and I thought you would also rather be at home.'

'You did well,' observed her husband. 'Bessie, close the door and fetch some more wood. I'm cold. I hope Sir Thomas does not make a habit of interrupting my dinner.'

Jane was absent from the Christmas celebrations that year. She was troubled, during the last six weeks of her pregnancy, with an occasional faintness which made any excursion inadvisable. Bessie attended most assiduously to her every comfort and soon learnt not to mention Miss Mary's forthcoming marriage to Sir Thomas.

Mary was too busy with delicious preparations for the event to visit her sister often. She found Jane very dull company and naturally spent most of her time at Ottercombe with Eliza and Sir Thomas. Every day Sir Thomas asked how Jane was, but never received an encouraging reply. 'Oh, I've not seen her for three or four days,' Mary would say. 'But she's grown very quiet and tedious, says almost nothing; just lies and reads. It seems a very tiresome business, to be expecting a child.'

On the second of February, a mild day of grey cloud and stillness, Jane gave birth to a healthy girl. Mother and baby were well, and William Harris expressed his relief and contentment very eloquently to Mr and Mrs Lockhart, though Jane herself detected a hint of disappointment in his manner that the child was not a boy.

William Harris suggested his daughter should be named Mary Martha, after his sister and Jane's. 'What's more,' he added piously, 'it has the advantage both of biblical precedent and alliterative music.'

'You can call her what you like,' said Jane, lying in bed and looking down into the cradle beside her, where a pair of enigmatic grey-blue eyes stared uncomprehending through the mysterious sunbeams. 'I shall call her Sarah.'

'That will not please our sisters so much,' fretted Mr Harris.

'I don't care what they think,' said Jane bleakly and turned her back on him. Mr Harris was dumbstruck. He did not wish to mar the occasion by an argument, so he went downstairs.

It was as if Jane had given birth not just to a babe, but to a new self, and one which was not nearly so submissive. William Harris shook off the unpleasant idea. Childbirth was of course a physical ordeal, no doubt most disturbing also to the sensibility. Jane would be herself again quite soon.

Jane, lying in her attic, had to endure visits from both Mary and Martha. Martha's was soon concluded, with the offer of smooth congratulations and an observation that the babe greatly resembled its father. Mary, for her part, declared that little Sarah was the image of Jane. Mrs Lockhart, who had reconciled herself to becoming a grand-mamma, soon arrived and insisted that the child was most like Mr Lockhart's sister.

Jane received these opinions without comment. It seemed to her that little Sarah's face was like none she had ever seen. The curious blankness of the infant's gaze was welcome. Here was somebody who was not watching, judging, suspecting, or condemning. It was a relief also to be able to nurse her, kiss her and play with her, and the babe grasped her mother's finger with what seemed like eager-ness and surprising strength.

She had wondered if the arrival of her child would sub-due the feelings for Sir Thomas which had persisted since his last visit. It seemed, however, that the tenderness she felt for her child could not quench that other passion, only intensify it. Soon after her confinement Mary called while she was asleep and left a bunch of violets and a brief note from Sir Thomas, which Jane found by her bed when she awoke, and read alone.

My dear Jane,
    Mary tells me you are safely delivered of a fine girl, who looks just like yourself. I cannot express my relief and joy at this news. I trust that you will permit me to bring my congratulations in person as soon as you are strong enough to permit a visit. Till then, may I assure you of my most tender thoughts and deep affection.
    T.B.

I found these violets peeping under a hedge yesterday, when I was thinking of you.

Tears flew to her eyes as she read; she crushed the letter to her heart. Then there was a curious tingling in her breasts, a buzzing almost, or a prickling, and Jane felt her milk come down. Hastily she seized her babe and little Sarah sucked obligingly, a sensation as delectable to her mother as the scent of the violets and the sight of his handwriting.

29

'We must find a wet-nurse for you,' said Mrs Lockhart, who called every day for ten minutes to admire her grand-daughter.

'No!' cried Jane. 'I shall nurse Sarah myself, for the present at any rate.'

Her mother sighed and looked about the bare attic with some disapproval. 'You've been in this cottage too long, my dear. I shall tell Papa to look for a house for you.'

'I like this one,' insisted Jane.

'What a case we are in!' Mrs Lockhart surveyed her fortunes with dry amusement. 'One of our daughters is to be Lady Burton and mistress of Ottercombe Park, and the other huddled in a wretched lodge like a peasant. Why, you could fit this whole cottage into Sir Thomas's hall. You should have seen it at Christmas, Jane. I've never seen anything so fine.'

'Is father reconciled to the marriage?'

'Oh yes. Though we were very shocked at first. But I think it will suit Mary to have an older husband. She's not as strong as you. She won't want to be gadding about.'

'Gadding?'

'I suppose you'll be off with your husband again in the spring, when he starts on his preaching tour.'

'That's hardly gadding, Mamma.'

'Well, I may as well speak my mind, Jane, though I know you won't like it. I don't think it suitable for a young woman to go jogging about over the whole West Country, not with a babe in arms.'

'I agree absolutely,' said Jane pleasantly. 'I have no intention of accompanying Mr Harris on any more of his tours. I'd rather stay here with Sarah.'

Mrs Lockhart was rather disappointed to be denied the chance for an argument, but gratified to find that the idea of Evangelism did not have such a strong claim upon Jane as the charms of motherhood. She launched therefore into a catalogue of complaint about the preparations for Mary's wedding. Every person concerned with the event had, it seemed, frustrated Mrs Lockhart's intentions and if the celebrations were concluded without mishap, Mrs Lockhart assured Jane, it would be entirely due to her own exertions.

'Don't fret, Mamma,' said Jane, for whom the wedding approached as a most painful ordeal. 'I'm sure everything will be very elegant and delightful.'

In the event, Jane proved correct. A spell of unusually mild weather culminated in a day of brilliant sunshine. Mr Harris seemed very willing to leave his work and put on his best shirt to adorn the wedding party of his sister-in-law. Jane wrapped the baby in many more shawls than might be supposed necessary to her comfort and spent more time adjusting her daughter's bonnet than her own.

Her husband did not look at her with impatience, however.

'I know I'm a sad fright, William,' she announced, to forestall what she supposed would be his dissatisfaction. 'But it's less than a month since Sarah was born and nobody will mind how I look – everyone will be admiring Mary.'

'On the contrary.' Mr Harris managed an authentic smile. 'I think you look very well and I'm proud of you, and of our daughter.'

There was something touching in this formal little speech, but Jane did not seize upon it with the desperate hunger she might have shown a few months earlier. She was too bruised by his previous rejections to wish to revive her old hopes of being loved by her husband. On this day she would be obliged to watch her sister marry Sir Thomas. Nevertheless, she would rather endure it alone. Her husband's arm felt like an extra burden, not a help.

Jane found her babe a most useful distraction, however. At church, she sat near the door, in case Sarah cried. Though at Ottercombe the tiny church held but thirty souls in comfort, fifty were crammed in to celebrate such an illustrious and propitious local alliance. The crowd of people, and the restlessness of her babe, occupied all of Jane's attention, though she was aware of the trembling whisper with which her sister made her vows and felt a pang of sympathy for poor Mary.

It seemed unlikely, however, that Jane would very long continue to think of her sister as poor Mary. As the happy couple passed out of the church, Jane was obliged to look up and though she had meant only to admire Mary's radiant face, somehow she could not avoid a brief glance at Sir Thomas. He was looking round him with a general public smile. Jane found herself offered nothing more particular and instantly withdrew her attention.

Out in the churchyard it was warm enough for congratulations and embraces. Luckily Sarah chose this moment to embark on a series of hungry screams, so Jane left her husband to present the compliments of the Harris family and accepted the invitation of the parson's wife to feed her child in the vicarage.

The wedding party then adjourned to Newington House, where every elegant refreshment was offered and the house trimmed out in its best looks, thanks to Mrs Lockhart's exertions.

'I don't know why she could not wait till the summer,' she complained to Jane, after her daughter had complimented her on the arrangements. 'Think how much more beautiful everything would have looked in June. Think of the flowers, Jane! And the vegetables and fruits. If she had waited, we could have had strawberries.' The mention of strawberries was particularly painful. Jane recovered by assuring her mother that she had never seen the house look so fine.

'Well, it looks better than for your wedding, dear, but as you took it into your head to marry a clergyman, something a little more modest was more appropriate. Sir Thomas is of course a fine gentleman. I suppose Mary was in a hurry to marry him because he is so old.'

'Nonsense, Mamma!' Jane could not help laughing, despite her wounded feelings. 'Sir Thomas is not old at all. I don't think he's as old as Papa. Sir Thomas has the air and grace of a man of thirty, no more, and I think Mary can look forward to many happy years with him.'

It took much secret courage to deliver this speech with the necessary flourish, but Jane felt her nerves so lacerated by it that she began to look about her for an excuse to escape from her mother's company. Mrs Lockhart, however, received her daughter's remarks with quite enough outrage to justify a modest argument and accordingly launched herself with relish at the subject of Sir Thomas's antiquity.

'What stuff you talk, Jane! Compare their figures. Look at Papa – there, they are together – why, Papa is a head taller, at least.'

'But being taller does not make him seem younger, Mamma.'

'No – why, you fool, Jane, I never suggested such a thing! I'm only saying how superior Papa is in terms of looks and youthfulness – why, Papa has twice the hair of Sir Thomas. And Sir Thomas is quite stout by comparison.'

Jane felt a reckless indignation kindle within her, and against every instinct, succumbed to it. 'Sir Thomas is not stout at all, Mamma – he is merely broad.' She recalled most vividly seeing him naked in his bathing pool, the solidity of his shoulders and breast providing, in her eyes, a perfect example of masculine strength. 'Indeed, many would say his figure was more manly than Papa's. And for all everyday purposes Sir Thomas has plenty of hair.'

'How can you reflect so poorly on your father?' Her mother was now at full gallop, in serene enjoyment of her fury. 'Papa has always been considered a handsome man – it was thought, when I married him, that I had the better bargain in terms of looks and I may say that the intervening years have marked him very little.'

'It's true that Papa still has a slim figure and a smooth face.' Jane was beginning to acknowledge the absurdity of the argument and tried to placate her mother. 'It's not so much in his looks that Sir Thomas seems the younger – it's more his playful manners and the liveliness of his mind.'

'Pah! What in the world does a gentleman want with playful manners?' observed her mother scornfully and swept away to greet a cousin.

Jane was relieved to be free. Sir Thomas had finished his conversation with Mr Lockhart and turned towards her. She averted her face and moved rapidly off, following her father. She could not face Sir Thomas, at least not on his own. He observed her escape soberly for a few seconds, but he was not granted many moments of solitary reflection. Everybody wanted to talk to him and congratulate him.

The sad loss of Lady Charlotte two years before had deeply affected all his friends and they saw in his alliance with this sweet, retiring girl the chance of some consolation in the second part of his life. Sir Thomas was much moved by the unanimous expression of delight. Only his sister-in-law avoided him.

'Papa!' Jane claimed her father's attention. She wanted her mother to see her paying heed to him, though she was never at ease with his severity. 'What a fine day! And what splendid hospitality you have arranged! Such a crowd of people. And all admiring your window.' Jane fell silent, having exhausted the remarks she supposed might be appropriate.

Her father looked across the throng of guests with a

pained expression. 'Yes,' he observed coldly. 'I'm only very disappointed I did not have time to erect my obelisk for the general admiration. If Mary could have waited a few months I might have contrived it. Whatever Sir Thomas has, he does not have an obelisk.' He turned and walked away through the crowd.

Jane sighed. After these conversations with her parents, to be for a moment on her own seemed a sweet liberation. She felt a gentle touch on her arm. Her heart leapt. It seemed she could not avoid him for ever. But she turned to find it was not Sir Thomas.

Her husband, instead, was smiling down at her. 'How are you faring, dearest?' he asked. 'Shall I find you a chair? You must not tire yourself.'

Astonished by his solicitude, Jane let him lead her to a sofa beside the library fire. Mr Harris sat down beside her and did not let go of her hand. The few people in the room greeted them cordially, congratulated them on the birth of their child and smiled benevolently upon their tableau of married bliss.

Jane could not attend to their remarks with anything more than civility. She was puzzled by her husband's solicitude till she remembered that he had always shown concern for her in public. On any other day, his parade of uxoriousness would have irritated her and she might have shrugged it off. Her sister's wedding, however, provoked such unbearable emotions that she found some relief in Mr Harris's show of affection after all. It seemed to defend her from her own agonies, in some public way at least.

Bessie arrived with little Sarah, who was hungry again. Jane withdrew to what had been her own room to feed the babe and found something melancholy in the thought that both Mary's room and her own wore now an air of disappointment. These were the arenas where the dramas of girlhood had been played out. Now, more imposing ceremonies had drawn their occupants away.

Laying the satisfied babe to sleep on her own bed, she

walked into Mary's room. A beautiful dress of coral-coloured velvet was laid out, in which Mary would, later that day, take her leave of Newington House. Sir Thomas had planned a wedding trip to the Mediterranean. They were to embark from Bristol directly.

Jane sat down for a moment on the bed and stroked the rosy velvet. Sir Thomas's hands would caress this cloth and beneath it, her sister's skin would feel his warmth. This bed would not receive Mary's body tonight. She would lie down with Sir Thomas. Jane closed her eyes, not to banish the idea from her mind, but to imagine it more intensely. She recalled, as she had a hundred times, the day when she had gone down to Ottercombe and discovered her sister's engagement and how Sir Thomas had embraced her, upon leaving, so fiercely that she seemed still to feel it. She seemed always to be feeling it.

The door opened. Jane awoke from her reverie to see Mary's face, flushed with happiness but anxious. 'Oh Jane!' she cried. 'I'm so glad to find you here. You are the very person – indeed you are the only person – to reassure me.'

'What about, dear?' Jane received her sister into her arms. There was something curious in the idea that this pretty neck, these glowing cheeks which she kissed and caressed now, would within a few hours receive Sir Thomas's lips. She shook off this distracting fantasy. 'How can I help you?'

'It's . . .' Mary hesitated. 'About tonight. I'm afraid.'

Jane was hardly in a position to reassure her sister. Her own experience of matrimonial embraces had been painful – and her recollections even of those occasions were now growing dim. It was more than half a year since her husband had offered any attentions of the kind. Yet she knew that her sister's experience would be very different. 'Think how gentle and kind Sir Thomas is,' she whispered into Mary's ear. 'No doubt he caresses you from time to time already.'

'Somewhat.'

'And you enjoy those caresses?'

Mary hesitated. 'I suppose I do. He's very kind. He's never done anything I did not like.'

'Then tonight will be no different. He has been married before, which is a blessing. He's not a clumsy young man. And he has a very loving temperament. He would not hurt you for the world.'

'No.' Mary stopped trembling. 'No. I think not. I feel better, Jane. You're a darling!' She embraced her sister heartily. 'I always feel better when you are by. Oh, how I wish you were coming with us to the Mediterranean. You would so love to see Naples ... I know! I will ask Sir Thomas if you can come with us.'

'Don't be ridiculous.' Jane laughed. 'The last thing Sir Thomas wants on his honeymoon is a third party. And it's the very last thing I should like, I promise you. No. Enjoy your intimacy with him.'

'As you enjoy yours with William?' Mary's need to be reassured forbade any hint of difficulty on that score. Jane therefore declared that she had the best husband in the world, and the best baby, and Sarah, feeling perhaps her mother's need for an excuse to withdraw, gave a lusty yell.

'Let's take her downstairs,' cried Mary eagerly. 'Let me carry her, Jane. I know how to. Oh, she smells so lovely! I adore her!' She kissed her niece's head with rapture.

Though it was only February, the warmth of the terraces below Newington House tempted the guests out to enjoy the promise of spring. The sun was strong and the cliffs protected the lower terraces from any hint of wind. The whole party, or such as were sound of limb, descended therefore and walked to and fro in the glade. The warm weather had encouraged the snowdrops to bloom and their sprawling clusters mingled with the drifts of aconites like a carpet of white and gold.

Jane, walking on her husband's arm, with Bessie behind them carrying Sarah, saw Sir Thomas approach, with Mary attached as joyously and firmly to his side as a pretty wallflower to a sturdy rock. She knew she must now speak to him and prepared herself.

'So, Jane,' said Sir Thomas when they met. 'What do you think of this glade? Have you ever walked on a softer carpet?' He looked at her for an instant with his old tenderness, then instantly turned aside to admire the surroundings.

'Indeed, it's like walking on clouds, I think,' said Jane. 'Something like being in heaven, I should say.'

'For confirmation of that', Sir Thomas suggested, 'we should apply to your husband.'

'As to heaven.' William Harris looked at Jane, and his face seemed almost to fall into a dimple, so demure and loving was his expression. 'I always feel, when I'm with Jane, that heaven could not offer any joy so exquisite.' And he bent down and kissed her cheek.

'Amen to that!' cried Sir Thomas. Jane emerged from her husband's embrace to find her brother-in-law's eyes fixed on her, glittering strangely: a look which aroused her so dangerously she could only return her gaze to Mary. Mary was staring up into Sir Thomas's face with a kind of nervous agitation and it occurred to Jane that not even her innocent sister, at that moment, enjoyed the flawless happiness which they were all assiduously claiming. The sun shone on their heads, the flowers blazed beneath their feet, but in their hearts were shadows and uncertainty.

30

Winter, having held off for Jane's confinement and Mary's wedding, now put in a belated appearance. A pitiless east wind drove across the valley. Sheep huddled on the western side of the walls. Mrs Lockhart complained to her husband that his fine new east window admitted more draughts than the modest old one. Miss Eliza Burton left Ottercombe Park to await the arrival of spring with her sister in Bath and Jane learnt to be a mother. Sarah nestled in her arms for many hours each day.

William Harris observed this with disapproval. 'Put her in her cradle. You will spoil the child.'

'She keeps me warm and I keep her warm,' replied Jane unflinchingly. 'It will be time enough to put her in her cradle when the spring comes.'

Mr Harris frowned, shrugged and went back to his pamphlet.

His disapproval was not so emphatic nowadays. Jane had acquired confidence from the return of her physical strength and mobility, and from a sense that, in little Sarah, an ally had arrived. Most of all, however, she had got beyond wanting her husband's approval. The desperate desire for it, which had driven her to so many humiliations, had been replaced with a wary indifference.

She knew that as her husband he could exact her obedience and thwart her inclinations. Not offending him too deeply was therefore necessary. But she no longer sought any reassurances from him and was brave enough to contradict him when provoked.

It might have been expected that William Harris would have welcomed this change. In the past, his wife's clumsy attempts to please, her transparent longing for attentions, had very evidently irritated him. Her self-containment now offered him every opportunity to pursue his studies with fewer distractions and increased purpose. But he did not seem at ease.

Jane found that at moments when she might have expected him to be immersed in his work he hovered near her. He came down earlier for his dinner and stayed longer at the table before going back up to his room. He seemed to want conversation, yet did not know how to initiate it.

'What are you going to do this afternoon?'

'Nothing out of the ordinary, William. It's too cold to be sowing seeds. I'll send Bessie out to ask Mr Allen for another load of logs and when she gets back we will be seeing to the laundry.'

'It is a pity the weather continues so severe.' He stood with his back to the fire. Jane nodded. She did not wish to encourage his meditations about the weather. They had already said too much about the subject on many weary occasions.

'In another month it will be April,' he continued. Jane did not contradict this *aperçu*. 'Time to resume the field preaching. The circuit.'

'Will you manage to finish your pamphlet by then?'

'Oh yes. I shall complete it in a week or so.' He waited for her to ask if she might read it.

Jane's curiosity about her husband's ideas had not quite evaporated. She knew, however, that the work on which he had been labouring all winter would offer no clues to the enigma of his character. She was not disposed to humour him. 'I'm not a great reader, as you know, William. But I hope it will be well received.'

'As to that—' A curious expression, half a smile, half a

233

frown, passed across his face, before he dismissed the subject with a shrug. 'I may enjoy a week or so of rest and repose, after the pamphlet is sent off and before we embark on the tour.'

'We?' Jane was alarmed. 'I'm afraid I can't go with you, William. I'm not strong enough yet. Dealing with an infant would increase the ordinary fatigues of travel to an insupportable degree.'

He looked surprised and displeased, but his tone was calm, even coaxing. 'But think of all our people in the West Country, eagerly awaiting the sight of our child. Wishing most ardently to see you restored to health and to admire our beloved daughter.' His tongue tripped slightly on the word 'beloved', awarding it an extra syllable.

'Well, I'm not at all sure I can accompany you, William. Mamma says it would be the height of folly.'

William Harris paused and picked his finger ends. 'We will talk of this later. I have no wish to impose upon you arrangements which you would find disagreeable.'

Jane considered that he had imposed disagreeable arrangements on her for the whole history of their marriage, but she bit her tongue and picked up some of his linen to mend. A buttonhole needed repairing on one of his shirts.

He watched her for a while. 'There is something very touching', he said, after Bessie had cleared the table and gone back to the scullery, 'in the sight of a wife mending her husband's shirts.'

Jane tried to hide her astonishment at this speech. 'I'm afraid I do the work very badly. I have little domestic skill, as you have often pointed out.'

There was a short silence. 'It was wrong of me to say so. I'm very much to blame.'

Jane was amazed, but said nothing.

'I'm afraid it has taken me some time to reconcile myself to married ways,' he went on.

'To reconcile yourself!' She could not help flaring out. 'If you found it so unpleasant, why did you embark on it at all?'

He got up and walked to the window. He looked out, not idly, but as if he was looking for something in particular. 'It is not – unpleasant. I cannot properly express to you my regret for the difficulties I experienced.'

Jane noticed that it was his difficulties, not hers, which were mentioned. All the same, the spectacle of her husband involved in a protracted apology was such a novelty that she put aside her work.

'As I said earlier, there may be two or three weeks between the completion of my pamphlet and the resumption of my duties on the circuit. I look forward to those days. Particularly I wish to spend some time at leisure with you and Sarah.' Jane tried to imagine Mr Harris at leisure, but the idea proved too much of a challenge to the imagination. 'Would you like that?'

The direct question felt almost like a blow, it was such a departure from his customary authority and indifference to her wishes.

'Of course,' she replied stiffly, unable to provide the enthusiasm which would have flooded into her heart seven or eight months previously.

He moved nearer to her and placed his hand on her shoulder. It did not feel like a hand, exactly, more like something inanimate. A glove, perhaps. 'I'm aware I have not treated you as I ought, or found ways to express my admiration and gratitude.'

Jane wondered how he might have responded if now she had been able to seize his hand, or leap to her feet and embrace him. She could not, however.

When she had longed for his attentions he had exhibited only indifference and irritation. At this time, when she wished to be left alone, he harassed her with his endearments. Another odd thing occurred to her: now she was beyond his power to hurt she had lost her clumsiness. He had become the clumsy one.

He withdrew his hand and went back upstairs. Jane

wondered whether he would persist in this curious, belated courtship, or whether her settled indifference would deter him. She anticipated supper with some apprehension.

At six o'clock it began to snow. The light was eerie. Twilight, which should have been deepening into darkness, seemed drawn the other way by the reflected whiteness of the ground. It was as if something was trying to drag the day back.

William Harris came downstairs. 'It's snowing.'

'Yes. I had noticed.' Jane was particularly irritated when he remarked on something obvious, as if she required his guidance to perceive it. But she also found her own irritation tiresome. It seemed as if he could say nothing to please her. She almost pitied his perseverance and wished she could find it in her heart to respond.

'I think we should send Bessie home early.'

'But supper might not be ready yet,' she objected.

'It doesn't matter. I want very little and I know your tastes are simple.'

'Bread and cheese would perfectly satisfy me, William.'

'I'll send her home then. It would be unfortunate if she had to stay the night.' He went to the scullery and Jane heard him speaking to Bessie. Presumably he had not wanted the girl to stay, in case he had to give up his bed to her and expose himself once more to the inconveniences of his wife's bedchamber.

But Jane was wrong in this conjecture. It became apparent, soon after Bessie had gone home, that William Harris wished to profit by this unexpected privacy. He first peered into the cradle where the child was asleep. 'Have you fed her recently?' he enquired.

'Yes.'

'She's unlikely to wake up, then?'

'Not for some hours, unless she has a dream.'

'It is hard to imagine the dreams of infants.' He contemplated the sleeping child with curiosity. Jane thought she might find it easier to imagine her baby's dreams than her husband's.

He drew up a chair and sat beside her. The chair legs shrieked on the flagstones. Jane was pretending to read, but he was sitting too close for her to continue with politeness.

'What are you reading?'

'*Tristram Shandy*.'

He pulled a face, and appeared to consider a remark, but decided against it.

'You disapprove?' she asked with calm certainty. He hesitated. 'I've never read it. Do you like it?'

'It's very amusing, yes.'

Jane set it aside. She hoped he would not question her more closely about it. She had not yet formed a clear enough idea of its contents. She had not Mary's ability to concentrate, to give up her imagination voluptuously to a book. For Jane, the real world seemed always to be providing more vivid distractions.

But Mr Harris showed no interest in pursuing the discussion of literature. He looked across at Jane for some time in silence and, though there was nothing exactly like admiration in his expression, she saw that she had become interesting to him.

'What are you thinking now, Jane?'

'Nothing at all. About the supper.' She got up, not wishing to indulge him.

But as she passed his chair, he caught her hand. 'Let the supper wait a moment. Sit with me.'

She obeyed. He continued to look at her. She took her hand away and stared into the firelight.

'I want you to come with me on the tour,' he said quietly. 'It would please me very much. I can't contemplate leaving you and Sarah here. However, I acknowledge your misgivings. Having an infant with us would certainly add to your burdens.

'But there must be some way in which this could be made

237

easier for you. We could take Bessie. And perhaps you could stay at Bristol, and Taunton and Exeter, while I travel to the remoter areas – and I could return to you very often.'

Jane's instinct to resist the idea was not in the least altered, but she felt she had to give the appearance of considering the matter and promised as much.

After supper, she declared her intention of going to bed early. Her husband carried up the cradle; Jane, the child. He watched while she settled the babe. Sarah had been only half roused and soon fell asleep again.

'Good-night, William,' said Jane, her eyes fixed modestly on the floor. He kissed the top of her head and went out. She made her preparations very quickly, got into bed, looked at the sleeping baby for a tender moment and blew out the candle.

She heard her husband go downstairs, bolt the doors and see to the fire. Then his footsteps sounded again on the stairs. At the top he seemed to hesitate. Jane heard the latch on her own door twitch as if it had been touched.

Instantly she was alert and fearful. Silence. He was standing outside her door. His indecision was palpable, but what emotions provoked it she could not guess.

The door opened and he came in, carrying an iron candlestick down which the wax from the tall candle wept and spilled, solidifying on his fingers. He sat down on the bed and looked at her. 'I would like to join you tonight, if you have no objection.'

'None.'

His hand came to the side of her face and touched her hair. She tried not to recoil. He bent down, his face growing larger until his breath beat in her nostrils. He kissed her, for the first time, on the lips.

Jane was so astounded that she could not move. To an observer it certainly would have looked like a kiss, but to Jane it was a peculiar experience, like a picture without colours, or a silent sonata.

He blew out the candle, got undressed and climbed in beside her. 'Turn to me, Jane.'

She obeyed. He took her in his arms and kissed her again, but he could not quite find her mouth in the dark, so she received his lips on her eye.

'William – I'm not yet well enough. I'm sorry. It's too soon.'

He became very still for a moment. 'I see. How long will it be before you are yourself again?'

'Not . . . not long, I'm sure.'

'Very well.' He lay still, but continued to hold her in his arms. Jane found the position awkward in its novelty. She did not, however, feel she could move quite yet. They lay together in silence, neither husband nor wife able to sleep, the thoughts of each of them wholly mysterious to the other.

The wind had dropped and the snow brought with it a peculiar atmosphere: a stifled, expectant stillness all around the house. Suddenly Jane heard what sounded like a footstep out in the garden. Instantly all her senses were alert. Another sound: the crisp protest of trodden snow. 'William! I heard someone outside.'

He raised his head. There were more footsteps and the sound of a body passing so closely to the house wall it could be heard brushing against the stones.

They both got quickly out of bed. Moonlight now flooded the room; it was an easy matter to cross to the east window, which overlooked the garden, and, as Jane slept on that side, she was there first. Peering down out of the window, she saw a figure loitering against the garden wall, looking up at the house.

Jane's eyes were sharp. She recognised the slight figure, for the moonlight flashed on his upturned cheekbones. 'It's Colin Watts,' she whispered. 'Look, William, I'm sure of it.'

Her husband glanced out of the window, then swiftly dressed and, without uttering a word, passed out of the room and went downstairs.

Jane returned to bed, somewhat reassured. The possibility of a stranger, a thief perhaps, no longer alarmed her. Though her husband had spoken of Colin Watts with the greatest vehemence and disapproval, she was sure he meant no harm, though why he was loitering in their garden she could hardly guess.

She heard the bolts drawn back and her husband go out. Then there were voices. She could not distinguish any words and the coldness of the night encouraged her rather to keep to her bed than tiptoe about, eavesdropping on their conversation. It seemed a protracted discussion. The voices moved further off, until they were no more than a murmur, and Jane, who was really very tired, drifted off into an uneasy and echoing sleep.

31

Jane awoke. It was already light. She heard someone attending to the fire downstairs. Sarah was asleep in her cradle beside the bed, but William Harris was not in the room. Jane had a curious feeling that he had not spent the night at her side. She had no memory of his return, or of sharing her bed with another body. She felt the greatest curiosity about Colin Watts's strange appearance the previous night. At times in the past she had experienced a feeling which returned, now, with some force: that Colin Watts wanted to tell her something.

Perhaps it was some elaboration on the message she had received while he was in his trance. Though she had at first been inclined to dismiss the idea that her husband did love her, his behaviour in recent days had become strikingly affectionate. Could it really be that he had always cared for her, but that some difficulty of feelings or spirits had prevented him from expressing it before?

That could not be more unfortunate. Jane no longer admired her husband – an admiration which could, if reciprocated earlier, have established a deep attachment between them. However, she felt that it was not just William Harris's apparent indifference to her, but also something in his character, which repelled her.

The extraordinary visit of Colin Watts must be accounted for. She fed the baby, dressed and carried Sarah downstairs. She could hear Bessie preparing breakfast in the scullery.

Her husband, having finished his exertions with the fire, was sitting by the window studying some papers. He looked up at her arrival with an expression of vivacity and satisfaction. 'Good morning, my dear! How is our daughter? I think she is almost smiling sometimes.'

Jane considered that progress towards smiling was rather more rapid in the infant than the father, but she replied cheerfully, 'She's very well and has been fed. I'm sorry I fell asleep before you came back in last night. What did Mr Watts want? Why did he come?'

'Oh, I dealt with him quite easily in the end, though it required a great deal of persuasion. He was in a state of agitation, and some confusion, which afflicts him at times. He's inclined to wander about without knowing properly where he is. It's a kind of sleep-walking, I think.'

'Like a trance?'

'Somewhat. I took him back to his lodgings and saw him comfortably settled there. By then he had recovered his full consciousness and I was able to have an entirely rational conversation with him. I convinced him to go back to Bristol, where his parents live. He would be much safer lodged with them there, than wandering about in this wild country. I think I can confidently predict that we shall not be troubled with any of his visitations again.' Mr Harris drew down his cuffs and looked out with an air of relief at the landscape.

The snow did not last long. William Harris returned to his manuscript with renewed vigour and Jane to playing with and talking to her babe. Though Sarah was still too young to do more than stare into her mother's face, she soon learnt to smile and, having acquired the gift, seemed inclined to exercise it at every opportunity.

Mrs Lockhart called each day to admire her grand-daughter and one morning when the first daffodils that grew beside the park gates were raising their trumpets to the sun, she brought a letter lately arrived from abroad.

'Oh Jane! We have heard from Sir Thomas and Mary! They have got safe to Portugal, and then they were to sail round to Seville and Granada. Here, you may want to read it.'

Jane seized the paper with great eagerness, recognised Sir Thomas's small handwriting, and felt herself blush with agitation. Luckily her mother was preoccupied with little Sarah.

My dear Mr and Mrs Lockhart,

We are pleased to announce ourselves safely arrived in Lisbon, and in excellent health and spirits. We hope you are well and think of you, and of Jane, every day. I suppose by the time you read this you will be enjoying a fine English spring. Here we have spring already. Mary and I have just been taking coffee out of doors, on a splendid terrace overlooking some lemon trees, beside an old moorish castle.

How Mr Lockhart would admire the architecture! Here are crumbling ruins to excite his greatest curiosity and a landscape full of light from the Atlantic, great trees already in leaf, even palm trees among the more elegant palaces.

And I am sure dear Mrs Lockhart's discriminating eye would find much to engross her among the very elegant ladies and gentlemen whom we saw at a concert last night. But I am proud to report to you that no young woman looked better than your Mary. I basked in her reflected glory, as she walked up and down on my arm and met with admiring glances on every side. All the ladies wished they were her, and all the gentlemen envied me and wondered how I could be in possession of such a pearl.

I have never seen her looking so well and am quite as besotted as a bridegroom should be. My gratitude grows daily, as her excellent qualities are revealed: gratitude to Mary herself for being prepared to endure me and to your good selves for permitting the match. I hope Mary is contented. She is at present reading, as you may guess.

We are sitting on our balcony overlooking the city. The power of the sun here in the south is extraordinary even at this time of year. Mary is wearing only a light gown and her silk shawl, and is perfectly comfortable. I sit here in my shirt like an old farmer, for no one can see me except my dear little wife and she is too lost in her novella to care what I look like.

I will ask her to add a few words. I bid you *au revoir* and send you my compliments and warmest good wishes. Please remember me particularly to Jane. Tell her I hope, when I return, she will find time for a conversation with her tedious old brother-in-law. Mary is too tender for teasing. I shall save all my satirical remarks for dear Jane.

Here ended Sir Thomas's part of the letter. There followed a series of exclamations, in Mary's hasty curling script, as to the beauty of Lisbon, the fineness of the fashions, the courtly manners of the Portuguese, the peculiar sound of their language and the delicious baked apples which scented the air at the corner of every street. Jane's eye fled across her sister's lines without receiving much of their sense: she was too stirred by the first part of the letter. Sir Thomas was obviously very much in love with Mary.

And of course this was excellent. This was what everyone would have expected and wished. She would not want Mary to suffer as she had done: she was glad Sir Thomas loved her sister. The message to her showed what she might expect from him in future. To be teased was her destiny. Mary was too tender to be teased. He cherished her. But Jane could receive his sardonic remarks and flinch if she dared.

Her spirits quailed in anticipation of such badinage. She feared that in this respect she might prove even more tender than Mary. The thought of seeing him again at some time – presumably in the late summer – now filled her imagination with a sense of pitiless exposure. She would see him next as her sister's husband: devoted, loving, cherishing. He would caress Mary, perhaps, in front of her; he would lavish his most gentle smiles on his wife. Jane would have to look upon their happiness and be glad.

She withdrew from such a painful contemplation at once. Her imagination contracted into the cottage again. Here were her mother and her daughter, playing together. This was where her happiness would have to be rooted. She gave the letter back. 'They seem very happy.'

'Oh yes! I'm sure they are. I wonder what they will make of Seville. Mary is so lucky. I wish Papa had taken me to see something of the world, but oh, no! He will never leave home. It's quite three years, I'm sure, since he even roused himself so much as to venture as far as Cheltenham.

'He speaks of going to admire the garden at Panswicke, but if he does not stir himself about it, if he keeps putting off and putting off every excursion, he will find he is too old, or dead, and it will be too late.'

'At least you are adventurous, Mamma. You do not let him clip your wings. You can go to Cheltenham whenever you wish, or indeed anywhere else, I'm sure.'

'Yes! That's a good notion. I might go to Cheltenham again quite soon. I could stay with Harriet at Panswicke on the way. Although Harriet is so very economical, I would not be surprised if she issued me with a bill for a night's lodging.'

Jane laughed and was grateful for the opportunity. Mrs Lockhart's elder sister, Harriet, was an old maid of austere habits, yet not without sympathy. Jane liked her. 'I might come with you, Mamma, at least as far as Panswicke, if you make your expedition in the second half of the summer. I should like to see Aunt Harriet again.'

'You're not going off with Mr Harris once more, are you, Jane? You'll regret it, I'm sure. What did he want to marry for, if he can't keep at home with his family like Parson does? Why must he always be roaming about?'

Jane forbore to mention that her mother had just expressed the greatest discontent at her own husband's disinclination to travel and was now berating her son-in-law for never staying at home. She knew that whatever she said would be contradicted and so confined herself to admiring her daughter. This was one subject upon which Mrs Lockhart was quite prepared to agree and accordingly they played with little Sarah and offered her enough compliments to satisfy a whole battery of babies.

Spring arrived suddenly. Warmth enveloped the land. At last it was a pleasure to open the door and feel the embrace of nature instead of an icy assault. Jane went out into her garden and began to mark out the flower-beds. She took Sarah with her and placed the babe in her basket underneath the apple tree. Blossom drifted down on to mother and daughter, and Bessie, glancing out through the parlour window as she swept, thought they made a very pretty picture.

William Harris completed his work and took it away to the printers in Oxford. This journey required his absence for three days. Jane welcomed the brief solitude. She had not been able entirely to dissuade him from his determination to take her with him on the circuit. At last she had arrived at a kind of agreement, which was that she would accompany him for the first six weeks and then come home, to spend the rest of the summer at Ottercombe.

When he returned from Oxford, towards the end of April, he would conduct the first field meeting, preaching in the fields below Woolton as in previous years. Jane could not shake off a feeling of heaviness at the thought that these pious exercises must be resumed. She had thought, when she had first heard William Harris preach, that some holy impulse had seized her, but she now feared it was not a glimpse of the Almighty, but some reflected glamour of his minister, which had worked upon her.

She did not think very often of the curious circumstances in which she had come to be Mrs William Harris. It was too mortifying. There was something sacrificial about it, and those who might have prevented it had stood back and succumbed to the operation of some inevitable process. She had herself wandered towards matrimony like a blind girl towards the edge of a beetling cliff. Now she had crashed down among the rocks and must try to piece together a broken life for herself and for her daughter.

There was no point in prolonging such gloomy thoughts, however. If the circuit must be endured, then at least she would not always be trying to please him. She would be more free, this time, to admire the beauties of the landscape – which seemed, this spring, to be more dazzlingly displayed than ever.

She was dreaming in the soft twilight under her apple tree, on the second evening of her husband's absence, when Bessie came out to her. 'There's a message, Madam – someone wants to see you.'

'Who is it, Bessie? It's rather late.'

'He's not here, he's in your father's garden – he sent word just now that he was waiting for you just below the cliff. By the glade.'

'But who is it?'

Bessie hesitated. 'Mr Watts.'

'Colin Watts? I thought he had gone back to Bristol?'

Bessie shrugged. Her look was ambiguous.

Jane felt the girl would like to say more, but did not dare. 'Do you think I should go, Bessie? He's not dangerous, is he?'

'Oh no, Madam – I'm sure of it. Only he said he had something very particular to tell you.' Bessie shivered suddenly. 'When he spoke in my father's voice that time and said "sell it" – my mother had been wondering whether to sell a brooch he had given her. I'm sure Mr Watts is genuine. I'll come with you if you like and stand nearby, in case you should need me.'

'Thank you. Yes. Fetch me my shawl.'

Jane was filled with the sense that something had arrived which she had been waiting for. She paused only to dress the baby in her bonnet and they set off across the park, Bessie carrying Sarah.

Jane did not wish to attract the attention of her parents in Newington House, so she skirted along the edge of the park, slipped out of sight behind the high yew hedges and across the upper farmyard. A quaint Gothic arch in the further wall gave way to a maze of narrow paths which, twisting to and fro, plunged down towards the lake. Trees dripped on all sides, newly in leaf, and though the light was thick and almost blue, the air was warm. She could smell the earth.

Colin Watts was standing under a kind of recess in the rock face – a geological phenomenon which Mr Lockhart had occasionally thought of making into a grotto. Jane had played here as a child and knew every stone of the path. She did not feel afraid and, at her approach, Mr Watts stepped out with a shy smile.

'Mrs Harris – you are very good, very kind to see me.' He looked behind her, where Bessie was standing a few yards away.

'You must not mind my servant coming,' said Jane. 'It is late.'

'Ah – your child,' said Mr Watts and Jane realised that he was not so much perturbed by the presence of the servant as intrigued by the babe. 'May I see her?'

Jane called Bessie forward and Mr Watts looked down on the sleeping infant. 'A beautiful soul,' he whispered with a sigh.

An owl hooted in a nearby tree and Mr Lockhart's peacocks, going to roost in the tall cedars, called to each other with unearthly screams which echoed up and down the valley. But the babe did not stir.

Jane shivered. 'You wished to see me, Mr Watts. How may I help you?'

Colin Watts looked pointedly at Bessie, who moved further off and turned to look up at the rising moon. 'It's a confidential matter.' Mr Watts spoke in a low voice, not looking in her face. 'There is something that I wish you very much to see.'

'What is it?'

'I can't say. It's better if you see it for yourself. You must, indeed you ought to see it.'

'Where? How?' Jane was irritated, but also beguiled by the mystery. 'Is it to do with the message?'

'What message?' It was Mr Watts's turn to be puzzled.

'The message you delivered me when you visited the lodge last September. When you went into your trance.'

He looked blank. 'I'm sorry, but I have no memory of any message. I can never recollect what I say on those occasions. I'm not aware of anything.'

'The message was, "He loves you, though he cannot show it." Colin Watts considered this for a moment. 'I can't understand it.' He frowned, shrugged and returned to his own purpose. 'As to that, I can offer no opinion, no explanation. But I can show you something which will interest you, if you come down to the Lower Barn on Friday morning.'

'Ah! My husband will be back by then. But he always walks for two or three hours very early in the morning. I could get away unobserved for an hour or so, at about seven o'clock.'

'Let it be seven, then.' Colin Watts smiled. She found the smile not completely reassuring. 'It's most important that your husband does not know of this arrangement, nor of my visit here to invite you.'

'I know.' Jane could imagine William's fury if he discovered that Colin Watts had dared to petition her like this – and that she had dared to accept his enigmatic invitation. 'I thought – William thinks – you are returned to Bristol. He assured me you had left Woolton and I'm afraid he will be angry if he finds you here again.'

'Then guard the secret closely,' urged Colin Watts. Jane assured him she would and they parted, promising to meet at the barn at seven o'clock on Friday morning.

32

Mr Harris returned from Oxford on Wednesday afternoon in good spirits, and set about clearing the papers from his study and putting his affairs in order. He immediately resumed his habit of early morning walks, leaving the house on Thursday morning at six o'clock and returning after nine.

'You should enjoy your walks more, I should think, now your article is finished, William,' observed Jane, watching him eat some bacon and eggs. 'It gives you an appetite and the exercise must be beneficial.'

'Yes,' he replied. 'I find that the early morning exercise has a stimulating effect on the mind. When I was struggling with a difficult passage of my work, two hours' solitary rambling often seemed to refresh my imagination.'

'And where did you go today?'

He looked startled for an instant. 'Down past the gates of Ottercombe Park, into the deep valley there and up the other side, towards Hartwicke.'

'It must be very beautiful there now,' said Jane. 'When I'm fully recovered, and not so fat, I may take some walks thereabouts myself.'

'My walks', said her husband defensively, 'are not so much for recreation as for the ordering of my thoughts. Though I have finished my pamphlet, there's a new season of preaching to consider and I shall be very busy for the next two weeks revolving ideas for my sermons.'

'Oh, I would not dream of intruding on your solitude,'

cried Jane with cunning gaiety. 'If I walked, I would go alone – or with Bessie. Have you walked towards Kingscombe, yet? Northwards across the plateau? There is a magnificent belt of woodland there. Great beeches. I'm sure you would admire them.'

'Perhaps I shall try that route tomorrow, then,' said her husband gratefully.

Jane took away the remains of his breakfast. 'Would you like some more coffee, William?'

'Yes, please, my dear. I should like that very much.' He smiled up at her and she looked benevolently down, though almost pitying him and regretting her own guile, which had made her suggest a direction for his walk tomorrow which would take him the opposite way from her own assignation with Colin Watts. She must keep her husband away from any risk of an accidental meeting.

All went well. She was feeding the child next morning when he got up. 'I shall take your advice, Jane, and go and admire the beeches at Kingscombe, I think,' he said and shortly afterwards she heard him leave the house.

The light was still weak and the land appeared half asleep when she slipped out some twenty minutes later. Sarah was fed and safe in Bessie's care, and the girl had been instructed, should Mr Harris return unexpectedly, to tell him that Jane had walked over to Newington House to take breakfast with her mother and to discuss some gowns for Mrs Lockhart's next journey to Cheltenham. Jane knew the mention of fashion would sufficiently deter her husband from any impulse to follow her.

Swiftly she walked along the edge of the park, took a wild path down the escarpment and crossed a belt of trees to the fields beneath. She took a route behind some walls that ran below the farmyard, so that her unusual early morning excursion was less likely to be observed by any farm workers, or anyone looking out of the windows of Newington House, which glittered on its high cliff in the morning light like a box made of glass.

Soon she had dropped out of sight of her father's house, below the lake, below the deer park, below the ha-ha, and now she found herself at the head of a vast and shadowy valley which plunged further down amid rocks and stones, fringed on each side by curtains of woodland. A stream leapt down the middle of this valley, to join the small river which ran along Ottercombe Bottom. Many times she had played here with Mary. They had made dams and pools in this little stream, picked cress and marsh marigolds and tormented frogs with their affectionate attentions.

Now she paused, feeling relieved that she was no longer visible from Newington House or the farm. Below her, a mist was rising from the valley in great cloudy domes and strange angled drifts. The sun, appearing on her left, cast majestic floods of light through the thick and swirling atmosphere. Gold and amber and rose and ochre, like chords on a sublime organ, seemed to announce the day with ceremonious solemnity.

Jane ventured on, moving easily across the damp grass, descending slowly into what seemed like an immense void of rosy vapour. A herd of cattle appeared and looked up at her with mild eyes. Their tawny flanks smoked, and their long horns caught the light and flashed like swords. But the bull, Jupiter, was a peaceable beast and recognised Jane, and only watched her with his small eyes as she passed some fifty feet away, offering him a quiet greeting.

Now she could see the outline of the Lower Barn. This was where she had come when she had fled from Henry in a temper, after his teasing remarks about Mr Harris before her marriage. She had wept on Sir Thomas's shoulder here and then walked back with him along the bottom road to Ottercombe. It was almost exactly a year ago.

Jane had not much time to reflect on the changes which a year had wrought. This meeting with Colin Watts was the first thing which had distracted her from her melancholy thoughts about Sir Thomas. Now she felt apprehensive certainly, but pricked into a state of alert anticipation. Mr Watts occupied in her imagination a role of almost supernatural promise. He was like a priest who was to reveal some mystery to her, she was sure.

A fleeting anxiety about her personal safety was brushed aside. Her extreme curiosity to know what he would show her banished all concerns of the sort. She trusted Mr Watts and as the barn loomed out of the mist she crossed the stream to it, leaping across the familiar stepping-stones with an easy grace, though her figure was no longer a girl's.

The great black doorway yawned and silently she ventured in. The faint scent of last year's hay was still perceptible, but the atmosphere was rather ecclesiastical than agricultural. The great rafters rose above her, shadowy and grey with antiquity. An absolute stillness possessed her senses. For an instant a shadow passed across her heart. Had he brought her here for nothing? 'Mr Watts?' Her voice trembled.

There was a sudden movement above her, high on the stacked hay: an exclamation. She looked up and saw, to her utter amazement, her husband's face appear and Mr Watts's next to him. They must have been lying together on the highest bank of hay, quite hidden from all possible scrutiny. Her husband looked as astounded as she felt. Mr Watts's face was alight with triumph.

She saw William turn to his companion with a look of absolute fury and Colin Watts receive it with rebellious defiance. Her astonishment and paralysis was pierced by a flash of energy: nothing coherent, only the wish to escape. She ran from the place and hid a short distance away in a hollow tree which had often sheltered her childhood games.

Mr Harris burst out of the barn in evident agitation and looked about him in all directions. Jane did not dare to move and struggled to control her panting breath, but her familiarity with the place, and her modest brown dress, were her escape. Such parts of her body which might have been seen were absorbed into the landscape and were not perceived. She heard her husband call her name. His cries echoed up the valley and were answered dimly by the peacocks on her father's terrace far above.

Mr Watts emerged from the barn also. Her husband rounded on him and a violent argument ensued, of which Jane could distinguish no details, only its alarming passion. Evidently thinking she had gone back up the valley, Mr Harris set off in that direction himself. Mr Watts paused as if in thought for a while, then followed him with urgent speed.

She watched them move further and further away, still locked in furious debate, which, when it ceased to be audible, still showed in their movements. At a certain point, however, they paused and faced each other, as if they had reached the summit of their fury, and at this moment her husband struck Colin Watts across the face with such intensity that Jane understood in an instant that she was watching the desperate rage of lovers.

Colin Watts ran away and disappeared into the woodland to the west. Her husband hesitated for a moment, faltered a step or two after him, then looked back up the valley as if torn between two impulses. Eventually he seemed to sigh, a sigh so profound as to be palpable hundreds of yards away, and set off uphill towards Newington House. Jane watched till he was out of sight.

She was surprised to find herself not inclined to tears, though greatly shocked. There was something in the discovery which consoled her. It was an explanation for the whole miserable charade of her marriage – though why William Harris should have proposed to her remained a deeper mystery than ever.

Wearily, and with much caution, she emerged from her hiding place and walked, hardly knowing where she went, except that it was away from the direction her husband had taken. She was so distracted that no coherent thought could be sustained for more than a moment. She tried to shake off the thousand taunting discoveries that crowded in upon this first great revelation: his lies, his excuses, his secrecy, culminating in that last barefaced deception this morning, the friendly confirmation that he was going to admire the beechwoods at Kingscombe.

She recalled bitterly now how guilty she had felt that almost for the first time she had deceived him. She had pitied his innocence – when all the time he was so very far from innocence that the whole of his conduct towards her, from the very beginning, had been a lie.

Jane found herself walking along the same lane which, a year previously, she had walked with Sir Thomas. Her pace slowed now at the memory. She had been upset, then, not only by Henry's teasing, but by her uneasiness about Mr Harris. Though they were engaged, he had gone away into Buckinghamshire and had not written. He had left her in an agony of uncertainty.

Sir Thomas had comforted her, she recalled, with an extraordinary speech about the intense longing which a young man would be feeling for the woman he loved and from whom he was absent. As Sir Thomas had spoken, her dejection had passed from her and she had felt more and more exalted. Whole cadences from his speech now flooded into her memory.

'He thinks of you night and day . . . he longs to hear your voice . . . he cannot pronounce your name without a physical thrill of joy . . .'

Tears came now, such hot, scalding tears that Jane quickly climbed over a stile and walked down to the riverside to avoid any exposure to the public road. She had accepted Sir Thomas's words as a declaration from the mysteriously silent Mr Harris, hardly noticing that it was Sir Thomas who expressed the sentiments. But William Harris had never felt anything of the kind for her.

Only now she felt the stinging truth of Sir Thomas's description of love. It was that violent longing she had come to feel for Sir Thomas himself. If only she had understood him – if only she had understood herself – she might have been walking with him in this valley now, in a state of perpetual enchantment. Instead, Mary was enjoying that happiness in the strong southern sunshine somewhere, in a city full of bells and palaces and orange trees.

Jane flung herself down by the riverside and wept heartily into the earth. Some of the tears were furious grief for the absurd and twisted farce of her marriage, and that she had let herself be so profoundly duped. But strangely, the occasion seemed to release a long pent-up torrent of distress: her futile longing for Sir Thomas, which despite her resolve to dismiss it from her soul seemed by the sudden revelation about her husband to have become more painful and more pointless than ever.

After a while all tears were spent and she became aware of the music of the water only inches away. Small insects threaded their way through the grass. Her head lay on the earth and for a moment she saw the world from their perspective. The blades of grass were as tall as trees. The small stones seemed great rocks around which the busy creatures scuttled. She herself was a giantess, a mountain, and her tears must have seemed a most curious aberration in the weather.

She sat up and leaned against a tree, and for a while stared dully at nothing, not so much at nature as through it. Suddenly a flash of blue jolted her back to full consciousness. A kingfisher was darting about at the next lazy loop of the river. Jane watched it, admiring its effortless beauty and the infallible simplicity of its courtship.

A moment later, however, her attention was drawn by the progress of a coach along the lane above and she recognised, with an incredulous leap of the heart, Sir Thomas's carriage travelling eastwards towards Ottercombe Park. She leapt to her feet, then recollected her appearance and bent down and washed her face in the stream, her thoughts thrown into wild conjecture. Was he come home now? So early? Was something wrong?

Fear and yearning drove her across the field and she gained the lane just as the coach was turning left some three hundred yards ahead, and embarking on the long climb towards Ottercombe Park. Jane found to her frustration that the plumpness of motherhood prevented the energetic progress she would easily have managed a year ago. By the time she reached the same bend in the road, the coach was just disappearing around the next bend, some half a mile distant. And so it went on. She arrived at the gates of Ottercombe very breathless, muddy and wild, provoking a look of surprise from one of the grooms' wives who lived in the small lodge there.

'Why, Mrs Harris! Are you—?'

'I'm well, thank you – but why are they come now?' She could hear the coach being brought round to the stable yard: the sound of horses, the cries of men, the barking of dogs.

'Because he's broken his leg, alas – and she's not well neither, they say she's fallen into a consumption, poor soul.' With a cry of horror Jane set off again, running more easily now along Sir Thomas's level drive, oblivious to her wild appearance, only full of dread for the two people she loved most in all the world.

She found the door still open and the footman Antony dealing with cloaks and a bonnet, and taking the liberty of bursting in, she only cried, 'Oh Antony – where are they?'

'In the drawing-room, Madam – shall I announce—'

Jane pushed past him and flew into the room, where two figures turned to her in astonishment. It was not Sir Thomas and Mary. It was Henry and Eliza. Henry lay on the sofa, looking pale and drawn, his leg extensively strapped up and laid out comfortably cushioned before him on a footstool. Eliza had flung herself into a chair, where her hectic red cheeks and thin face suggested a body racked with fever.

'Henry! Eliza!' cried Jane, quite unable to account for herself. 'Forgive me – I thought—'

'Dear Mrs Harris!' cried Henry, recovering from the shock of her appearance. 'And looking wilder than ever. Is the mud on your face some Evangelical fashion? Are dust and ashes no longer the mode?

'Tell us what has been happening here, or I'll give you the whole story of my leg, which has been known to move strong men to sleep. Antony, ask them to bring us some tea, if Mrs Harris will grant us the honour of her company?'

Jane felt at first disappointment that it was not Sir Thomas and Mary, then relief, for she would not have had them return ill or injured. Immediately she felt guilty at such thoughts. Sympathy for Henry and Eliza, real pleasure at seeing them again and concern for their condition soon followed.

Such a hectic race of emotions would have been enough to endure, without all she had suffered at the Lower Barn. Jane felt quite exhausted, though glad enough to take tea with her friends, though she knew she could never mention to them the extraordinary anxieties into which she had been plunged by the morning's events. She knew that as soon as she had passed a half-hour here she would have to return to the lodge and a dreadful conversation with her husband.

33

Henry was evidently very glad to see Jane. She suspected that he had suffered a lot of pain on the journey – and perhaps from having to act as nursemaid to Eliza, when it might have been more suitable for him to be nursed himself. Eliza did look very ill. She seemed fretful and in answer to Jane's enquiries she declared she missed Papa exceedingly, and she did not understand why he had got married and gone away and left her all on her own for so long. It was most unfair.

'Nonsense, Eliza.' Henry was always quick to detect a remark lacking grace or courtesy. 'You're only saying that because you've had a fever and you miss Papa and Mary more than if you had been quite well. You're delighted that they have married. You told me so yourself. And when they come back, which will be very soon, you'll have two devoted slaves to answer your every whim instead of one.'

Jane asked about his injury. He told her the accident had come about on board ship, and the surgeon and Henry's commanding officer had agreed that sending him home for six months would offer the best prospect for a complete recovery. He had accordingly been conveyed back to Portsmouth on another vessel and had travelled from there to Bath, where he had found Eliza ailing, Eleanor's baby Thomas struggling with the double challenge of a bad cold and several erupting teeth, George spending far more time than might be advisable at the gaming-tables and Eleanor herself getting rather fat.

'So you see, our whole family is going to the dogs!' He smiled. 'But how is yours? I hope your parents are well. But bless me! You're a mother yourself since we last met. Eliza told me you have a fine daughter. I must see her. I shall fall in love with her immediately. May I be the first suitor to ask for a lock of her hair?'

'You must give her a chance to grow some first.' Jane laughed. 'For Sarah is quite bald at present.'

'Bald ladies have always been my favourite! But how is Mr Harris? Is he pleased with paternity?'

'Very well and very pleased.' Jane blushed and, after a few more minutes of Henry's diverting company, felt she ought to leave. She dreaded returning to the lodge, but it must be faced. After expressing sympathy at Henry's and Eliza's afflictions, and declaring her intention of helping them as much as she could, Jane left Ottercombe Park, promising to call again the following day.

She found her husband sitting alone, reading. The fire had gone out, but he did not seem to be aware of it.

He looked up as she took off her bonnet. 'Where have you been?'

'I came round by Ottercombe Park. Henry and Eliza have just arrived home. He's broken his leg and she has been ill with a fever. Shall I ask Bessie to mend the fire?'

Mr Harris looked distracted by so much information. He seemed sunk so deep in his own thoughts that he could scarcely understand a sentence on any other subject. 'No. I have given Bessie the day off to go and see her mother.'

The babe, hearing her mother's arrival, stirred and whimpered. Jane picked her up and started to feed her.

'I did not want a servant to be in the house to hear us talk.'

Jane began to dread what must follow. She could not think what to say and could only look down into the infant's eyes, which steadily returned their mother's gaze.

'I have done you a great wrong,' William Harris announced suddenly, standing up. He sighed and paced about the room, looking first out of the western window towards her father's house, then out of the eastern window at the back, towards Sir Thomas's. 'There is no doubt I should not have married. But I want you to understand how it came about. I did not entirely know myself – my own nature.

'It was thought I should marry. Friends and my sister said so. I wished myself to be married. I had wanted this for some years, though I had never met anyone suitable. As you know, my work is unrelenting. There is little time for social engagements. I never meet anybody.'

'But you meet hundreds of people! And many of them admire you exceedingly.'

He stopped for a moment beside the hearth, picked up the poker and stabbed at the extinct coals and ashes. 'That is a burden. My preaching sometimes excites a kind of admiration beyond rationality, and as a single man I was in some ways painfully exposed to the consequences.'

'Ah! You married me, then, to protect you from your admirers.'

He gave her a sharp look. 'Please don't speak bitterly to me, Jane.'

'Some might say I have good cause.'

'Please hear me.' He looked for a moment almost helpless, and her anger subsided. 'When I first met you I was most struck by your innocence and integrity. You're a serious, intelligent young woman. You have a conscience. You're more interested in helping the poor than dressing a bonnet. And your family enjoys comfortable circumstances.'

Jane wondered what that was to the purpose and he saw her expression.

'You think perhaps a minister should not interest himself in such things. It was for your sake I made the calculation. As I said just now, I was not entirely confident I would be suited to the married state. Though I wanted it, I was very much afraid of failure. In such circumstances I wanted to be sure that my wife's family would be able to support her.'

'In what circumstances?' She could not help herself. He seemed jarred, by her interruption, into silence. 'Failure?' she persisted. 'Have we failed, then, William?'

He seemed entirely unable to speak for a moment, then, 'I would . . . be obliged', he faltered at length, 'if you would hear me out before making your observations.'

She understood he had prepared a speech.

'You ask . . . if we have failed.' He struggled to address her question none the less. 'If I look at our daughter I cannot think so.' He stared at the babe on his wife's knee. Sarah, having fed, was now drifting back to sleep. 'We must rejoice in our child. She is a blessing.'

Jane nodded.

'I don't find it easy to express affection,' her husband continued. 'But I can assure you that I feel as devoted to her happiness as any father could.

'However, I would ask you to consider me for a moment as two persons. One is the private man. In this respect I am very much to blame. My conduct has exposed you to unhappiness. I regret this more than I can say. And I am willing to make amends in private in whatever way you require.

'In public, however, I am convinced that our best course is to remain together – unless my company is absolutely insupportable to you. My reasons for saying so relate to my other life. My public responsibilities: my work. It must continue. It's not for my own sake I say this. If I have a gift for utterance, it is not something for which I take any personal credit. The gift is God's.

'It brings responsibilities, however. If conscientiously exercised, such a gift could bring hundreds – perhaps thousands – into a state of bliss, of spiritual enlightenment. You are a young woman of great moral sympathy. You know, and deplore, the poverty into which so many of our fellow-creatures are born and you understand what a great comfort to them it must be to live in a state of spiritual grace. I hope you will acknowledge, therefore, the importance of my work.'

'Oh, certainly. The state of mind is everything.'

'Anything, therefore, which might damage that work is most scrupulously to be avoided. Whatever our private difficulties, they must remain private. I'm sure you will agree. What could be worse than reading insulting conjectures in the newspapers about our marriage? I'm sure the idea revolts you, as it does me.'

Jane shuddered.

'Very well, then. I have only one more observation to make. It has often been mentioned, by your father and mother particularly, that they might find us a larger house. I think that would greatly assist matters. We might then have separate apartments, yet dine together and enjoy the company of our child together, with every appearance of married contentment. What do you think of this idea?'

Jane felt complete blankness. 'I don't know,' she said dully. 'I'll think about it.'

'Good. Then I have no more to say. This painful conversation is at an end.'

'At an end? Why, I've said nothing yet!' Her indignation burst out at last.

'I beg your pardon. Of course you must have some observations to make.' He sat down with a nervous air. 'Please let me know your thoughts.'

Jane did not know where to start. 'You astonish me,' she began, struggling to control her agitation. 'You declare the conversation is at an end and you have no more to say. Yet you have not mentioned Colin Watts.'

He flushed deeply, got up and resumed his pacing. 'He played a cruel trick upon us,' he said. His words came rapidly and raggedly now. This was very different from the measured cadences of his prepared speech. 'It's true, I've had some private conversations with him. I wished particularly to convince him to give up his dabbling in necromancy and trances and so on. It works upon superstitious minds. It arouses fears and distracting thoughts.

'I wished also – as you will understand – to persuade him to go away. As you know he's not . . . he is in some measure unhinged. He's not rational. He would not go back to Bristol. He was forever lying in wait for me upon my walks. There is some . . . some fascination he feels for me. I'm continually attempting to hold him off, send him away. But he's gone now. I will refuse absolutely to see him on any pretext whatever. You must understand that despite the difficulties he has placed me in, with his continual opportuning and manipulation, my conduct has never been other than entirely decent and proper.' He stopped pacing now, looked down at Jane and blushed again.

'I thought it looked as if you loved him,' she said boldly, feeling that if she did not speak now, she would never find the courage.

'Love him? Absurd!' cried her husband. The blood left his face suddenly. He looked waxen. 'It's not . . . my difficulties with you are not that . . . the case is rather that I seem not to be able to love anybody.'

'You don't love me, then? Or Sarah?'

'I do love you both, very dearly, in my fashion. Only I can't express it.' He was trembling. Sweat broke out on his lip. He sat down. 'Fetch me a glass of cordial, Jane. I feel faint.'

She ran to get it; he drank and was revived. 'This has been a terrible conversation,' he whispered. 'I feel utterly spent. I'm going to lie down.' He dragged himself upstairs. Jane heard the boards creak above her head. He had gone into his own room, which was directly above the parlour.

She got up, put the sleeping babe into her cradle and considered what to do. Lighting the fire was the first task. Jane found a curious pleasure in the simplicity of the act, after the exhausting struggle of talking. As the tiny flame kindled around the dry sticks and grew to a heart of warmth, she felt grateful for its heat and light. She sat beside it and felt soothed by it, without thinking of anything at all.

34

Mr Harris proved so upset that he had to keep to his bed for two days afterwards, suffering from a sick headache of such exquisite sensitivity that the least sound distressed him. Jane had every excuse, therefore, to leave Bessie to wait on him and to take Sarah out all day. The season invited it, for the sun was growing in strength. At Newington House Mrs Lockhart welcomed her granddaughter with joy and Mr Lockhart condescended to inspect her from a safe distance.

At Ottercombe Park, however, Jane felt she could do more than simply call. The invalids required diversion. Accordingly, after passing the morning at her mother's house and stopping by at the lodge to find that Mr Harris was no better, she set out for Ottercombe Park at about two o'clock. She was glad enough to get there ten minutes later, for Sarah was now three months old and had grown so bonny that carrying her any distance was beginning to require some exertion.

'My dear Mrs Harris, this is extraordinarily kind!' cried Henry at her arrival. He immediately admired the babe and asked for its hand in marriage. Jane laughed and was grateful for his silliness. Laughing made her feel better. The relentless seriousness of Mr Harris was something she was only now beginning to be aware of. It was as if all her customary spirits had gone into a kind of suspended sleep while she was with her husband. Laughing with Henry reminded her of the person she had been before she married.

The mildness of the air had encouraged Henry to lie out on the terrace, sheltered from the wind and facing south. It felt almost as warm as June. He was arranged on a day-bed, his leg laid out before him and a glass of brandy on a small table at his side.

Jane enquired about the health of Miss Eliza. Henry's face grew troubled. 'She's not at all as well as I would like,' he confided. 'She has kept to her bed today. They tell me she's not feverish, only rather low in spirits. She misses Father dreadfully.'

'I'm sure she depends upon him more acutely because of the loss of her mother,' mused Jane.

'Indeed. But I'm persuaded she will soon pick up. I'm sure his return would do wonders and till then we must do our best. This delightful baby would make her smile – but I believe Eliza is asleep at present.'

Servants brought a chair for Jane, an old cradle was found in one of the attics for Sarah and soon a very happy picnic was contrived from cold ham and apple pie.

'Now,' said Henry, wiping away the last crumbs, 'you must excuse my manners, Jane, for having to lounge about like this I'm become rather like a great baby myself. I'm afraid I have dropped food on my shirt and if I don't get what I want I shall scream and blow bubbles like Miss Sarah there.'

'Well, what do you want?' enquired Jane with a smile. 'Let's avoid this tantrum.'

'Gossip!' cried Henry. 'Of all social arts the most pleasurable. And let's begin with our own families, my dear, for they have done their best to provide us with a feast of scandal. My father marry your sister! What! I could not believe my ears. However did it come about? I blame you – you should have knocked their heads together, and tied 'em up by their kennels and given 'em not so much as a bone till they had promised never to speak of marrying again.'

'My fault! How impudent of you to say so!' cried Jane, playfully but not without conviction or pain. 'It was your responsibility entirely. I returned from my honeymoon' – she pronounced the word with bitter sarcasm – 'to find my poor sister almost wasting away in despair at your departure. You played with her affections, Henry, don't deny it.' Her real anger now broke through. 'You gave her every encouragement, then left without a word. The poor girl was almost dying of a broken heart when I came home. All I did was lay the problem before your father and beg him to do what he could to amend it.'

'This is a fairly radical solution of his, however.' Henry still tried to joke.

'Confess it! You knew you were toying with her affections and that she was becoming most attached to you, and you left abruptly and without any kind of understanding.'

'How could there be an understanding?' Henry had grown sober now. 'I never felt anything particular for your sister. I never offered her any courtesies that I did not express to a dozen other young ladies.'

'Well, Henry, you are a sad flirt, I think we may agree upon that. And a most determined one, too, considering even I have received your compliments at times.'

'I never flirted with you,' cried Henry, a flicker of light returning to his eyes. 'I meant every word I said. Indeed, I meant a great deal more than I ever dared express.'

'There! You are off again. Stop it! Away with you!'

'No, pardon me, Mrs Harris, and hear me if you please. There can be no harm in a respectable married woman being informed of things which are long past.' His tone dropped and manner grew exceedingly confidential. Jane somewhat reluctantly drew her chair a little closer. 'From the first time I met you I was intrigued by your manner. It was different from any other girl's I had met. You seemed full of thoughts. Your eyes, my dear . . .'

'I find them convenient for seeing.' She laughed, determined to outwit him and prevent his chivalry.

269

But he would not be prevented. 'No, I'm going to tell you something you won't like. You'll be disgusted with me, but you must hear it. Because you have accused me of trifling with Mary's affections and that is a serious charge. I was never in the least attracted to Mary. I was always most exceedingly intrigued by you. But that rascal Harris was hovering, and I could see very well that his dark looks and his damned magnetism had quite captured your poor little heart. I could only offer you Henry Burton, but he could offer you the kingdom of heaven. Not much of a contest, unfortunately.'

Jane was struck by something authentic in his tone and could not think what to say. It surprised her exceedingly that Henry had expressed a serious interest in her. She had always taken his attentions for frivolity.

'Nobody takes me seriously, however.' Henry sighed theatrically. 'That is my tragedy. Light girls and flibbertigibbets flock around me. Serious girls – clever, witty girls with satirical eyes – those I long for and they despise me.'

'The solution is in your own power. You must cultivate a more serious manner.'

'Ah! You want me to be serious, then, like your husband. I confess I envy him mightily. I wish I had been able, like him, to offer you serious embraces. Serious devotion. Sombre admiration. Here, let me practise.' Henry fixed her with a look of such dour veneration that Jane could not help laughing, though she was feeling less and less comfortable.

'Stop it. You look like an old dog who wants his dinner.'

'But I do want my dinner, dear Jane. I'm quite desperate for it, don't you see?'

'I don't understand you.' She was disturbed by his words, and could not quite dismiss them.

'I envy your husband to the point of madness,' Henry whispered, with a smile which did not contradict a tone of great candour. 'To think that at any time he can reach out his great serious arms and enclose you in a devotional embrace! Ah, the ecstasy of it. A religious ecstasy! I break out into a sweat, imagining it.'

Tears burst from Jane's eyes. Henry, seeing them, looked stricken, sat up and reached for her hand.

'My dear, what's the matter? If I've offended you, please do me the kindness of a firm blow between the eyes with your fist. Dear Jane, do stop. Oh! I'm a villain! I would not have upset you for the world. I admire your husband exceedingly, but I do envy him. And I did fall a little in love with you and could be in love with you again at thirty seconds' notice. So I can't help being somewhat jealous of the idea of his embracing you.'

Jane looked up. It was time to tell somebody and it had to be Henry. He might be the very worst person to tell; he might be the best. She almost did not care. 'Then allow me to reassure you, Henry. My husband never embraces me and he never will.'

Henry grew pale and said nothing for a moment – a most uncharacteristic stillness.

'Indeed, he informed me yesterday', Jane went on, finding inexpressible relief in the simple act of revealing her unhappiness, 'that he felt our best course was to live together as man and wife, but to get a bigger house so that we may have separate apartments. Then he won't have to suffer the inconvenience of my presence in his private moments.'

'What – is the fellow mad?' Henry looked wild with mystification. His eyes went to the cradle. A question too delicate to frame passed across his face, but Jane saw it.

'When we first married he made some effort to behave as a husband might be expected to behave. But I've come to feel that it was all a charade: that he did not marry for himself or me, but for his congregation. So that they might see their minister a happily married man – with a child.'

'But—' Henry stumbled to understand. 'How can he . . . not like you?'

Jane began to tremble and dreaded the course the conversation must now take. But also she longed to say the things which were so deeply shocking she had been unable to imagine ever expressing them to anyone. 'I fear, Henry – if you will forgive me, I don't know how to express it – I fear William does not like women much at all.'

'Good God! He's not a damned molly, is he?' Henry recollected himself and stifled his exclamations. 'Dear me! I can't believe it. What makes you think so?'

'There's a young man', Jane hesitated, 'who has haunted the area for some time. He came with us on our tour last year, although I thought nothing of it – he rode with William, while I went in the coach with Martha, and during the winter he has been at Woolton and I have reason to think he meets my husband every day in the mornings when he goes on his long walks.'

Henry grew very serious and reflective. 'But are you sure you're not imagining it?'

Jane was obliged to tell him how Colin Watts had come to her and invited her down to the barn, and everything that followed, including much of her subsequent conversation with her husband. When she had done, she felt almost physically lighter, purged of some burden which had weighed upon her for weeks, even months.

Henry, however, looked more shocked, and more subdued, than she had ever seen. 'This is common, of course, in the Navy,' he said quietly and, for once, without any intent to amuse. 'You'll forgive me, Jane – I would not normally think of mentioning such things to a woman.'

'It's a relief to me to be able to speak of it.'

He looked at her with great concern and overpowering sympathy. 'My dear, I cannot adequately express my horror at your situation. But what can be done? You are surely not going to acquiesce in this hideous proposal of his to live as man and wife for the world's sake? I cannot bear to think of you having to endure such loneliness, such separation. Agonising to contemplate! – And your poor daughter! How could she grow up happy in such a house?'

Jane could not answer. She could only shrug. 'My

husband is convinced that any other course would harm his reputation and his work, and since he considers he is doing God's work it is difficult to make any objections.'

'Tell me, my dear . . .' Henry fixed her with a look which was half serious. 'Would you like me to arrange an accident? I could invite him to a shoot. He would have to oblige me, out of civility, and I'm such a terrible shot! Indeed, I think I would probably shoot him even if I were trying not to.'

Jane was convinced that, for Sarah's sake, any father would be better than none, and declined the shooting. 'I have to confess, Henry, that though Mr Harris has caused me more unhappiness than any other person in the world, I would not harm him for anything. I think he suffers from his difficulties just as much as I do. Perhaps even more – for he must feel guilty at marrying me and there is nothing worse than guilt. He can't help his own nature. I would not wish to harm him in any way.'

'You dear, good creature!' cried Henry. 'Well, if you ever change your mind, let me know instantly. I shall be happy to challenge him for you, with any weapon of your choice, from a hairbrush to a blunderbuss, I promise you.' For once in his life, Henry did not quite have the heart to jest further. He contemplated Jane's future with distaste. 'So you are reconciled to wasting your life in a frozen solitude?'

'What else can I do? Ladies can't sue for divorce.'

'No, no . . .' Henry considered the proposal for a moment. His eyes soon kindled to a brightness. 'But wait – he could sue!'

'He has no grounds.'

'Allow me to offer my services. Though I would make but a poor husband, it has often been remarked that nature framed me for a lover. I know you find me abhorrent, but not more abhorrent than Mr Harris, surely, for though he may be cold, my heart is on fire for you, Jane.'

'Stop it! Don't be silly!' She could not help laughing, however.

'No, no, I mean it!' His eyes were large and his manner convincing. 'I'm in earnest. I told you I could be in love with you again in thirty seconds. It was a lie: I'm in love with you already. I thought of you more often, on board ship, than any other woman. I thought of you so vividly, as I travelled up from Portsmouth, I could hardly take a passing interest in any pretty girl, and now I consider myself enrolled as your faithful knight. I shall not be content until I have slain the dragon and cut you free from the rock.'

'It's time I went home.' Jane looked about her for her things, though she was very reluctant to go back to the cold lodge and leave this warm terrace, this entertaining nonsense. 'Your conversation is quite indecent, Henry.'

'You're smiling, though. Don't deny it. A little indecency, Mrs Harris, is what you need – and you need it desperately. Wait! You can't go yet! My leg's hurting!'

She had got up, but now was obliged to hesitate. 'I don't think your leg is hurting you at all.'

'How can you be so cruel! Not content with breaking my heart, you refuse to sympathise with my leg! Go on, break the other one! Having a leg broken by you, Mrs Harris, would be more enjoyable than having one's hair caressed by a thousand other beauties.' He winced, however, with some conviction, and Jane was rather sorry for him and sat down again.

'Where does it hurt, exactly?'

'The knee. Just above the knee. Would you do me the honour – the great kindness – to stroke it? My mother used to console me greatly, when I was little, by stroking.'

Jane was tempted to help, but hesitated to stroke him above the knee, though the grey silk of his breeches looked very fine and inviting, above the bandage. She extended her hand timidly and placed it below his knee, on the white stocking.

'Well, that's a start,' said Henry. He sighed a little in pleasure. 'The touch of your hand on my leg is beginning to work a cure. Could you not . . . stroke me a very little? I can assure you it is not forbidden in any book of the New or Old Testament. Your husband can have no objection.'

Reluctantly but gently, Jane began to stroke Henry's leg. He fell silent. His large blue eyes played admiringly over her face. She felt he was getting more pleasure from her attentions than she was investing in them, yet there was gratification in it also for her, to see the lines of pain clear from his brow. 'Are you feeling better, now?'

'Yes – but don't stop. If you stop now, having started the treatment, I can assure you I'll rapidly fall into a fatal decline.'

'You're extremely naughty, Henry.'

'Bad dogs can be stroked into submission,' he murmured.

Jane thought it was fortunate he did not resemble his father at all, for she had been fighting off all afternoon a sense that Sir Thomas was somehow in the house and would come out at any moment to surprise them.

'Higher up.'

Jane stopped stroking and hesitated. 'What do you mean?'

'Place your hand above my knee. Just for an instant. That's where the worst pain is. If you were a true nurse, you would not withhold treatment.'

Jane placed her hand on his thigh. The silk was warm. Henry seemed to catch his breath. 'Did I hurt you?' she asked anxiously.

He shook his head and only looked at her with the most enigmatic smile. 'Stroke me,' he whispered. 'Just a very little.'

Jane felt disturbed. It was as if she were being lured into an infidelity. Curiously, she felt it was not her husband she would be betraying, but Sir Thomas – even though at this moment in some beautiful Italian or Spanish city Sir Thomas was probably offering caresses to her own sister. Jane removed her hand.

'Ah, my dear,' said Henry with a long sigh. 'You have given me much to think about.'

'Well, I hope you will have improving thoughts.'

'Spoken like a true parson's wife! Oh yes, my thoughts will all be improving. They will improve my own condition and my state of mind. They will also be busy all night with rehearsing the scenario by which I'm to assist your escape.'

'What escape?' She laughed, getting up and reaching for her shawl.

'Briefly – I seduce you, much against your will, because you do not naturally incline to me, I know. Your pity for my broken leg, however, will excite you to even more kindly acts than that you have just performed. And perhaps I dare hope that after such a bitter experience as you have just had to suffer, the experience of being adored will not be so very hard to bear. For I adore you, Jane.'

She pulled a face and snapped her shawl at him. 'I'm going now.'

'Wait! Do you not wish to hear how I contrive your escape?'

She could not help wanting to hear it, though preparing to disparage its nonsense immediately.

'Here's the plan, then. We become lovers. Mr Harris is informed of the fact by a sympathetic friend. No doubt he has one. If not, I can lend him one of mine. He's enraged, but perhaps also relieved. This gives him an excuse to cast you off, without any damage to his own character. Indeed, he will only appear more saintly as a wronged husband.

'So – he accuses me of having enjoyed Criminal Conversation with his wife and sues me for damages. I'm very happy to pay whatever sum he requires. As a clergy-man his rapacious instincts will perhaps be modified. We must hope so. The divorce is granted. Neither of us needs appear, by the by – it's all conducted by the lawyers, while we sit under a tree somewhere, crowning each other with daisy chains.

'As soon as the divorce is granted, you do me the in-expressible happiness of marrying me. I know you don't love me, but I think you like me and that is far better for our purposes, Jane. A wife who doted on me would be made miserable by my flirtations. A wife who liked me might forgive them. You would forgive me the odd little indiscretion, I hope?'

'Oh, certainly – if I'm granted one myself.'

'By all means take a lover, after you've given me an heir. It's a most agreeable custom which is pursued in many European countries. The ladies go about squired by their lovers, for their marriages are mostly arranged, you know. I've seen them myself, in Venice.'

Jane was amazed and shocked, but somehow not offended. Indeed she found herself wanting to prolong the game. 'I shall be allowed a lover, then?'

'My dear, of course. But one proviso: he is not to be younger than me, or better looking.'

'I accept your terms. My lover must be older than you and not so handsome. Why then, I should like to have your father.' She could not pronounce the words without a hidden shock of feeling, but she managed to keep her manner calm and playful.

'My father? My dear, a stroke of genius! Nothing could be more agreeable. The gossips of the country would be most infinitely obliged to you. This choice of yours exhibits a refinement of scandal which is altogether exhilarating. You shall have him.'

Jane now really felt she must go. She picked up the baby and hesitated only a moment longer. 'You forgot to mention just one thing, however, Henry.'

'Oh! And what's that?'

'I should be ruined. We should all be ruined, and damned.'

'Ruined? Hah! What of that?' He picked up a leaf which had fallen on to him, and tossed it in the air. 'We can live here a life of perfect happiness and seclusion. Our friends will not merely forgive us; they will congratulate us. We can cultivate our own little society here. I've danced enough in the ballrooms of Europe. Would you not rather be ruined and radiant, than fade away in a cold, heartless mockery of a marriage merely for the sake of reputation? As for the damnation – we could get Mr Harris to intercede for us with the Almighty, I'm sure.'

Jane merely shook her head and smiled, then turned away and walked off slowly down the drive. She could feel Henry's eyes watching her all the way to the bend. Indeed beyond the bend, as she passed through Sir Thomas's great iron gates and took her course up the lane, she felt as if Henry were still watching her, long after she knew she was out of sight.

As she arrived at the lodge she saw by Bessie's expression that something had happened.

'Is Mr Harris worse?' asked Jane anxiously.

'No, Madam – he's asleep. But this letter came for you an hour ago. Delivered by young Fred Smith.'

Jane took the paper quickly and broke the seal, walking out into the garden to avoid Bessie's curious eyes. She did not recognise the handwriting, but a glance at the signature told her it was from Colin Watts.

Dear Mrs Harris,

I wanted you to know that I never intended to hurt your feelings. Quite the contrary. As you might guess from my own work it is my hope always to bring comfort and to ease suffering. I cannot bear to cause pain.

But I have been very concerned about you. Mr Harris first mentioned the possibility of his marrying four years ago. I was always against it. I thought it would be very unfair to the lady.

But he was under great pressure from some in his church and he would not listen to my arguments. He said it would make relations between us easier. When he met you and told me what he intended I felt the bitterest blow of my life.

Not merely for myself. I knew his marriage could not thrive. I knew his nature better than he did. He thinks because his work is about transforming people, that he could transform himself. I knew he could not.

When I met you, I began to feel a deep sympathy for you. I have always felt more at ease in the company of ladies and you are a good woman. I felt no jealousy because I knew he could never love you. Instead, I felt very sorry, especially as I could see in your face the beginnings of that unhappiness which I knew you must suffer.

His own burden was also very great. To live in that way required many lies of him. He could not persist in such deception without great damage to his soul. His lies, and his perplexities, were an offence to all three of us.

It caused many terrible passions between us. Many a time he threatened never to see me again. He has banished me from his presence again and again, but then welcomed me back with the most exquisite relief after. There is an understanding between us which I am convinced will last until one of us dies – and perhaps even beyond.

I felt that you should be told about it because otherwise your life must drag on in mystery and frustration. I supposed – I hope not wrongly – that understanding would bring you some relief. Believe me I feel the greatest horror at the possibility that you are tormented by the discovery. If you are, I beg your forgiveness. If there is anything I can do for you please do not hesitate to send for me. I lodge above the Pelican in Woolton.

He has said he will never see me again. No doubt he has told you this. But I know he will relent. I urge you not to believe him or entertain any hope that he will change. Your happiness will only come from abandoning hope altogether.

Your devoted servant,
    Colin Watts

Jane felt a curious satisfaction in reading the letter, freed from the last shreds of some oppressive condition. She supposed she would continue to live with Mr Harris, but without any of the torturing doubt and uncertainty. She found a spade, dug a small hole and buried the letter beneath the apple tree.

35

Several times during the following week Jane went to Ottercombe Park, but she did not see Henry alone again, for Miss Eliza was somewhat improved. Jane and her baby daughter were the best company to encourage Miss Eliza's recovery and Jane was very glad to find, after the passage of seven days, that the invalid had abandoned her couch and was rambling among her father's rose-beds.

'You've nursed my sister with great skill and devotion,' said Henry, who was in his favourite place on the terrace. 'Now you must dedicate yourself to my welfare, else I shall start hurling things about in jealous pique.'

'I'm sorry.' Jane was obliged to deliver some unwelcome news. 'Mr Harris has informed me that we must set off for the tour on Friday. I'll be very busy tomorrow, packing and making ready. I'm afraid I've come to say goodbye.'

'Damn it! And how long shall you be away?'

'Perhaps six weeks. No less, at any rate.'

'You don't want to go. Elope with me instead. Let's go to Italy. You, me and little Sarah – I don't know that the most abandoned rake has ever eloped with two ladies, mother and daughter.'

'Well, we may elope with you one day, Henry.' Jane laughed. 'But not till Sarah is old enough to give me her opinion on the matter. Besides, I don't think you're fit enough for elopement at present. I hardly think you could elope as far as the drawing-room without assistance.'

Henry fell into a subdued mood, in contemplation of her departure. She could not say anything to comfort him, so swiftly prepared to make her farewells.

'Eliza must be your nursemaid now.'

'Eliza! She's no more use than a kitten. But dear Jane, I've sunk into a melancholy, without ever considering how you are to suffer. Travelling about on hot, dusty roads, horrible inns and Mr Harris not offering you the adoration you deserve.'

'Oh, I'm perfectly content,' said Jane. 'I shall enjoy looking at the scenery. I find old buildings interesting.'

'You don't!' cried Henry, looking up helplessly as she prepared to go. 'You want diversion and life and vigour and jokes and jollity. Old buildings be damned. I tell you, Jane, I'm going to devote every ounce of my energy to repairing my leg while you are away and I hope to welcome you back with a country dance.'

Jane returned to the lodge more miserable than she had confessed to Henry. She was going to miss his vivacious company very much and dreaded the long hours of journeying with Mr Harris and his sister.

At least Bessie was to accompany her. Jane found great relief in the girl's presence. Bessie had long sensed the coldness between her master and mistress, and her loyalty to Jane was expressed in a hundred imaginative contrivances for her comfort and convenience.

Mr Harris sometimes rode, sometimes travelled in the coach with his family. The summer season was rather dark and rainy. They seemed often to be riding through a vast green abyss, hanging among hills made indistinct by mist and low cloud. The ways were muddy, the inns dirty, the coachmen and grooms in a bad temper. Everyone whose work was out of doors found themselves inconvenienced by the weather. The haymaking was universally acknowledged to be a disaster and Mr Harris's own work, the saving of souls, suffered too, being also a harvest customarily conducted out of doors.

'When we get to Exeter, Madam, I should like to have leave to see an old friend of mine who lives there,' remarked Bessie one evening, over cold pigeon pie in an inn near Taunton.

'Of course, Bessie. Who is it?'

'A girl I knew in London, Hannah Morley. She worked with me at Primrose Hill, but she came from Exeter, Madam, and now I heard she's returned there to marry her childhood sweetheart, Mr Turton. I have her address and I took the liberty of sending word I might be in Exeter and should like to see her.'

'I have no objection whatever, Bessie.'

Mr and Miss Harris were not in the room, or Bessie might not have had the courage to make the request, or Jane to grant it. Mr Harris had retreated, since the tour began, into his grave and preoccupied demeanour. Despite his apologies to his wife some weeks previously, Jane found she still feared him, most especially here, where he was continually exercising his considerable powers over congregations of several hundred souls.

In most places where they stayed the household occupied two rooms: one for Jane, Bessie and the babe, and the other for Mr Harris. It was understood he must not have his rest disturbed by Sarah, who was developing a strong pair of lungs and a disinclination to sleep. Bessie and Jane, therefore, struggled through the nights, singing themselves hoarse with lullabies, and dozed in the daytime whenever they could snatch a few moments of repose.

Miss Harris shared a room, when necessary, with a travelling companion of hers, a Mrs Marsh, who was newly recruited to the company of the blessed, an enthusiastic admirer of Mr Harris and particularly ingratiating to his sister. Mrs Marsh was a widow without children and was therefore at liberty to follow the touring party and pray and sing with ostentatious loudness.

Her devotion was not in the least discouraged by the rain. Indeed, like a duck, she seemed to be noisier and more completely herself, the more violently she was assaulted by the weather. Jane could not help being very irritated by her, although as a companion for Miss Harris she spared Jane what might otherwise have been long and tedious hours in her sister-in-law's company.

Jane's spirits were vexed by the weather, by the discomforts of travel, by the exertions and fatigues of motherhood and, beyond all these mundane difficulties, the painful charade of her appearance at every field preaching. In a succession of fields throughout Somerset and Devon, Jane stood listening again and again to the same sermon, holding in her arms the significant babe. Sarah was much admired as Mr Harris's daughter, almost as if she had sprung from his head like the daughter of Jove, without any assistance from a mother. Jane wryly assumed that Mr Harris would have much preferred that method of propagation, had it been available.

She endured all this, somehow, by not thinking too closely or continually about it. There was no sign of Colin Watts. Mr Harris treated her with remote kindness in private. In public his courtesies were just emphatic enough to be convincing to the multitude. She bore them demurely, thinking of almost anything else: her old girlhood days, wondering if Henry's leg was any better, or if her mother was gone to Cheltenham or Panswicke to visit her Aunt Harriet. She never thought of Sir Thomas at all if she could help it.

They were to spend a fortnight in Exeter, at an inn which the inclement weather had made damp and unpleasant. Mr Harris made several excursions into the adjoining country to preach, but Jane did not always accompany him. On the third day she gave Bessie permission to go to see her friend, Mrs Turton, and stayed on her own in the dirty bedchamber, dozing as best she could in a great old worm-eaten chair, while the wind hurled handfuls of rain against the window-pane. Sarah slept in a small cradle. Her face seemed the only flawless thing in the room and her tiny breaths soothed her mother's ears as Jane drifted in and out of sleep.

At five o'clock Bessie returned and brought some tea, and Jane roused herself, though her solitary afternoon had plunged her into a deep melancholy. She had not been able to avoid reproaching herself for the ignorance with which she had fallen into this unhappy situation in life and wondered how long she would have to endure it. There seemed no escape. She was plucked from her stupor, however, by observing that there was something unusual in Bessie's expression.

'Well, Bessie,' she asked, yawning, 'how did you find your friend? Was she as well and happy as you would have hoped?'

'Oh yes, Ma'am, entirely. But her husband said something which upset me rather and I think I should confide it to you, if you will permit me.'

'Of course.'

'It's . . . he said, Mr Harris's pamphlet is out, what he was working on all last winter, Madam, and Mr Turton hadn't seen it himself, but he's heard folks say it's treasonable like what Mr Paine wrote about getting rid of the King, and Hannah did fear Mr Harris might be indicted for seditious libel as Mr Paine was.'

A thrill of horror ran through Jane, but her instinct was to allay Bessie's anxieties if she could. She assured her that the worst she expected was perhaps Parson's disapproval of the pamphlet and distracted Bessie by a request for an early supper, which the girl instantly set about providing.

Two hours later, Jane heard the sound of many voices out in the street. Her senses were instantly aroused, as it seemed there might be an argument or an affray, for the cries were angry and increasing.

'What's that noise outside, Bessie? Is there a fight?'

Bessie rose and went to the window. Almost as she bent her face to look out, a stone shattered the glass and fell not six inches from the cradle. Now the crowd's cries grew louder and Jane heard with terror her husband's name shouted, together with insults and hoarse yells of 'Hang him! Hang him! God Save the King!'

There was the sound of more stones being thrown and other windows broken. Jane did not stop to think, only snatched up the babe and ran in great terror from the room.

'This way, Ma'am – the back stairs!' Bessie knew the service passages that led away from the front of the building and out to a quiet yard at the back. The rain, driving down with punishing force, lent some assistance, for it was impossible for anybody to raise their eyes much, or see through it. Bessie led them through a warren of old lanes until they reached a wider street, from which the cries of the mob could be only faintly heard.

'Come – come, Madam, we'll go to Mrs Turton's, she'll be very glad to give us shelter I'm sure.'

Jane looked back for a moment, over the huddle of steep old roofs to where the sounds of riot were still audible. 'Oh! God preserve William, if he is there!' she murmured. 'I think he was out at Newton Abbott, however; he was not due back yet. God grant he gets away safe.' Whatever her husband's personal difficulties or political persuasions, she would rather he were not torn apart by an angry mob.

Mr and Mrs Turton were very glad to offer hospitality to Jane and her child, and though their house was very small, the contrast between its clean cheerfulness and the dismal inconveniences of the inn increased Jane's grateful sense of escape and rescue. Mr Turton promised to go to the inn the next day to retrieve such of Jane's things as might have escaped the riot and to enquire after Mr Harris.

At breakfast, the rumour was that he had fled to France. Mr Turton went out at about half-past nine, and returned an hour later with some of Jane's belongings and a suspicion that Mr Harris had been warned not to return to the inn the previous night, had escaped the attentions of the mob and was widely supposed to be already embarked for France, and his sister and Mrs Marsh with him.

'I'm sure he'll write to you as soon as he can,' said Mr Turton, 'and no doubt he will make arrangements for you to join him, but I think for the present your best plan would be to return home to your parents, perhaps travelling under another name. I'd be very happy to escort you if you wish. There is a coach leaves for Bath every morning from The Crown.'

His wife added that if Jane would like to stay longer, they would of course be more than delighted to entertain her, but Jane was grateful for Mr Turton's suggestion and resolved to act upon it, only insisting that there was no need for him to accompany her. She would travel alone and call herself Mrs Black.

The journey to Bath was uneventful. The conversation of the other passengers touched but fleetingly on the radical priest and his shocking pamphlet, which everyone condemned, but nobody had read. The company then settled to the more scandalous subject of the effect of the weather on the harvest and the price of bread. Jane looked out of the window at a countryside almost rotten and mouldering with damp. Mildew hung upon the leaves and every brave wayside flower hung its head, sodden with water and spoilt with mud.

There was something novel, however, in the idea of travelling alone. Nobody could impose arrangements upon her but herself. Her husband, whose authority had been absolute in matters of travel and accommodation, had gone. Jane could do what she liked. As the journey proceeded and she overheard her companions making plans to stay in Bath, she suddenly decided to spend a few days there herself. Dry lodgings, and a little leisure, would enable her and Bessie to recover slightly from the fatigues and alarms of their journey. Accordingly, upon arrival in Bath she sent word to her parents that she and Sarah were quite safe and coming home soon, but had decided to rest for a few days first.

Jane had her own money with her. She had learnt that

important lesson from observing her parents' marriage. Lodgings were acquired with relative ease, as it was not the busy winter season. A comfortable house not far from the Abbey offered a modest suite of rooms which Jane secured for a week and as soon as a bed was ready she fell into a great sleep for almost twenty-four hours, dimly aware of Bessie moving about and taking care of the baby, who was put into the bed with her at intervals to feed.

At length Jane's body seemed to have drunk its fill of sleep and she awoke. It was very early in the morning. She counted the strokes of a bell. It was five o'clock. Too wide awake to want to stay in bed, she got up and silently washed and dressed. Little Sarah was fast asleep in the adjoining room, next to Bessie's bed. Bessie was muttering in her sleep something about walnuts. Jane found herself inclined to exercise and slipped out of the house.

The very early mornings of this wet summer had often been the only time when the sun shone and now it was casting up into the clouds behind the Abbey a mysterious coral light. Jane wandered for a while idly enjoying the recovery of her strength, but she could not walk these streets for long without the most vivid recollections of Sir Thomas, and lamenting how different Bath was without him.

Then, the winter season had seemed vivid and full of warmth and colour. Now, in his absence, the summer seemed wan and forlorn, the streets as abandoned as herself. She refused to shed any tears of self-pity, but as she turned into the Abbey Square she thought she might step inside the Abbey, if it was open, and offer a prayer for her husband's safety and for the safety of Sir Thomas and Mary too, for the world seemed a fragile place this morning, as if the inhabitants of the earth had been swept away, leaving their houses all empty, as sea-creatures leave their shells.

A man was standing before the Abbey church, looking up and admiring the West Front, above the door. His back was turned towards her and Jane smiled at the fondness of her imagination, for haunted as she was by so many tender memories of being with Sir Thomas here, she could not help thinking that the gentleman's figure very closely resembled his. As she approached, he turned, hearing her footsteps, and to Jane's great astonishment she saw that it was indeed Sir Thomas. They both hesitated for an instant, unable to believe their eyes, then walked slowly across the forty yards which separated them, staring in amazement at each other.

Sir Thomas reached out his hands; she took them; he kissed her ceremoniously on both cheeks, then on both hands, and stood and looked at her in disbelief, through glittering tears, squeezing her hands again and again as if to assure himself that she was not a phantom, or a figment of his imagination, but warm flesh and blood.

36

'Jane! But how extraordinary – I was in the act of praying, to whatever gods there may be – is it you? Can it be you? I've not slept all night. We heard yesterday of your husband's flight to France, or so it is supposed. I've been in the greatest anxiety about you – and here you are before me.' Sir Thomas finished this incoherent speech with an air of disbelief. Jane could scarcely speak rationally herself, but recovered her composure, after a moment or two, so far as to ask about Mary.

'Mary is well. At least, she . . . she's expecting a child.' He looked away and blushed. 'Not with any great enthusiasm, it must be said. She's enduring the customary discomforts, I'm afraid, made worse by travelling. She insisted on coming home early. I thought it might perhaps be better to spend the summer quietly in Italy, and promised her she would feel better and more able to bear the journey home in September, but she would not listen.

'Mary sometimes . . .' He hesitated. '. . . sometimes seems to fear the worst, to flee from some imagined catastrophe and it's of no use whatever, I find, to persuade her otherwise. She can argue me quite into a corner when she's in the grip of a fear. It quite defeats me.'

Jane recognised, in this description of her sister, her parents' worst characteristics unhappily united. 'So you've not had a very happy journey, then?' she enquired timidly. Her feelings were most uncertain. She wanted Sir Thomas to have been happy, she wished her sister to have made him so, and yet some small demon so worked upon her most private thoughts that she found some comfort in the idea that Sir Thomas could not be made happy by anyone except herself.

Though ashamed of this sensation, she could not quite rid herself of it, despite being perfectly aware that as Sir Thomas was married to her sister, and she herself married to someone else entirely, the opportunities for her to make Sir Thomas happy were significantly curtailed.

'Oh, we had some fine times early on,' Sir Thomas conceded. 'Lisbon, the great limestone cliffs at Sintra, the wild palace on the hill there, the moorish castle with its view of the Atlantic, oh yes, very fine.' He sighed. 'Not that poor Mary finds any great delight in the landscape. But I think there were occasions – balls, concerts, parties – which she did enjoy.'

'I saw a letter from you both in which she seemed very happy. It was the first letter you sent, I think, from Lisbon. You wrote it on a balcony. Sitting in your shirt in the sun.'

Sir Thomas seemed struck by the exactness of her recollection. 'You are extraordinary, Jane, to have the command of such details. It's as if you had been there with us.'

Jane could not say how ardently she wished she had been. Sir Thomas could not express the thought either. They were both quiet for a moment, sensing another conversation, requiring no words, which seemed to be running beneath their present talk like an underground river.

'You look well, my dear, but you are grown thin.'

It was true. The fatigues of the circuit and the despondency which had dogged her relations with her husband had affected her appetite. Only her bosom retained the plumpness of motherhood. Jane's maiden figure was otherwise restored, but what troubled Sir Thomas was the evidence in her face of abiding sorrow and frustration.

'Will you give me your arm and let's walk for a while, my dear,' he said. 'Then I'm sure Mary and Eleanor won't forgive me unless I take you back with me for breakfast. Where are your lodgings? We could go there first and collect young Sarah.'

Jane was grateful for these initiatives, especially the opportunity to walk for a while with Sir Thomas first in the morning air. The stones sparkled, for it had rained in the night, and now the early sunbeams seemed to mantle the city in frail golden light.

She took his arm, rejoicing in the warmth of his body, and he caressed her hand as they walked for a while in quietness.

'When I got here three days ago,' said Sir Thomas, 'I found a letter waiting for me, from Henry.'

'Oh! How is his leg? And how is Eliza?'

'She's much better and he seems to be mending, I thank you. He's off crutches, at any rate – walking with a stick, now, I believe.'

'Will he have to go back to his ship this year?'

'Jane, Jane . . .' Sir Thomas stopped for a moment and reproached her with a tender look. 'I'm trying to talk about you and you will always be fretting about someone else's welfare. Henry told me the whole history of your marriage, as you had related it to him. I'm sorry if he has betrayed a confidence, but you know Henry – he can't keep anything to himself, he has a worse tongue than a washerwoman.'

'I'm glad he's told you,' said Jane, looking across the paved space of the Circus, where they had now arrived. 'It would have been very hard to have to tell you myself.'

'You can imagine the horror with which I learned of it.' Sir Thomas looked earnestly into her face. 'The thought of you so abused, so neglected, so unloved, quite broke my heart.' Tears stood out in his eyes.

'I have found comfort in my child,' said Jane quietly.

'Yes, yes, my dear, and I'm glad of it. But maternal feelings should not have to be a solace of that kind. Your marriage has been a wilderness. I see it in your face. I suspected it before we left, but was ignorant, until Henry's letter, exactly what you were enduring. Good God! I blame myself. To think of you suffering so, when any man of feeling would have loved you, cherished you, adored you and thanked the gods every day for such an exquisite blessing.'

Tears broke from Jane's eyes. Sir Thomas offered his handkerchief and she covered her face. The city was beginning to come to life around them. The first carts and carriages were trundling across the Circus, boys were running on errands, dogs chasing each other, tradesmen's messengers making deliveries, but Jane heard nothing, and Sir Thomas saw nothing, of the surroundings. They felt entirely alone.

Jane cried for a while and Sir Thomas, steadily holding her hand, waited till she was done. 'I'm a villain to upset you so in the street.'

'I don't care where we are,' said Jane, wiping her eyes. 'And I'm extremely happy.'

They walked on and came at last to the Royal Crescent. Here they stopped to admire the immense sweep of the building, the airy space it embraced and the folds of land dropping away beneath, a pastoral scene of fields and beasts, down to the River Avon which glinted below.

'My dear Jane,' said Sir Thomas suddenly, 'would you like to dance with me tonight?'

'I should like nothing better!' cried Jane.

'Let's wipe away these tears, then, and banish all regretful thoughts for a while. Eleanor has bullied me into agreeing to a ball tonight – nothing elegant, only country dances. Mary can't dance at the moment and Eleanor is grown so stout I'm sure she won't last more than ten minutes, so I shall be without a partner unless you do me the great honour to stand up with me?'

Jane happily agreed. She could think of nothing more delightful.

Now they returned to Jane's lodgings to collect Sarah. As Jane walked into the room, Bessie, who had been attending to the baby, looked up and caught in an instant the change in her mistress's expression. 'Oh! What is it, Madam? What's happened?' she cried eagerly, and Jane knew her face must betray the uncommon happiness she felt.

'I met Sir Thomas in the street, Bessie, and we're going now to see Mary – she's expecting a child. They came back early from Italy – they are staying at his daughter's. And we are to go to a ball tonight.'

'Oh! Madam! I'm so glad for you, so pleased, pleased beyond words.'

It was but a short step to Eleanor's house, where Jane was received with surprise and great affection by Eleanor and George. Mary was feeling very sick and had kept to her room, but Jane was invited to go up by herself and was grateful to have the chance of a private reunion with her sister. It would have been difficult to see Mary with Sir Thomas standing by.

Mary looked up from her bed with the greatest astonishment and delight. 'What, Jane! How did you come here? How are you? Poor thing, we heard about Mr Harris's pamphlet – I feared you would fly with him to France. I was afraid I should never see you again, Jane, I was afraid I would die in childbirth and never see you again ever in my life. Oh, how terrible that would have been!' She clung to her sister with such extraordinary strength, Jane was immediately reassured as to her sister's well-being.

'Well, I'm here now, dearest, and you are not going to die in childbirth either, but have a bonny baby to play with mine. Sarah's downstairs. If you feel well enough, you must come down and see her.'

'Oh, the darling! I must see her now! Tell Bessie to bring her up directly!' Mary was half out of bed already.

'No. I don't think she should be allowed to fret you if you're not well enough to come downstairs.' Thus artfully did Jane contrive to tempt her sister into her clothes and down the stairs.

'Oh, Jane, I've been feeling so ill!' cried Mary as she dressed. 'You can't imagine – well, perhaps you can, for you have been in the same case yourself. Such weariness! And such sickness! I tell Sir Thomas I shall never forgive him. Poor Sir Thomas! I'm sure he would rather be married to a hyena.' She grew contemplative for a moment. Jane was instantly alert. 'I'm afraid I have made his life quite a misery in the last few weeks. I refused to stay in Venice, I was quite sure I should die there. It was so hot, there was a storm, and I was sleeping with the window open and awoke to find my bed covered with hailstones. I'm afraid I was in such a terror I blamed Sir Thomas for everything.'

'Sir Thomas is a man of considerable powers,' remarked Jane slyly, 'but as far as I'm aware, he is not responsible for the weather.'

Mary laughed heartily. 'Oh Jane! I'd forgot how funny you are! You make me feel better! And I'm sure you must do your best to make Sir Thomas feel better, for he likes your company, he told me, better than anyone's and I have nagged the poor man almost out of his wits.'

Jane heard this with a silent jolt of the heart, but said nothing, only smoothed her sister's hair.

'There!' cried Mary. 'Am I in order? Oh, I don't care! Baby will not mind what I look like, nor will anyone else.' She plunged downstairs to embrace her niece.

The infant Sarah had been introduced to Eleanor's child, young Thomas, who had begun to totter about and lisp. Mary played with both children with great pleasure. Her delight in the infants was unfeigned and inexhaustible.

'She will make a good mother,' remarked Jane quietly and Sir Thomas nodded, though he seemed not anxious to add any observations on the subject, nor was Jane eager to hear any.

After an hour or two of celebration and reunion, the company parted to rest, bathe and dress for the ball that night. Jane made her preparations in a state of exultation.

Eleanor had lent her a gown, which Bessie soon altered to fit by raising the hem some three inches. It was made of rosy silk, a colour and a cloth much finer than Jane would have chosen for herself.

'Oh, Madam!' cried Bessie, standing back to admire her, 'it's wonderful! You look quite like a princess! Look, look there in the glass!'

Jane saw her face so transformed with happiness she hardly recognised herself. She looked a hundred times more alive than the sad reflection she had been used to seeing of late. Her eyes sparkled and the colour of the dress seemed to set off her face and figure to an extraordinary degree. She could not help being delighted with her appearance for the first time in her life.

Sir Thomas's carriage was soon at the door. Jane's landlady hovered in a state of avid curiosity and was rewarded with some courtesies from Sir Thomas. At the first moment of their meeting Jane felt a shock of admiration. He was dressed in grey, black and white, with a simplicity which suited the healthy colour of his skin, touched by the southern sun.

His eyes glowed at the sight of her. 'Why, Jane,' he murmured, 'I've never seen you look so beautiful.' He blushed.

She felt an exultation run through her body, but only bowed a little and said, 'It's Eleanor's fine dress, I'm afraid I don't do it justice,' and hastened out to the carriage.

She was welcomed, and admired, by the whole party, though Mary had stayed at home. Nothing could be more natural, in the indisposition of his wife, than that Sir Thomas should take the hand of his sister-in-law and lead her on to the dance floor to forget her troubles for a while. Of course, Jane's identity was known to many present; her story had a poignant and sensational appeal and many pairs of eyes scrutinised the abandoned wife of the preacher who had published such a seditious pamphlet.

Jane, however, felt nobody's gaze but Sir Thomas's. She had been unhappy for so many long months together that merely to be in his company at last was reason enough for joy. But to be dancing with him, to turn from him, then turn back and meet again, to feel the touch of his hand, then lose it, then have it restored, to float towards him, buoyed up by the cadences of the music and to feel his eyes, skin, breath, all brought her to a pitch of exultation beyond speech.

They danced all evening in a kind of delirium, almost without exchanging a word. Somehow they managed to be civil and cordial and to exchange compliments with others when it was necessary, without ever leaving that enchanted space which they shared and to which they returned instantly whenever their eyes met, whether they were standing close, or separated by a crowd.

Jane did not permit herself to worry about what these extraordinary sensations meant. She could only dance, and be happy.

'What are you thinking?' he asked in a murmur, at a moment when they were moving in harmony down a set of people all so busy with their own talk as to offer a curious privacy.

'I dreamt we were flying together once,' confessed Jane suddenly. 'It was like this.'

They were separated for a moment by the demands of the dance and stood facing each other across the set. Other dancers passed between them. His look, so tender and voluptuous all evening, had now acquired a quality of painful longing.

When the moment came for them to take hands again he whispered, 'I dream of you every night, Jane. Whether I'm asleep or awake.'

She heard it with a shock and understood at last what she had hardly ever dared to contemplate as a possibility. Sir Thomas loved her.

He spoke no more to her in the public rooms. They had danced almost to the end of the ball. Eleanor, very sleepy, was to be conveyed home by her husband in the carriage.

'I think Jane would prefer to walk,' said Sir Thomas to his son-in-law. 'I'll escort her back to her lodgings.'

'She must be damned fit, then.' George yawned. 'For I'm almost dead on my feet and I've done nothing all night but sit and play cards.'

'I would like some air,' acknowledged Jane quietly, receiving her cloak.

They left the Rooms and walked slowly back through pools of gaslight cast by the fine new lamps and through pools of darkness between them, and Jane seemed to feel every particle of light upon her face and every atom of darkness, as if it was the moment of creation and she was the first creature ever to have lived.

Suddenly they were at her door. Sir Thomas sighed in exasperation. 'Oh no,' he said. 'This is too soon to say good-night.'

'Will you come in?' Jane asked quietly. 'Bessie will find you a glass of brandy, I'm sure.'

Sir Thomas seemed to be very grateful for an excuse to stay in her company.

Bessie received them and took their cloaks, though stumbling with drowsiness. The babe was safe in her cradle. Sir Thomas sat down on one side of the fireplace, Jane opposite. They did not speak.

Bessie soon brought the brandy and hesitated, half-asleep. 'Will you call if you need me, Madam?' she asked. 'Shall I stay in the next room?'

Jane was suddenly aware of a sound outside in the passage. The landlady had heard their return. Jane became intensely irritated not to be in her own house.

'Please be so good as to stay with us, Bessie,' she said clearly, then added quietly, 'go and lie down on the sofa, my dear.'

Bessie gladly obeyed and within two minutes was snoring with perfect tact: distinctly enough to guarantee oblivion, but not quite loudly enough to be heard out in the hall.

'Well,' said Sir Thomas, for the benefit of any eavesdropper, 'I shall just drink my brandy and say good-night to you, my dear, for poor Mary has had some wretched nights lately and I'm anxious to see how she has fared.'

'Please be so good as to give her my love,' said Jane. 'And be sure to tell her I'll call tomorrow as soon as I have slept.'

They heard the landlady's skirts rustle away and a door closing in some dim recess of the house.

'Tomorrow?' smiled Sir Thomas, glancing at the clock. 'Why, it is tomorrow already; it's past midnight. You must be tired.'

'I've never felt less inclined to sleep.' Jane's heart raced at the idea that they were now almost alone.

'Nor I.' She looked at him and found in his face that eloquent admiration in which she had floated all night. 'Well, well, Jane. We are almost in private. So soon as we can contrive it we must get back to Ottercombe and have done with other people's houses.'

Jane began to shiver.

'Are you cold?' he asked. 'Shall I come across and warm you, Jane?' His voice sank almost to a breath.

'No, no—' She was alarmed. 'I'm not cold.' She ached to touch him, but not with Bessie so near.

'Shall we go into the next room?'

'It's my bedchamber.'

'Let me put you to bed, then. Let me do Bessie's office, as she is exhausted. I shall only stroke your hair and leave you to sleep.'

She felt almost dizzy at these possibilities. 'No – not here. I can't – I want only to sit here with you just now.'

'It's almost impossible for me to sit two yards away from you, Jane.' His voice shook.

'Why did you marry my sister?' The question came soaring out of her like a rocket. She had not felt it coming herself and Sir Thomas flinched at it. For a moment he was silenced. 'You said, when you came to see us at the lodge last December – you said you wanted a private conversa-

299

tion with me. You wished to explain how your marriage came about.'

Though Sir Thomas had had seven months to consider his explanation, he appeared not very eloquent on the subject. 'It was an idea of Eliza's, at first. A silly tease, but somehow Mary took to it, and would not let it go, and between them both they would give me no rest until it was settled.'

'You speak as if you had no wishes in the matter. No desire. Did you not love her, then?'

'Who could not love Mary, in a way?' he retorted uneasily. 'Everybody must love her.'

'So you did fall in love with her?' Jane found herself racked with mysterious anger.

'I was in despair, Jane. It did not seem to matter to me what I did.'

'Why?'

'Because you had married Mr Harris.'

Jane's anger left her for an instant and was replaced with a sickening remorse. But frustration drove her forward. She spoke from despair, hardly knowing what she would say next. 'But why did you let me marry him? You could have stopped me, but you stood aside. If you had felt any misgivings you should have said so. You seemed not to care what happened to me.'

'How can you say that?' cried Sir Thomas. 'I know I was very much to blame, but I did nothing not because I did not care, but because I cared too much.'

'What do you mean?'

'I had come to want you so very much myself.' He fell silent. She could not speak either. It was so still they could hear the candle flame writhing in its pool of wax.

'I dared not intervene,' Sir Thomas went on. 'I was astonished to find you had formed an attachment so quickly. I could only conclude you did not feel anything extraordinary for me. It was agonising. But I was paralysed by wanting you so much myself and feeling I had no right to.'

He had been looking into the distance; now he bowed his head and seemed to stare into the floor. 'I have such a horror of tyranny that I have often refrained from asserting my will,' he admitted quietly. 'And so much of my life has been spent in an effort to please others that sometimes I act as if I have no desires of my own, or no right to gratify them.'

He looked up at last and at the desperate longing in his eyes all Jane's anger vanished. She only wanted to touch him, and stood up.

But at the rustle of her skirts, Bessie awoke. 'Oh – am I – I beg your pardon, Madam—'

The awkwardness of Bessie's sudden return to consciousness filled Jane with dismay. Sir Thomas saw it and got up too. Bessie herself, sensing something curious in the atmosphere, hastily excused herself and went into the next room, closing the door very quietly behind her.

'Promise me we may have more conversations at Ottercombe. In greater privacy – at greater ease.' He glanced about him in frustration. The sounds of Bessie's movements seemed an unbearable intrusion. It was someone else's house, the door unlocked, unlockable, the key in someone else's keeping.

'Yes. At Ottercombe.' Jane could not say more. Now there was the painful business of parting.

Sir Thomas advanced a pace, then hesitated. 'May I kiss you once?' he murmured. Jane felt her heart rock and her limbs shake.

He drew near. His mouth, which had never failed to please her with its words, now touched hers at last. He only held her arm lightly as they kissed, though she felt him tremble and feared she might fall down, so great was her agitation and her pleasure. She felt the faintest roughness of his chin, for it was many hours since he had shaved. She tasted for an instant the edge of his tongue and felt the backs of her legs burn with longing to do more.

The kiss ended. He bowed and, with a great sigh which

301

flew all down the alarmed skin of her neck, he left the house without a sound. She stood still for ten minutes afterwards, lamenting the emptiness of the space where a moment ago he had stood and consoling herself with the possibility that, by breathing in, she might recapture his parting sigh, that air which had once been in his body.

37

Before they could leave Bath, a day of rest and a day of preparation were necessary. Jane hardly saw Sir Thomas, paying only brief calls on her sister, whose spirits were always much improved by the arrival of little Sarah. Mary was also encouraged by the thought of being soon at home, although she dreaded the journey.

'And when you arrive, my dear,' Jane reminded her, 'you will find yourself mistress of Ottercombe Park – think what a pleasure that will be, to have such an elegant and comfortable establishment at your disposal.'

At these words Mary cheered up a great deal, though they had the opposite effect on Jane. She was, however, looking forward to stepping across the threshold again of her own dear little lodge and the thought of it was the more beguiling because Mr Harris would not be there.

At least, she supposed he would not be there. In the absence of any convincing evidence of his whereabouts she had been forced to accept the general conjecture that he had fled to France. He could, however, be in hiding anywhere in England. Jane was haunted by a ridiculous but unsettling idea that she would find him at the lodge, crouching in his room under the eaves. The thought of having to share a house once more with her husband was insupportable.

His irritation with and neglect of her would have been enough to make the idea unbearable. Her misgivings about his private passions and his political ideas had increased her alarm, and now she had met Sir Thomas again she could not imagine spending even a few hours in her husband's company. If she could not be with Sir Thomas she would rather be alone. She would sooner sleep under a hedge in a storm than endure bed and board with Mr Harris.

But she hoped not to be driven to such extremes. She had an instinct that her husband had fled the country and she had already imagined the possibility that she might never hear from him again. There was a sadness in this thought, despite her repudiation of her marriage. Jane did not wish to live with Mr Harris, but it would relieve her heart to learn how to be friends with him. Nor did she feel her life could settle into any kind of pattern without communication between herself and her husband. She was most anxious to hear from him, therefore, but with very different feelings from what might normally have been expected of a wife.

The rain continued, though as Sir Thomas's carriage began the long climb out of Bath some faint gleams of sunshine pierced the clouds. Shafts of light fell on the land, raced across fields and hedges, then died, plunging the countryside into sudden shadow. An atmosphere of uncertainty, of joy and despair, seemed to hang over the landscape and reflect Jane's agitation.

Sir Thomas was seated opposite her. Mary and Bessie were happily engrossed in playing with the baby and Jane found herself at liberty, for the first time since the ball, to look frankly across at him and find in his face the same understanding, tenderness and desire which had by degrees stolen over her senses and, at the last, utterly captivated her.

Sir Thomas said very little. As the journey progressed he remarked occasionally upon the appearance of the land; the attempts at a harvest, despite the weather, or the curious effect created by the thick green light on a landscape already voluptuously overgrown. But he seemed inclined rather to admire Jane than study the topography of the south-west of England.

They shared a rapturous contemplation of each other which was at first completely intoxicating and drove out every other thought. As they continued on their way, however, and they passed through villages with more familiar names, a sense of their imminent separation began to bear in on them. Jane now saw in Sir Thomas's look a painful desire to prolong the fleeting moments. Mary had begun to feel uncomfortable, then very tired. At length she fell asleep, her head resting on Sir Thomas's shoulder, and Bessie dozed also.

There was something unnerving at the sight of Mary, spent and unconscious, enjoying the convenience of Sir Thomas's body as an instinctive right, almost without even being aware of it. Jane began to feel her lonely separation from him most acutely. He still gazed at her with the same tender eloquence, but Mary's blank face alongside his seemed a disturbing emblem of possession which Jane could not ignore. However, despite these uncomfortable sensations, the journey, which to poor Mary seemed interminable, was to Jane's unhappiness all too soon concluded.

Now they were travelling along the valley bottom at Ottercombe. Mary awoke and recognised with excitement the familiar hedges of her own parish.

'Oh! Soon we shall see Papa and Mamma!' she cried. Jane felt that if she were Mary, nothing would have given her greater pleasure than to settle with Sir Thomas into their own home at last. Her parents' health and spirits would of course have been a first consideration and messages sent instantly. But she would not have rushed to see them immediately. She would have wished to take possession of her kingdom first.

She reflected, however, that it would prove something of a torment to her if she were very often to think how differently she might have felt or acted, if she had been Sir Thomas's wife. She therefore tried to prepare herself for the separation from him which, in a very few minutes, would be required, and to console herself with anticipation of her lodge and garden.

Mary was desperate to get out, so the carriage called first at Ottercombe to discharge her. Eliza ran out across the gravel to greet her beloved Papa and Jane was glad to see Henry hobbling out after her. A mêlée of embraces took place. Jane expressed delight at her friends' evident health and received with resignation their sympathies as to her husband's behaviour.

'What shall we do now?' whispered Henry mischievously. 'Mr Harris has quite trumped us. I was resolved to offer myself to him as a supposed lover of yours, so he could sue me and divorce you. Now I shall have to limp my way across France, and by the time I find him we'll all be in our dotage and our wedding night will be a sad disappointment to you, my dear.'

Jane brushed him away with impatience. Her heart was so full of Sir Thomas that his son's whispers were particularly empty. Yet there was something agreeable in Henry's vivacity and she sensed such an authentic sympathy beneath his banter that she could not help feeling glad to see him.

'I shall escort Mrs Harris home first,' said Sir Thomas to the groom, and the horses were persuaded, with much ado, to convey a reduced party the further half-mile or so to the lodge. Bessie was very busy about the baby's things, which permitted Jane and Sir Thomas to share a moment of intimate contemplation which was now almost unbearably bitter, but their sudden arrival at the lodge provided a most unexpected distraction.

'Oh! Madam! It's all boarded up!' cried Bessie, whose quick and unengaged eyes were first to see the damage. Jane looked out with horror to find her small house horribly ravaged. There were signs of fire and of attack. Window-panes were shattered, the guttering was hanging half off and at the back, part of the roof had gone, leaving blackened and exposed timbers to witness what could only have been a fearful assault.

'A mob must have come up from Woolton,' said Sir Thomas at once. 'Don't cry, my dear, your little house will soon be put to rights, I'm sure.'

He leaned forward and took her hand, but Jane could not help weeping as the carriage jolted off across the park towards her father's house. Her dreams of independence and solitude were at an instant shattered. She must become a dependent daughter again. Her heart rebelled at it.

At Newington House, Sir Thomas told Bessie to get out first with the baby, to give Jane a few moments to compose herself. The instant they were alone, he spoke. 'I'd imagined I could call on you at the lodge – I'm desperate, Jane, for some private words with you – the sweetness of that thought must be our consolation for a few hours. I shall contrive something. I'll come to you.'

Jane nodded through her tears, though it seemed to her that she and Sir Thomas must be parted, now, by waves of other people and be tossed by those waves further and further apart, drowning for a glimpse of each other.

'Come, my dear. Be brave. You must reassure your poor mother.'

He raised her hand to his lips and kissed it with a desperate fervour, then handed her out of the carriage. Jane found only her father waiting on the gravel, however. Mrs Lockhart had been visiting her sister in Cheltenham, and though she had been sent word of Mary's early return and Jane's dilemma she was entirely unable to return home at present, as she was suffering from a severe sore throat and fever.

John Lockhart greeted his son-in-law with the necessary civility and made a discreet enquiry as to Mary's health, though dreading Sir Thomas might supply unseemly details. Sir Thomas, however, seemed anxious to be gone and the rain, which had held off for an hour or so, now returned with sudden ferocity, driving Sir Thomas back into his coach and Jane into the damp, echoing hall of her father's house.

'If you would care to repair your appearance for a few moments, I shall be glad to take tea with you in the drawing-room,' he said, bowed and walked away. Jane was most struck by this example of her father's reserve, following so close upon Sir Thomas's ardent and expressive nature. She shivered and went up to her own room to make such adjustments to her dress as she supposed her father might require. For a moment she looked out of the window, but the grandeur of the valley was quite blotted out by a thick squall of rain.

Fifteen minutes later she presented herself for her father's inspection, with little Sarah, but the child grew fretful and began to offend her grandpapa's ears with a series of painful shrieks.

'Take her out, Bessie,' said John Lockhart. 'Take her up to the gallery at the top of the house. She may make as much noise as she chooses there. It served well enough as a nursery for you and your sister, Jane. We might think of fitting it up again for your daughter.'

Jane was obliged to thank her father for this kind thought, but the assumption behind it, that she would now be returning to live at Newington House, filled her with a sense of oppression. Once they were alone, Mr Lockhart sighed deeply and steepled his fingers. The sounds of Sarah enjoying the echo of the grand stairwell soon faded into quietness. Jane sipped her tea soberly and made every effort to confine her thoughts to this household and to what her father might consider ought to be said.

'Well, this is a sad business of Mr Harris,' he said at length. 'I suppose you've not heard from him? We have not either. I'm sorry now that I ever gave my consent to the marriage. You can imagine my feelings a week ago, to see my eastern lodge attacked by a mob and almost destroyed. It will be a most expensive matter to repair. The damage was so bad that I thought at first of leaving it a ruin – but that does not look well in a lodge and besides, I have resolved to make a kind of retired hermitage out of the Smiths' old hovel in the wood.

'I've quite left off my plan for an obelisk. The idea of a boathouse has occurred to me, though. Down by the lake. I've done some preparatory sketches. You might like to see them. They are in the library. Very simple – just a Gothic window, nothing ostentatious like Sir Thomas's bathhouse.'

'Sir Thomas's bathhouse is not in the least ostentatious!' cried Jane, provoked into indignation by her father's determination to talk about architecture and to ignore her own most delicate and painful circumstances. 'It is of classical simplicity, nothing could be more modest and neat.'

Her father was shocked by her outburst and looked at her for a few moments with foreboding. 'You're beginning to look like your mother, Jane,' he observed. He meant this as a rebuke.

She swept it aside. 'As I have always considered Mamma to be very pretty I am honoured by the comparison. If my feelings are to be considered in the matter, Papa, I would be most grateful if the lodge could be repaired with all possible speed. Though it's most kind of you to welcome us here, I'm anxious to resume my life there and not to be a burden on you, nor to impose the noise and inconvenience of a child upon your tranquillity.'

Sarah assisted her mother's argument at this moment with a remote scream from above.

'But surely you do not expect your husband to return?'

'I suppose not. I believe he would be in danger of arrest if he did.'

'What an absurdity it has turned out, this marriage of yours,' her father observed scrupulously. Jane was silent. Her marriage had been infinitely more absurd than her father could ever imagine. 'I deeply regret giving him my consent. Marry in haste, repent at leisure,' he concluded, with such a grim sigh that Jane was reminded for an instant that her parents' own marriage had been somewhat hastily concluded.

'I was not in a hurry,' she observed bitterly. 'It was Mr Harris. He seemed to do with us what he wanted.'

'He was a very fine-looking man,' observed John Lockhart, as if this was reason enough for him to have acquiesced instantly in Mr Harris's every wish. 'And what gave him a far greater authority was this tiresome business of his being a clergyman. One does not dare to obstruct a clergyman. One feels somehow intimidated by his office.'

Jane agreed, though privately. She recalled how once she had felt overwhelmed with enthusiasm for Mr Harris's eloquence. She had desired nothing more than to be at his side in charitable works and in his efforts to bring his congregations closer to the kingdom of heaven. Now she felt that if she heard even the distant echo of a hymn she would be sick. She had been prepared to put all her youthful strength and intelligence at the disposal of Mr Harris and his God and she had found herself held in contempt.

'I suppose you will go to join him abroad, if he writes to suggest it?'

'No, Papa. I utterly repudiate my marriage and feel no obligation whatever to obey Mr Harris.'

Her father looked startled and began to be afraid that his daughter might alarm him with more vehement outbursts. 'Well, he has written treasonably. Your sentiments do you credit. There is no need to tell me more. You can be quite quiet and comfortable here with us.'

He got up, in his haste to avoid further exposure to emotion. Jane also rose, pitying, in all her wretchedness, his deeper inability to express or receive the affection which every human being, she supposed, must long for. He bowed, she curtsied, he withdrew to his library, leaving her to ponder his last words. Jane was reconciled to some time spent at her parents' house, but she could never be quiet or comfortable here.

Over the next few days, visits were exchanged between the households. John Lockhart was relieved to find Mary in reasonable spirits, and when at last his wife recovered enough to return from Cheltenham the encounters became more animated and vivacious. Sir Thomas presided at Ottercombe Park over a family glad to be reunited, but whose spirits were troubled by being very much out of sorts.

Henry was impatient at being denied the activity which his youthful energies required. Healing a broken leg seemed an eternity to him. He was somewhat embarrassed by the return of Mary, whom some thought he had once jilted, as his stepmother. His spirits were further lacerated by a kind of remoteness he encountered whenever he attempted to tease Jane. The intimacy which he had enjoyed in their talks on the terrace in April seemed to have vanished. Jane was subdued, withdrawn. She seemed almost a different person, but her altered mood only increased Henry's feeling that of all women she was the one whose company was most agreeable.

Miss Eliza was much improved in health, without being quite as completely recovered as everyone would have wished. This irritated her, and though she was delighted to be reunited with her Papa and with Mary, her jealousy at having been excluded from their honeymoon was often revived and she was obliged to wrestle with the discovery that she no longer enjoyed an absolute priority when it came to her father's attention. She must share him with Mary. This inflamed her demands, rather than qualifying them, and Sir Thomas found himself caught between a spoilt and ailing daughter and a young wife very apprehensive about her own health and prospects.

Mary was in a dread of childbirth and her discomforts, which time appeared rather to augment than repair, seemed to feed her anxieties. She blamed Sir Thomas for her condition, as if she had not recognised that bearing children was a possible result of matrimony, and Jane was astonished to see how irritating Mary found his attentions, which would have proved so delectable if offered to herself.

Observing Sir Thomas in the midst of so many competing demands, Jane could hardly blame him when first a week passed, then two, without his having managed to arrange the private conversation for which she longed more intensely every passing day. Occasionally their eyes met in the midst of some noisy talk at his house, or her father's, and for an instant a silent assurance was exchanged that their feelings had not altered since they had last enjoyed a moment of privacy.

But it seemed impossible that they would ever find the excuse to claim a private interview. It began to appear that some kind of ruse was necessary, for Sir Thomas seemed quite at the mercy of his family's demands, and Jane was obliged to sit on the edge of the company and wait patiently for the glance he might at some stage find it possible to offer her, much as a dog sitting below the table at a feast might hope, in vain, for a scrap to be dropped.

The unsatisfactory summer began to disintegrate. Mildew cloaked the blackberries. Spiders' webs flashed in the cooler mornings, like a thousand looking-glasses. Jane stared out at the great vista below Newington House and saw the first leaves turn yellow, a month before it might have been expected. She shuddered at the thought of the approaching winter, but understood it must come.

38

'I wish your precious Mr Harris were here with us now. I could cheerfully wring the fellow's neck!' Mrs Lockhart fanned herself in an ecstasy of indignation. Jane sighed and began to hem another small shift for Sarah. In the three weeks since her mother's return she had heard Mrs Lockhart rehearse many vehement proposals for the painful despatch of Mr Harris, or, in more benign moods, for his humiliation and punishment.

'To leave you and our little babe without a word, without a scruple – and I don't suppose we shall ever hear from him again. You're neither one thing nor another, Jane. Neither a married woman nor a widow. I don't know what we shall do with you.'

'I hope there is no need to do anything with me,' remarked Jane mildly. 'If Papa could be persuaded to repair the lodge I'll happily resume a solitary life there. I could make myself useful in all sorts of ways, I hope – to you and Papa, of course, and to some of our more needy tenants, perhaps.'

'And to Mary,' said Mrs Lockhart. 'Don't forget Mary. She is working herself up into such a silly state, I think your calm good sense would be most welcome there.'

Jane almost smiled to think her anguished perturbation of spirits could be mistaken for calm good sense.

'But don't think I shall ever let you go back to that horrid lodge, even if Papa repairs it,' her mother went on.

'What! Live alone there, like a cottager, with a row of beans by the kitchen door! It was all very well for a bridal bower, a pastoral interlude, but I was never entirely happy about your staying there more than a few weeks.'

'I was perfectly comfortable there, Mamma.'

'Not as comfortable as Mary is at Ottercombe Park; I'm sure you would not contradict me on that point. For the time being, Jane, I want you here. Nothing could be more natural. You have suffered a great deal. You have been abandoned in the cruellest manner by a hypocritical rascal. Prating of God and heaven all the time, while secretly resolving to tear down the Government and kill the poor King!'

'I'm sure Mr Harris was in earnest whenever he preached, Mamma.' Jane felt a perverse inclination to defend her husband. 'And as you never either heard him preach or read his pamphlet, I think your judgement might be a little hasty.'

Her mother was on the point of launching a robust attack on this impudence, when she seemed struck by an unexpected pang of tenderness. 'Ah! You still love the fellow, Jane. Poor, dear girl! Always so tender-hearted. So kind, even to snails and toads, I remember. You must try not to love him any more, dearest. Root it out. Look about you. There are a hundred worthier fellows – but dear me, you are not widowed; how can it be done?

'A Deed of Separation perhaps – but I'm not sure that can be agreed in his absence. A divorce is impossible, I fear, unless a husband sues and you, dear Jane, are above reproach – and much the worse for it. It is curious, and very irritating too, to think that if you had been unfaithful Mr Harris could sue your lover for Criminal Conversation and obtain damages and the marriage be dissolved, and you could be free to marry. As it is, you are blameless and trapped. I'm sure the law is a nonsense – is it not, Mr Lockhart?'

Her husband had chosen this inopportune moment to

come into the room. He looked dismayed at his wife's greeting. 'What, my dear?'

'Is it not a monstrous injustice that Jane can't get a divorce?' Mr Lockhart winced. 'Here's the poor girl utterly abandoned and betrayed, and by a traitor to his country. What is the law on this point, Mr Lockhart? Could not we sue for desertion? How can poor Jane have the marriage dissolved?'

Mr Lockhart shook his head and moved backwards towards the door again with some urgency. 'I neither know, nor desire to know,' he said. 'The position is most unclear and I'm sure Jane would never wish to attract the conjectures of the impertinent by any reckless exposure of her private history to the courts. And think of the expense.'

This last inspired thought silenced his wife most effectively. 'Well, well,' she lamented, as her husband disappeared, 'I suppose Papa is right. I shall have to ask Sir Thomas when I next see him. He is a good deal better informed than Papa. If only we could free you of this tiresome marriage, my dear, I'm sure Henry Burton would pay his addresses to you on the instant. I've observed him the last two times we have gone to Ottercombe, and he looks at you with such admiration!

'Perhaps he never did seriously care for Mary. Perhaps he was always more drawn to you. You are both of a merry disposition. And Mary and Sir Thomas are so well suited. I never saw anyone so devoted to Mary as he is. When we were there last Wednesday he was so attentive. I'm sure Sir Thomas is quite madly in love with her, don't you think so, Jane?'

Jane was obliged to concur.

The conveniences of living at Newington House were welcome. The torments, however, were inescapable. Not only was Jane denied any private quarters in which she might enjoy a conversation alone with Sir Thomas, but she was obliged to endure her parents' company beyond the occasional half-hour which might have proved agreeable.

She did not know which made her more uncomfortable: her father's terror of emotion, or her mother's vehement and painfully inaccurate conjectures about everybody's feelings.

Mrs Lockhart did offer a suggestion which Jane found useful, however. Sarah was now more than six months old and a plan was brought forward to wean her, with the assistance of a local woman, whose own child was now being coaxed off the breast, as a wet-nurse. Jane acquiesced in these arrangements with some fond regret, but to be relieved of the necessity of nursing every few hours would greatly increase her freedom to go out and walk, and escape for a few hours the constraints and irritations of her parents' house.

She felt her strength increase. Nature seemed to offer a small encouragement to her after so much suffering, for the summer, which had seemed likely to dissolve away in rot and mildew, recovered and September saw several serene days of sunshine, which tempted Jane out among the fields. One fine day towards the end of the month she set out, hardly knowing where she was going, only wanting to feel the air on her body.

Ten minutes' walk brought her to the gates of Ottercombe Park, where she hesitated. The possibility of glimpsing Sir Thomas tormented and tempted her, but the certainty of having to soothe Mary, defend herself against the flirtatious entreaties of Henry and observe the sulks and demands of Miss Eliza forced her to conclude that she was more inclined to solitude at present.

She continued, therefore, down the lane, plunging more and more deeply into the valley. She did not like to see Mary and Sir Thomas as they seemed now, uneasy with each other. Although to see them delighting in each other's company would perhaps have been worse. As to the harmony so desirable in marriage, Jane reflected ruefully that almost every couple of her acquaintance failed to exhibit this happy quality.

Living with her own parents again, she had become most

struck by their entirely separate existences, patrolling different territories within the same house, their conversations taking on a symbolic quality. Her mother would assert something, her father acknowledge it almost without listening and proceed in due course to some observation of his own, entirely unconnected with his wife's remark. Their talk was like the singing of birds, designed aggressively to defend their own territories rather than to create an harmonious ensemble.

Jane recalled that it was the poet Humphrey Axton, whose cottage she would pass in five minutes or so, who had informed her many years ago of the habits of songbirds. She wondered if she might call, for she had scarcely glimpsed either the poet or his sister for months, they lived such a very retired life. Indeed, she thought the last time she had enjoyed anything like a prolonged conversation with either of them must have been at Miss Julia Burton's wedding, almost two years ago.

She wondered if Julia Burton's experience of matrimony had been any more encouraging. Sir Thomas hardly ever mentioned her. The couple had made their home in London and Jane had detected, in the few remarks Sir Thomas had let fall, that he considered his daughter somewhat vain, preoccupied with the demands of fashion to the exclusion of much else and a good deal less amiable than the indolent and greedy Eleanor. Julia's husband, Mr Francis Lloyd, was thought to be intolerably proud and preoccupied with the breeding of horses to a tedious degree. Perhaps they were peculiarly well matched in their selfishness. This might be considered the nearest to a happily married couple of all Jane's acquaintance.

But what of Sir Thomas himself? Though his marriage to Mary appeared often uncomfortable, perhaps his first marriage had been more fortunate. Jane had often wished to ask Sir Thomas about his wife, but as she had become attracted to him herself, she had begun to avoid the subject. Jane's feelings about Lady Charlotte had grown into a kind of painful knot which she suspected would not easily be untangled.

Jane was hauled from her reverie by a cheerful greeting and looked up to find she had reached the poet's cottage. Miss Axton was picking apples from a tree and her brother was seated at his easel, busy with his water-colours. They begged her to step in and offered her refreshment, and Jane was very glad to accept.

Miss Axton was most anxious to show her the improvements which an ingenious and tasteful intelligence had contrived. 'Humphrey has put up a shelf here; and look, he has built a bookcase in this alcove, where my old plates used to be, and invented a new home for them over there above the stairs.'

Jane looked about her and admired everything, though the Axtons' habits were not the most orderly and she was obliged to remove some embroidery, three books and a cat from the chair where she was urged to make herself comfortable.

As Miss Axton and her brother busied themselves about the place, Jane admired how long custom, and scrupulous fairness, had divided the domestic labour. Mr Axton mended the fire, swept the hearth and filled the kettle. Miss Axton busied herself joyfully among her gleaming cups and saucers. They were evidently delighted to see her, although when at last they all sat down together a moment of perplexity seized Miss Axton.

'My dear Jane, we were so very sorry to hear ... your poor husband, harried out of the land – and only for writing what enlightened opinion has long held, and advocating a more just and humane society. Alas! You must miss him most dreadfully, I'm sure.'

Jane was surprised at Miss Axton's tone, but determined to avoid any misunderstanding. 'I have to confess that I've not yet read William's pamphlet. He gave me a copy, but in the hurly-burly of travel, and with the baby always distracting me, somehow I lost it.'

Mr Axton got up and went to the bookcase. 'Here, my dear,' he said and handed her a copy. 'Do borrow mine. You ought to read it so soon as you can find the time, for we both feel that your husband has met with most unjust vilification, when he should have been praised for his humanity and courage.'

'Yes! Read it!' cried Miss Axton, her curls shaking with enthusiasm. 'You will find it will only make you love and respect him the more.'

Jane hesitated. A terrible urge to be candid quite over-came the scruples of etiquette. 'I think I always did respect William,' she ventured cautiously. 'And I'm sure that if what you say is true my respect for him will be augmented and I am grateful to you for the opportunity. But love—' The word lurched awkwardly in the air, and seemed to hang and ring for a moment among the teacups. 'I wished very much . . . but in the event . . . I'm afraid we were not suited in that way at all. Indeed William could not . . . I seemed not able to . . .'

'We are not all suited to marriage, alas,' said Humphrey Axton quickly. 'I can assure you, he felt it very much. He was guilty and remorseful beyond anything.'

'What?' cried Jane, astonished. 'He spoke to you of it?'

'He often called here on his morning walks,' said the poet. 'Indeed, we got to know William through a common acquaintance, shortly before he met you in Bath. I hope it will not offend you to think that he discussed his feelings with us.'

'No, it's some kind of relief to me to know he had friends to whom he could confide . . . his unhappiness.'

'His greatest unhappiness was in his conviction that he had wounded you,' murmured Mr Axton, inclining his long body in his chair as he spoke and half closing his eyes, as if to minimise the intrusion of his presence on the room. 'He married you with the greatest hopes of being able to make you happy, but alas – as I said, we are not all suited to matrimony.'

319

'No,' said Jane. 'And the misfortune is we cannot tell if we are suited or no until it is too late.'

'My dear.' Miss Axton touched her hand. 'One must keep body and soul together. A ginger biscuit?'

Jane took one, though she felt little appetite. There was a short silence, in which Jane chewed her biscuit as quietly as possible. The poet and his sister seemed at a loss what to say next.

'Is anyone ever suited to matrimony?' asked Jane suddenly, returning to her previous preoccupation. 'As I walked down the hill just now I was trying to think of a happily married couple – in vain.'

'Ha, ha! Yes! Very good!' Mr Axton seemed grateful for the diversion. 'History presents us, however, with many examples of unmarried felicity. Indeed, I think my sister and I could claim some distinction in that number. For here we are in perfect harmony. We share all the daily tasks, we have no children to tease our tempers and arouse our anxieties. We're not cursed with that jealous possessiveness which afflicts those passionately in love. Ah no! I think I may say we are quite snug here together, aren't we, my dear?'

His sister laughed. 'No wife would ever put up with your foolishness, Humphrey,' she said fondly. 'Always stalking birds and painting mosses and sitting up till midnight trying to find a rhyme for wolf.'

'There is no rhyme for wolf, by the by,' added the poet. 'To spare you the fatigues of research.'

'And have you seen any unusual birds recently?' asked Jane, for she had always been very interested in them herself.

'Well, I saw a most exciting thing the other night, up at the church,' said Mr Axton. 'I'm sure there are some barn owls nesting in the tower there. I saw a white shape float across in the gloom and you know, it would be most extraordinary if it proved to be true, for there are all tawnies around this valley, and I had always thought the tawnies drove the barn owls away.'

Jane promised she would make some observations herself and report her findings.

'Do so!' cried Mr Axton gratefully. 'And be sure to record for me the last day on which you observe a swallow. They will be gone in a few days.'

'So sad.' His sister sighed.

After a further ten minutes in the company of this contented pair Jane made her farewells and promised to come back soon to return the pamphlet. Miss Axton insisted she must bring the baby to be admired and to taste some of her apple and honey compote.

She now addressed herself to climbing the hill again and, though tempted by the thought of rambling up through her father's fields, she decided at last to retrace her steps and go up by the road past Sir Thomas's gates. She would pass them without going in today, however. She was thoroughly weary of seeing Sir Thomas surrounded by his family. It was more than a month, now, since they had returned from Bath, and Sir Thomas had not succeeded in finding a moment for her. Indeed, she was beginning to fear that he never would and that the feelings she had been encouraged to share with him had on his part been obliterated by the demands of his wife and children, or had perhaps been set aside by him in some determined way as too dangerous and threatening to his comfort.

'Jane!'

She was not half-way past his gate when she heard his voice. She turned and found him standing with his gamekeeper.

'How can you pass my gate and not even turn to look at it?' he cried, half joking, but with an undertone of real indignation. 'Come in, I beg – Mary has been so fretful today, we were hoping you would appear to take tea with us, but you disappointed us.'

'I walked down to the valley and took tea with the Axtons,' Jane informed him. The gamekeeper stood by, watching and listening. A groom was visible twenty yards away and two gardeners, occupied in the western terrace, had noticed her arrival. So many pairs of eyes watching her! And she had not been exposed to his family yet.

'Come in, I beg you.' Sir Thomas walked up, took her arm and turned back towards the house, dismissing the game-keeper. He would not be denied.

They set off down the drive towards the house. At the touch of his arm, Jane's heart was too full to speak. She had before her two hundred yards in which to enjoy his company and she was sure these few precious seconds of intimacy would be interrupted by someone wanting his attention, and that every word she spoke would be over-heard by the gardeners or the groom.

'Stay till it is dark, Jane,' he said suddenly, with a quiet vehemence which quite startled her. 'Endure the infernal fussing of them all for my sake. Stay till it is dark and I will see you home. And we shall wander in the dark together and see if we can get lost together and stay lost for a hundred years.'

39

Jane stepped into the drawing-room of Ottercombe Park to find herself instantly engulfed by the promised bedlam. Everybody greeted her with delight and reproach. Mary was cross with her for not coming earlier and not bringing Sarah. Henry rebuked her for taking the selfish exercise of a solitary walk, when she might have limped with him around the terrace a couple of times and speeded his convalescence with some badinage. Eliza had acquired a small pug-dog puppy which tumbled over everybody, scratched the furniture, tore at curtains, cushions and clothes, and excited the jealousy of Sir Thomas's spaniel Suzy.

Jane placed her husband's pamphlet on a high shelf for safety and promptly forgot about it, for she was obliged to admire the puppy and receive its robust attentions with pleasure. Sir Thomas sat silently amidst the noise and watched while Jane made friendly enquiries as to everybody's health and delivered a few messages to Mary from her mamma.

'So you paid your compliments to the great poet.' Henry grinned. 'And he instantly set about a sonnet in praise of your beauty, I suppose?'

'No, Henry. Mr Axton is more interested in birds. Indeed he told me he thought he had seen a barn owl flying about our church tower here the other evening. A white shape in the gloom. He was convinced it was a barn owl.'

'Or a ghost!' cried Mary, shuddering. 'Perhaps it's an omen. I have never liked the churchyard, even in daytime. What could be more gloomy than all those tombs?'

Jane was aware that Lady Charlotte was buried there and was afraid that Sir Thomas might have been upset by this thoughtless remark, but he spoke only of owls and without a trace of a sigh. 'It would be unlikely for barn owls to be nesting here. Our tawnies would see them off. But I shall be most interested to see. If you give us the pleasure of your company until dark, Jane, I'll escort you home myself and we can stand quietly in the churchyard for a few minutes first and look for barn owls.' Sir Thomas pronounced this invitation with a determined air.

'Can I come too, Papa?' cried Eliza, who had no interest in birds, but wanted to be included in everything.

'Let's all go,' said Henry. 'I can certainly hobble that far, if Jane will do me the honour of giving me her arm.'

'You'll stay at home, Sir!' cried Sir Thomas sternly. 'It's a foolish idea for you to think of stumbling about in the dark upon uncertain ground; and you, Miss' – he turned to his daughter – 'the night air could work untold mischief on your lungs. And you both quarrel and prattle like a crowd of starlings. The owls would hear your noise and never come out at all.'

'I could be quiet,' retorted Henry, who was still obstinately cherishing the hope of leaning on Jane's arm in the dark.

'Quiet! The only time you will be quiet, Sir, is when you're in your grave.' Sir Thomas delivered this rebuke with a snarl. He got up and looked round at everybody except Jane with evident irritation. 'I shall conduct Jane home myself and enjoy the tranquillity of her company – a blessing I have not experienced for more than a month.' He walked out of the room in a deadly silence.

'Poor Sir Thomas! We've driven him half mad with our fussing,' said Mary. 'Do try to soothe his spirits, Jane. You know he values your company above anyone's.'

'Not above mine!' cried Miss Eliza. 'Papa always says I am his great favourite; and after all, I'm his daughter and Jane is only his sister-in-law.'

Henry said nothing for a while.

There was a moment of some difficulty, in which the puppy now provided a useful diversion.

Jane's thoughts, however, had gone out of the room with Sir Thomas. 'Has your father been in poor spirits?' she asked Henry. 'Has he been overwhelmed with business and had no time for refreshment or repose?'

'He's been busy with a thousand things. Repairing tenants' cottages, agitating over his investments, conducting intermittent warfare with his beloved wife, making plans to cast his tiresome children adrift in the Atlantic in a barrel . . .'

'And the bathing pool!' cried Eliza. 'Papa has had an idea, which he got in Bath, of heating our pool, so he's having a furnace put in and when the water is warm he will be able to bathe there even in winter.'

'He says he likes the idea of lying in hot water and watching the snowflakes fall down on his head!' cried Mary. 'I think he is quite mad, sometimes! I would not want to join him for the world. Would you, Henry?'

'I think the idea might prove vastly agreeable.' Henry smiled, casting Jane a significant look. 'If one could enjoy the tranquillity of a quiet friend.'

Jane looked away. She found her attention drawn to the window and saw it was growing dark.

For the next ten minutes or so she half listened to her companions' idle talk, but she could only feel the darkness increasing outside and an agitation gathering within her at the thought that Sir Thomas would soon appear to escort her home. The clock struck the hour. The door opened and Jane's heart leapt. Sir Thomas stood dressed for the outdoors, looking directly at her and ignoring the rest of the company.

Hastily she got up and made her farewells. She accepted

the loan of a cloak which Sir Thomas thought it would be prudent to place on her shoulders, and together they left the heat, noise and light of the house, and found themselves in the cool darkness of the garden.

'Give me your hand,' he said.

Even when they had first been acquainted she had admired the masculine size and warmth of his hands. Now she reached out and with a flash of joy received his touch. It was what she had spent so many lonely hours imagining and Jane felt almost giddy with gratification. They stood for a moment in silence. The garden smelt of decay, but the night was mild.

'Come,' murmured Sir Thomas. 'Come and see the owls.'

They needed some subject unconnected with themselves to carry them away from the house. They could not immediately plunge into the intimacy they had been so long denied. Jane appreciated his delicacy and followed him through the intricate spaces of his garden. Some tobacco plants were still blooming. Their white flowers gleamed like stars and Jane felt as if she passed through an invisible cloud of their scent, a sweet, voluptuous, smoky vapour.

Sir Thomas led her through a small gate in the wall and into the churchyard. Before moving out into the moonlit space he looked about him for an instant, listening intently. 'I trust we are unobserved,' he murmured.

Jane did not dare speak. She was so happy to be alone with him at last that for a moment she required nothing more.

Yews loomed, their dark blocks sinister, like shapes from a dream. Tombstones cast long shadows across the dewy grass. The tower glowed coldly in the moonlight. Sir Thomas led her to it. They stood beneath it.

'If they are here,' Sir Thomas whispered, 'we'll see them fly out soon like ghosts, to pounce on some poor innocent mouse.'

Jane gazed up. The clouds floating across the moon, and the stars pulsing far beyond, made it look as if the tower was moving. 'It seems as if it will fall and crush us,' she said, moving instinctively closer to him. 'It makes me feel dizzy.'

Sir Thomas drew her gently to his side and Jane rested her head on his shoulder, looking down upon his waistcoat, which was half undone. The stitching of a buttonhole gleamed in the moonlight. It looked like a silver mouth. Jane felt his arm steal about her and his other hand moved tenderly to her face. He touched her cheek. She looked up into his eyes.

'Are you still dizzy?' he whispered.

She felt his breath on her eyelashes. 'No – yes – a little. I thought it was the clouds moving which made me feel giddy. But perhaps it's not that.'

'What, then?'

'I think you know.'

'Yes. I feel the same.' He rested his brow against hers and they stood together for a moment thus, with racing hearts. 'I had not thought to kiss you here,' he whispered. 'I thought it would be too near the house. But I find I must.'

'So, have you been thinking of kissing me?' enquired Jane with shy playfulness.

'My difficulty, dear Jane, has been to think of anything else.' Still they held back from each other in rapturous contemplation of their moment, which seemed to have come at last. There was but a bare inch of air between their burning faces. 'I could stand like this for a year,' he whispered. 'But it's much more than a year since I first longed to touch you. I've waited enough.'

Now came the kiss at last: a kiss so tender and so prolonged that she felt as if she had been taken up into the air. The owls were quite forgot. Jane herself was flying. This kiss was mightier than the first they had shared in her lodgings in Bath. It released a passion far too long tormentingly concealed. At length Jane was obliged to break off and pant for breath.

'If the grass were not so wet, Jane,' murmured Sir

Thomas, 'I'd pull you down upon it and tumble you about so, we'd wake the dead.'

He crushed her in his arms and she enjoyed for the first time a man's enveloping strength. She felt the cold stones of the church tower against her back; before her, his hot body, beating heart and racing breath.

But his last words brought distracting anxieties into her mind. She was more concerned that their embraces might be witnessed by the living than wake the dead. But Jane could not drive out the thought that the mortal remains of Lady Charlotte lay somewhere very close and that her offended spirit might be watching from the shadows.

'Sir Thomas!' A woman's voice floated suddenly through the night. Jane leapt in horror, dazed by superstitious fear, but renewed shouts from the direction of the house identified the intrusion as the work of the living.

'Damn it! Damn it!' Sir Thomas was in a fury. 'Not a moment to ourselves – what in the name of God is it now?' Hastily he released Jane from his arms, stood back and smoothed his hair and clothes, and returned the call. A servant stumbled out of the gate.

'It's your wife, Sir!' she called. 'Lady Mary – she has been taken very ill.'

Sir Thomas and Jane ran in horror back to the house. They found Mary ghastly pale and in agony on the sofa, Henry attempting some clumsy assistance and Eliza in hysterics. The physician was sent for and Jane took her sister in her arms, supplying every endearment and reassurance she could muster, despite the terror she felt.

Messages were sent to Newington House and Mrs Lockhart arrived. Her mother's presence seemed to offer Mary some comfort and together they kept a vigil of the most desperate anxiety, until the dawn light revealed that Sir Thomas's wife was fallen into a shallow sleep and, though deathly white, was still alive. She had lost the baby and the following day the physician issued a stern warning that she must never attempt a pregnancy again.

The days passed. Jane returned to Newington House to sleep, but otherwise never left her sister's side and was rewarded every day by some small but significant sign of improvement. Sir Thomas stood by helplessly, seemingly paralysed by events and not able to offer anything more than his presence.

As Mary recovered a little vigour, however, she seemed averse to his company. Sir Thomas felt himself an irritation to his wife and withdrew. When Jane arrived in the morning, and when she left in the evening, he would exchange a few words with her. Jane did not look into his eyes and he did not encourage her with any kind of remark beyond the subject of her nursing duties and Mary's progress.

This was partly necessary because Eliza and Henry were almost invariably present. But even on the occasions when they happened to share a few words alone their manners were oblique and wary. The brutal interruption of their caresses by this dreadful event had utterly crushed their spirits and Jane felt she would find it very hard to contemplate a private conversation with Sir Thomas again until long after Mary was completely recovered. Indeed, she shrank from him at present and when she went home each night was so exhausted by the daily task of coaxing Mary back to life that she could do no more than fall on her bed and sleep.

Jane's exertions were not in vain. Mary felt well enough in time to leave her bed, then her room, and six weeks or so after the night she had been taken ill she was able to walk about the terrace, if the weather was fine, and respond to Henry's teasing with some healthy laughter, which everyone was very glad to hear.

It was November. The leaves still hung on some of the trees. It had been a quiet, damp season, without storms, which was unusual. The lanes smelt of mushrooms and damp moss and woodsmoke, and Jane began at last to notice these small signs that though her own life had been thrown into an anxious suspension, nature had continued in her habitual rhythms. Here in the countryside the world grew darker and darker, a mantle of leafmould thickened beneath Sir Thomas's beeches and the frost came at last, turning the frail surviving flowers to corpses overnight.

'I'm very tired,' admitted Jane to Sir Thomas one evening as she left. 'I shall rest at home for a few days, I think. Mary seems so much improved. I'm sure there is no danger now. I've told her I shall not come again till Sunday. But I shall send Bessie over with Sarah for Mary to play with.'

'You have saved her life, I think,' said Sir Thomas soberly. Jane looked past him, down the drive. They were standing at the door. 'Look at me, Jane.' He spoke quietly. A servant was carrying coal through to the drawing-room. Jane shook her head dumbly. She could not face him.

'I rather think I almost killed her,' she whispered, her exhaustion and dejection suddenly flooding over her, now Mary did not need her any more to exert herself.

'That's nonsense,' Sir Thomas said in a fierce undertone. 'You must not think so. It is ignorant superstition and not worthy of you.'

'I'm tired. Forgive me.' Jane pushed past him and walked out.

'Let me walk with you back home.'

'No. Please. Not today. Stay with Mary. Goodbye.' Jane plunged on down the drive, indicating with a desperate gesture her disinclination to his company.

She did not hear the door close behind her. The drive seemed long and her legs heavy. She struggled on westwards, where a dismal sunset was struggling against the approaching night. The short climb to the gates of Newington House felt like twenty miles and she paused by the lodge to survey its continuing dilapidation. The weather, animals and birds had continued the work begun by the mob. Her dear little house, which she had come to love almost instead of her husband, looked beyond repair,

330

its boarded-up windows like blind, bandaged eyes. She wept bitterly as she walked on across the vast cold spaces of her father's park.

Her mother welcomed her with concern, gave her broth and put her straight to bed. For once, Mrs Lockhart did not indulge in prolonged reproaches. She was very concerned that her younger daughter, in nursing the elder with such devotion, might have become really ill herself. In practical matters Mrs Lockhart was a very capable manager. For the next few days she insisted that Jane slept as much as she wished to and ordered all her daughter's favourite dishes to tempt an appetite which had all but disappeared.

Within a week or two Jane had recovered much of her strength, but her spirits remained very low. She could not hide her dejection and Mrs Lockhart, attributing it only to the shocking possibility of her sister's sudden death, began to feel it would do Jane good to go away for a while. Accordingly, she began to frame a plan. At Ottercombe, however, Sir Thomas was also very busily considering possible arrangements for Jane's welfare, and so it came about that on the morning of the second of December Jane received two very different proposals for a complete change in her circumstances.

40

Jane felt a need to embrace her child, but could not for a while do more. Sarah's growing energies and unpredictable moods were difficult for her mother to tolerate. Bessie managed the child entirely and was glad to spend many hours up in the gallery with her young charge, for Mrs Lockhart's housemaid Hetty had still not forgiven her for her usurpation of what should have been Kitty's place. The atmosphere in the servants' quarters was no more easy than among the Lockhart family.

Mrs Lockhart fretted while her daughter brooded. During the past fortnight she had been able to persuade Jane only to a very brief call at Ottercombe Park and could not understand why the cheerful spirits of the neighbouring household, with Mary, Eliza and Henry all robust at last, could not persuade Jane out of her melancholy.

Mr Lockhart refused to discuss his daughters' health. The terrifying episode of Mary's illness had fulfilled all his worst fears. He lamented that the arrangements nature had contrived for the propagation of her species were not merely undignified but dangerous and wished with all his heart that grandchildren could be acquired by engaging the services of an architect, enjoying the perusal of drawings and researching the pattern books of Italian masters for the selection of desirable eyebrows and noses.

Jane walked alone in the glade. It was the beginning of December. Weak sunshine visited the rocky cliff now and then, bringing a fitful gleam to the windows of her father's house above, like eyes weltering with tears. She found no consolation in the landscape, which winter had now revealed in its bare shapeliness. In another mood she might have looked for any brave flower that bloomed in this dark season, or collected the different sorts of evergreen leaves, but she was entirely unable to escape her own painful reflections.

In the year since she had first understood that she loved Sir Thomas, the urge to see him and enjoy his company had been so powerful, and the opportunities for gratifying it so few, that she had been almost oblivious of any moral reflection. Now she had been made to accept that he was her sister's husband. Nor was her own husband entirely absent from her thoughts. Jane was married, which made her feelings for Sir Thomas doubly aberrant, even though she neither loved her husband, nor was loved by him.

She felt no guilt in that regard. Mr Harris had not wanted her love, had offered nothing lovable of himself, and to persist in loving him could have been perverse and destructive. In any case, it had proved beyond her. However, she could not help wondering where he was, whether he ever thought of her, and if she would ever hear from him or see him again. Others expressed sympathy for her plight. They could not know that to be abandoned by Mr Harris was in some ways a relief to both parties. Yet she was still legally his wife and in her blackest moods she felt that if she could not be liberated from this paradox she would just as soon not live.

It was the dead season. She paused above the lake to look down across her father's land. At the eastern edge of the lake, foundations were being dug for Mr Lockhart's Gothic boathouse. She almost had to admire the persistence of her father's architectural energies. In her present mood of dejection any exertion seemed impossible. The sun dimmed now. The landscape seemed to shrink and grow flat. Pheasants, startled in a hawthorn brake below, uttered their harsh, choking cry. The echoes died against the cliff.

Jane wondered why she had been given feelings which it was a crime to exercise. She could not think her passion for Sir Thomas base in any sense. It had grown from an admiration for his manners and his morality. He was always observant of others, always ready to exert himself for their comfort. An exquisite sympathy and understanding had developed between him and Jane. This swift and glorious communication must excite her body, which longed in its own way to express its rapturous enjoyment of his company. Indeed, this was what nature required. It was, however, forbidden. Jane felt alienated from her God, her society, her landscape and the most pleasurable impulses of her own consciousness.

The lake glittered invitingly below. Jane began to walk down towards it. Conscious thought had now fallen away exhausted and given way to a blank impulse. Feelings which had for so long subdued her spirits now seemed to require a literal descent. She walked joltingly, only wanting to find oblivion from her pain. Stones tripped her, dead brambles caught at her clothes, but hypnotised by the shining water, she lurched towards it.

From far above – it seemed to come almost from the clouds – a baby's cry rang out. Jane stopped abruptly, shaken from her deadly trance, turned and stared up at the façade of Newington House with awakened concern. One of the topmost windows was open. She could see Bessie looking out and Sarah's tiny face on her shoulder.

'Oh, my baby!' she sobbed aloud. She felt horror at the stupor she had allowed to slide over her. Her child was up in the house, requiring in her helpless innocence every attention Jane could give. She called out to alert Bessie to her presence and to announce her intention of returning, and received an echoing cry in return to the effect that it was almost time for dinner. Jane scrambled back up the cliff in desperate urgency to see her child again. They were united in the drawing-room, and Mrs Lockhart observed the feverish tears with which her daughter embraced the baby and quietly requested that Jane might grant her a private interview after dinner.

'I heard from Aunt Harriet yesterday,' said Mrs Lockhart with cheerful vigour, closeted in her salon with Jane at three o'clock. 'She has acquired some land behind her stables at Panswicke and has plans to make a garden there. It is but an acre, but that is enough for a woman of her age to manage on her own, with only Ben to help. I think it would divert you to go and stay with her for a week or two, Jane. You're interested in gardens. You could be very helpful to her.'

Despite Jane's lethargy the idea had a faint appeal. 'But Aunt Harriet does not like children as I recall – babies even less.'

'You could leave Sarah here with us,' her mother went on briskly. Jane began to understand that every impediment had been anticipated. 'She's weaned now, after all. It will do her no harm whatever to be with Bessie for a week or so. If you miss her too much you can always send for her. If Harriet does not wish to accommodate her she can be lodged with Bessie in the town.'

'I should miss her very much.' Jane felt a tear steal from the corner of her eye.

'My dear, it will be a refreshment to you to be away from Ottercombe for a while and away from baby too. You're doing her no favours, clinging to her and weeping sentimentally over her as you do now. You've suffered a very shocking alarm over Mary's case and acquitted yourself nobly in nursing her, but I can see you are quite worn out and cast down by it and a few weeks at Panswicke will do you good.'

Jane was on the point of asking for some time in which to reflect on the proposal when the bell rang loudly in the hall. Mrs Lockhart started. They heard Hetty answer the door and then the servant's feet came clattering upstairs.

'Sir Thomas is below,' said Hetty, 'and requests an interview with Mrs Harris.'

Jane felt most agitated and immediately leapt up.

'See him in the drawing-room, dear – your father is in his library, I'm sure.'

'No – tell him to come up to the gallery, Hetty – I'm sure he would like to see Sarah.' Jane felt alarmed at being plunged into a conversation with Sir Thomas without any preparation and at a time when her spirits were so uncertain.

'You can't ask him to climb all the way up there!' hissed Mrs Lockhart. 'The poor fellow will have a seizure. Don't be so eccentric, Jane.'

'I believe Sir Thomas climbed the campanile at St Mark's in Venice,' observed Jane with rebellious ingenuity. 'Our few flights of stairs will offer him very little challenge after that. You greet him first, Mamma – and send him up.'

Jane flew upstairs and Mrs Lockhart descended, prepared to suffer defeat in this small matter in the conviction that her more significant plan to send Jane to Panswicke would be accepted without strenuous objection on her daughter's part. Jane arrived trembling in the gallery, where Bessie was sewing and Sarah slumbering in her cradle.

'Sir Thomas is coming up in a moment, Bessie,' she whispered. 'Please stay with us.'

Bessie nodded and after some moments, during which Jane was aware only of her thudding heart, they heard Sir Thomas's steady tread upon the stair. Jane moved away to the window which offered the loftiest and most soaring views across a countryside beginning to feel the approach of evening. She heard Sir Thomas's clothes rustle as he drew near.

'Good-afternoon, my dear.'

She must turn now, she knew. She offered him her hand. He kissed it, but she did not look into his face. Her eye fell instead on to his breast and recognised the same waistcoat, now neatly buttoned, on which she had laid her head when they had stood together in the churchyard. At the sight of it she was seized with a throb of recollection which quite took away her powers of speech.

'Bessie,' said Sir Thomas pleasantly, 'would you be so good as to take the child downstairs?'

Bessie looked at Jane with distress to be obliged to disobey so soon, but Sir Thomas's orders had an authority beyond any Jane could give. Jane nodded her agreement and Bessie withdrew, removing the child so gently that her sleep was not disturbed.

'You're not well,' said Sir Thomas quietly. 'I can see that. May we perhaps sit down?'

'Oh yes. I'm sorry—' Jane looked about her distractedly. 'Here are only old nursery chairs—'

'Jane!' He smiled reproachfully. 'Do you think I care for such trifles? Old chairs are best in any case. Let's sit here by the window. Your father's view is stupendous, is it not? You want something better to look at than my worn old face.' Jane sat down and stared in agitation over the tumbling valley, touched by this immediate evidence that he understood her feelings, though she found it hard not to contradict the gentle joke. Of all nature's works, his face was what she most ardently longed to admire.

'We've had a very great fright,' said Sir Thomas. 'But happily Mary is restored almost to her old health and spirits.' Jane nodded. 'However we at Ottercombe Park are denied the one thing which could complete our happiness.'

'What?' asked Jane, made stupid by her nervousness.

'Your company.'

She was silent. Tears gathered in her eyes. She stared down into the valley. A deer ran out of a clump of trees and disappeared into a plantation some fifty yards away. Pheasants were startled by it into flight, giving voice as they escaped.

'Why do you keep away?' asked Sir Thomas. 'We all miss you. Henry has nobody to tease. Mary longs for the company of her dear sister very much. As for me—' He broke off and his silence forced her at last to turn and look at him. 'I'm quite desperate, Jane. I think I shall go mad if I am required to live without you. I shall become a wild man and live in a tree, and wear animal skins and everybody will say, "That is Sir Thomas; he used to be a gentleman, but love has reduced him to the condition of an ape." '

His words were a feverish attempt at banter, but Jane found his expression so exactly reflected her own agony that she could not bear it. Tears flowed down her cheeks. Sir Thomas stirred in his chair and reached out to her. She recoiled from the possibility of his touch, but accepted his handkerchief. It carried to her senses the same faint emanation of Sir Thomas which had brought her the revelation, a year ago, that she loved him. Now she felt in its comfort a cruel assurance that she would love him always.

'How can I come?' she said at last, when she had found her voice again. 'Mary is your wife.'

Sir Thomas sighed. 'I am tormented sometimes, Jane, by the thought that when I first took you and your sister to Bath I was a widower and you were a maid. But there is nothing to be gained by such reflections. You were carried off by William Harris; I came in due course to be married to your sister. We did not find each other soon enough. But we have found each other now.' His words were pronounced with a determination which roused her from her hopelessness.

'But what can we do?' she cried. 'Every teaching forbids it. You're Mary's husband; I'm William's wife; and there's an end of it.'

'The very pious, and the simple, may need the guidance of external authority in these matters,' said Sir Thomas quickly. 'I hope you are not so stupid as to mistrust your own intelligence, Jane.'

'What do you mean?'

'You say you are married to Mr Harris. Where is he? Where is the comfort, the society, the affection he should provide? You might as well say you are married to a draught of air. As for my case . . .' He sighed. 'Even before her miscarriage Mary had begun to doubt her choice of husband. Now she recoils from me in the most pitiable way. Even if the physician had not forbidden it I should have felt obliged to retreat to my own quarters. I have contrived a kind of bachelor suite of rooms on the eastern side of the house.'

Jane heard this with a kind of forlorn triumph. If she could not have him, there was comfort in the idea that nobody could.

'I retire to my quarters to read and to rest, and to think of you. Nothing could be more misleading than to describe you as William's wife or myself as Mary's husband. These are mere legal anomalies.'

'Some would say they were bonds forged in the sight of God.'

'Ah. You're still of the religious persuasion?'

Jane hesitated. 'Hardly.'

'Do you think our actions are subject to divine scrutiny?' Sir Thomas pursued his subject with energy and indignation. 'Do the gods look down, as we do now across this tract of land, and observe our actions and condemn?'

'Some would say so.'

'I'm not interested in the opinions of anybody except yourself, Jane.'

'I don't know what to think. It seems a cruel trick to play on us.'

'Indeed. Let me give you my opinion. We cannot know what is beyond this world, therefore we must do our best to be happy in it, without making others unhappy. Priests have tried to explain suffering by suggesting it ennobles. We all have to endure our share of it, but I think life punishes us enough. We should not unnecessarily punish ourselves.'

He paused and drew a deep breath. 'I want you to come and live with us, Jane.'

Jane was too shocked and confused to speak.

'I would never impose my company on you if you did not desire it. By degrees I think we would discover how to behave to one another. Your situation would require the most delicate consideration on my part. I require only not to be exiled for ever from your understanding. Your presence – being able to share your thoughts – would reward me beyond anything. I can offer but little in return except my complete devotion.' Sir Thomas shrugged as if this were not very much.

'But there is something so very awkward about it.' She struggled with the ambiguous invitation. 'And after your first marriage, which I understood was so very fortunate and which I have always supposed must have been an ideal of the married state, such arrangements as you propose must seem a sad compromise.'

'My marriage?' Sir Thomas grew grave and got up. He walked up and down the gallery for a moment. Jane immediately sensed a change in his mood. She almost wished she had not mentioned Lady Charlotte. But she had often wondered about Sir Thomas's first marriage. It had, after all, fully occupied over twenty years of his life. Her own two years' acquaintance with him seemed in comparison very insignificant indeed.

'My marriage was not what it seemed, my dear.'

'What?' Jane was astonished. Sir Thomas paused at the far end of the gallery and looked soberly at her.

'You should know the truth. You should not be encouraged to persist in illusion. Lady Charlotte was never in love with me. She married me most reluctantly, for she had been in love with a Marquis, who had disappointed her. Her family and friends thought I was a steady prospect; and I was in love with her, so she accepted my offer in the end.'

'But she came to love you, I am sure? How could she not love you?' cried Jane, to whom these revelations were peculiarly upsetting in being, somehow, secretly welcomed by a primitive part of herself of which she was ashamed.

'She came to care for me somewhat in the end,' Sir Thomas conceded. 'But I had always to indulge her whims. It was not so much an appetite for finery, such as Julia and Eliza display. It was rather a desire for conquests. She could not meet a new person, man or woman, young or old, but she wished them to find her the most extraordinary, the most attractive person of their acquaintance. Her appetite for adoration was quite exhausting. And in the case of young men, as she got older, her desires grew more reckless.'

'Her desires?' Jane could hardly dare express the questions this suggested.

'Her desires, yes,' Sir Thomas continued, now very pale. 'Reckless and imprudent. I would not have minded if she had confined herself to a discreet liaison. After all, I am myself rather dull, and she was of a rare beauty and vivacity. Our children were unaware of her indulgences, for she distracted them by indulging them too. Besides, they were all almost fully grown. There could have been no harm in a quiet partiality, diplomatically allowed. But I discovered – to my great dismay and anguish – that she was intriguing with the footman.'

'What?'

'Yes. And it was the height of folly in her, for that sort of thing upsets the whole household and lays one open to the risk of unscrupulous manipulation – quite apart from its effect on the young man, who finds himself horribly torn between his loyalty to his master and his infatuation with his mistress. It was an act of the greatest imprudence and the instant I discovered it, I could not help myself, I had to confront her – the greatest convulsion of feelings erupted and in the midst of it all she fell dead at my feet.'

Sir Thomas was silent now for several minutes, recovering his composure. Jane could only guess the horror and distress which this account had awakened in him. At last, however, he seemed to be himself again, and came and sat beside her. 'And so, my dear Jane,' he said, in a voice quite spent and bleak, 'you must accept that my first marriage was very far from being a pattern of happiness. You must not feel your own claims to my company wither before some imagined perfection I might have experienced in the past. Charlotte brought me great joy, but great grief also.'

'At least you could console yourself with the knowledge that you were true to her.'

Sir Thomas did not answer. An uneasy silence gathered in the room, which seemed suddenly seized with darkness. Outside, the sun had set. Indoors, Jane began to dread something further that must be revealed. 'I must disabuse you of that idea too, I think.'

'Oh no!' cried Jane in horror and jumped up from her chair.

Sir Thomas got up too. 'Jane, it was nothing. But once or twice I found some consolation. When she was at her most indifferent to me she could shrivel all my good humour with a careless word. She did not mean it, but I was so vulnerable. Twice I did involve myself with another party – it was nothing significant, it was more than ten years ago. Do not hate me for it, Jane.'

Jane backed away towards the stairs. This, more than anything else he had said, wounded her beyond endurance. 'So I'm nothing very much to you,' she burst out, hating herself for the foolishness of her jealousy and her rage. 'I'm only the latest of your distractions.'

'Jane, stop! This is nonsense and you know it. You were a child when these things passed. They were transient consolations to me only. No woman has ever meant to me what you do.'

'I can't come and live with you in any case.' Jane trembled, violently offended with him and dismayed with herself. Lady Charlotte she accepted, even his marriage to Mary she could endure, but the thought of these other women he had touched drove her into a frenzy of revulsion. 'I'm going to my aunt's at Panswicke. Pray excuse me.' She ran away down the stairs and locked herself, weeping, in her room.

She heard his footsteps hurry down the stairs. He paused on the landing, and she dreaded he might call, though she knew he did not know which was her door and would not commit the impropriety of trying to find her. She almost heard his thoughts whirling and at last, seeming to resign himself to this most painful estrangement, he hastened down to the hall and strode out of the house.

41

❦

Harriet Fletcher had lived by herself in Panswicke for more than twenty years, had developed strong opinions on every subject and had acquired the happy conviction that she was never mistaken about anything. For Jane, enfeebled by anxieties and uncertainties, her aunt's brisk and confident manner was at first a reassurance.

'Save the tea-leaves, Jane – we use them twice and then I give them to Hannah for her old mother.' Jane, who had thought the tea very weak on its first appearance, was helping her aunt to clear the dishes. Aunt Harriet's servant was out on an errand and Jane was glad to be of use. Any activity was preferable to the painful business of sitting and thinking. 'So, I suppose your mother must be very anxious, with one daughter abandoned and another quite an invalid.'

'Mary is not an invalid, Aunt. She had regained most of her health and spirits before I left.'

'She was always the delicate one,' mused Aunt Harriet. 'Always with her head in a book and reading most unsuitable things, in my opinion. But Anne would never listen to me. Oh, no! And then of course Mary's imagination would flare up at anything. She was in tears half the time as a child. Dear me! The vexations we had with her.'

She sighed at the memory of these ordeals.

'You were always the stolid one, Jane. Oh, yes! You were a deal less trouble. Mary was always under our feet indoors, working herself up to her next bout of hysterics. You always played outdoors. Yes. Even then your temperament was very placid and as it has turned out, you're fortunate to be blessed with such a mild and phlegmatic constitution, for I'm sure it has helped you in your present circumstances.'

Jane polished the spoons and placed them back in their box, trying to imagine what it might be like to be placid, stolid and phlegmatic for even five minutes. She was glad that her present circumstances were but very partially understood by her aunt, whose censorious spirit would find much to blame in Jane's recent conduct.

'Come, my dear, I want you to inspect my new parcel of land, for as you know I am utterly without any aesthetic sense and your mother tells me you have got quite a taste for gardens, so I'm impatient to hear your ideas.'

Jane protested a little at her ignorance, but was glad to put on her cloak and go out into the late afternoon light.

Harriet's house was of a trim, square design, erected some forty years previously in the middle years of the century. It was situated in one of the side-streets of Panswicke, on the higher side of the town, above the busy valley where the sound of mill-wheels could be heard now as a distant hum beneath the spare and glittering winter song of the robin. Before the house was a quiet square of gravel, with box hedges clipped in sober symmetry to resemble globes. Behind it, a small walled garden offered some roses, vines and figs upon the walls, and a knot garden set out in lavender, with herbs growing in between. It was all very old-fashioned and in the summer quite charming, but in December offered very little to the senses.

'The new land is through the gate,' explained Harriet, and led Jane into an extensive wild area where brambles and stones contended. It was a sloping site, the ground climbing in rugged contours to a belt of hanging beech trees at the top.

'It's quite out of order.' Aunt Harriet sighed irritably.

'But one must try to subdue the wilderness of nature. Do you think we could contrive here an avenue of pleached limes, with perhaps a gravel walk, leading to a gazebo? And I should love a neat kitchen garden with trim beds of vegetables and fruit. Some espaliered apples, perhaps. What do you think?'

Jane hesitated to give her opinion. Her first instincts were that the area would be best left rough, as a home to a few ducks, poultry or sheep, with a couple of beehives. 'It will require a very great deal of work,' she observed.

'Oh, yes, but my Mr Franklin can get some strong fellows in – there's always casual labour in winter.' Harriet had practised such a strict frugality for twenty years that she had accumulated an encouraging superfluity of funds, and having no children to dissipate her fortune she was resolved, while she still had health and strength, to enjoy herself in this project.

'I suppose the first thing would be to survey the land, or make some sketches of the area, to scale,' pondered Jane, though without any very clear idea how this could be done.

'Ah! Yes! You're so like your father in your ways.' Harriet smiled, seeming more confident of pleasing, the more insulting her comments on Jane's character. 'It might prove a source of ideas for you to walk round the gardens of Panswicke House, my dear. They are perhaps a little in the old-fashioned style, but I like that. It is of course quite on another scale – very grand indeed. But you might find illumination there. I shall make enquiries on your behalf and arrange a little expedition. It's only a short step up the road.'

Jane awoke the next day to find a severe frost had seized the land. She lay in her bed for twenty minutes, trying to summon up the courage to get out, for Aunt Harriet never permitted fires upstairs. At length the servant arrived with some hot water in a jug and Jane felt she must stir herself. Her body felt stiff and weary from the unfamiliar bed. She had not slept well. She missed her babe very much, though aware that Sarah was very likely too young to suffer reciprocal yearnings. Jane also missed her mother's generous provisions for her comfort: the fire in her bedroom, the varied table, the clean linen, the spiced wine.

But most of all Jane was tortured by the thought that Sir Thomas had invited her to go to Ottercombe Park, and if she had not recoiled with such anguish from his revelations she could be there now, before his great fire. Mary would be petting her, Henry would be teasing her and Sir Thomas – here Jane's imagination failed her and she shed some bitter tears, observing ironically that if she could not help weeping, it was at least convenient to do so at a moment when hot water was at hand.

She dressed, went downstairs, was offered oatmeal porridge by an adequate fire and began to feel a little better.

'Here are some water-colours and paper and pencils.' Aunt Harriet brought some very ancient and worn specimens out of a drawer. 'As the weather is so bitter, I think we should keep indoors today. You might like to amuse yourself with some sketches. Or would you prefer needlework?'

Jane hastily declined the needlework and, having finished her breakfast, spread out her materials and tried to work.

It was extremely hard to confine her thoughts to garden design. She sketched an arbour, but was tormented by the thought of Sir Thomas in it, whispering endearments to an unknown lady. She cast it aside and put down instead a rough outline of a pergola, but Sir Thomas seemed to saunter beneath it, the lady's head on his shoulder. He extended his mischievous behaviour by offering his mistress an apple from Jane's espaliered trees, kissing her in the kitchen garden and pleasuring her in the gazebo.

Gasping with anguish, Jane tore this last design across and cast it in the fire.

'My dear! Please don't waste paper!' cried Aunt Harriet, who was darning a shift which, like an old soldier, had served bravely at the front for almost as long as the Thirty Years War. 'There are a thousand uses for a piece of paper, even if it's quite written over. You seem very discontented with your efforts. Do not cast things aside so soon. Reflect before you put pen to paper.'

'My difficulties, Aunt, spring from too much reflection,' Jane could not help declaring.

Her aunt looked surprised at this departure from placid stolidity. 'Don't think of your husband, my dear,' she said suddenly, with an air of one who has received a shaft of divine inspiration. 'Try not to think of him at all.'

Jane could hardly inform her aunt that it was her sister's husband, not her own, who was so distracting her. The advice was capable of secret translation, however, and Jane resolved indeed not to think of him at least until dinner time.

Instead of thinking of Sir Thomas, she consulted her memories of his garden and found relief for her feelings in a series of small sketches of details of the grounds at Ottercombe. Gradually her imagination kindled to the project and her attention soon became more general and hypothetical, and by half-past one she had accumulated several very pleasing sketches of walks, beds, gazebos, avenues and vistas, and felt a peculiar satisfaction in what she had achieved.

Aunt Harriet was very pleased. Dinner, a modest stew of mutton and dumplings, was at least hot and savoury, and Jane settled down for the afternoon to clean her aunt's silver and listen to her recollections.

'Your father wished to visit Panswicke House, I recall. Of course this is the very worst time, the dead of winter. He will want to come in the summer.'

'Papa is more interested in the architecture of a garden than the plants,' Jane remarked. 'I think he might like to come very much.'

'Well, perhaps he will. I'm sure your mother will call on us soon, on her way to Cheltenham.'

'Do you think she has plans to go to Cheltenham?' Jane was surprised. 'She never said so to me.'

'Oh, she will, my dear. Mark my words. Since you and your sister were off her hands she has spent a vast deal of time there. I'm sure she would rather celebrate Christmas at our father's house in Pittville, with all the diversions of the town, than stuck in that cold house of yours, with nobody to talk to but your father.'

Jane acknowledged some truth in her aunt's words. Her mother had indeed spent a great deal of time in Cheltenham recently.

'I would not be surprised if she gets into the habit of spending whole winters there,' Harriet went on. 'Summer is of course pleasant in the country, but she has never really taken to country life. She's too inclined to the pleasures of society. And your father is such poor company. I've known him sit down to dinner among friends and never utter a syllable from soup to dessert.'

'Papa is quiet.'

'He's worse than quiet, Jane. He's only happy on his own.'

Jane consulted her own recollections on this subject and had to agree that her father was more inclined to display anxiety than pleasure at the arrival of another person. 'I feel sorry for Mamma sometimes,' she acknowledged. 'But she can go and see her old friends at Cheltenham and if he is content to be left behind, I suppose there's no harm in it.'

'Oh no, my dear – no harm in it now.'

Jane was struck by the emphasis her aunt placed upon this last small word. 'What do you mean, Aunt, no harm in it now?'

'When they were young he was so horribly jealous he would not let her go anywhere. If he but fancied he saw some admirer of hers across the room at a ball, he would sulk for a fortnight. Anne had plenty of beaux, as you may imagine – she was the prettiest of us – and even after her marriage she liked to flirt a little. But your father had quite a devil of jealousy in him. Indeed, he persecuted her so much about it, it quite spoilt her happiness with him. And there was nothing in it. It was all his imagination.

'I'm always particularly pleased that I have never married when I consider your parents, my dear.' Aunt Harriet snapped off a thread with complacent energy, as if it might have been the head of a hopeful suitor. 'No jealousy, no tantrums, no children to drive me distracted. I've always kept strict control of my finances and enjoyed perfect liberty.'

She smiled at Jane with an air of convincing contentment. 'I have, of course, no heir.'

This announcement seemed to have something portentous in it. Jane's senses were alerted, though she went on polishing the candlesticks. 'It has been suggested from time to time that I should take a companion. Some younger person. The idea always revolted me. But I will be candid, Jane. I like your quiet manners and if this project of my garden appeals to you, you might like to stay here some months. Indeed, I think I may say I would be very happy for you to stay as long as you wish. You might come to feel at home here. It's a lively town, more stimulating for a young person, I should think, than Ottercombe.

'What would a young widow do at Ottercombe? Of course you're not a widow, my dear – I don't mean to upset you, but there is something in your case which must be considered. You could live with me here, make friends in the town and be almost half-way between Cheltenham and Ottercombe.'

Jane put down her work. 'I'm very much obliged to you for these generous thoughts, Aunt,' she said. 'But my child—'

'Goodness!' cried Aunt Harriet. 'I had quite forgot your infant! Of course, you're a mother yourself. Well, well . . . I had not considered that properly. Arrangements would have to be made . . . but I'm sure . . . we will talk of it again.'

After ten days of maidenly pursuits, Jane found herself missing her baby very much. The business of designing her aunt's garden had begun to occupy a significant part of her imagination, however, and a quietness had descended upon her spirits. She no longer tormented herself with thoughts of Sir Thomas's early infidelities. She avoided thinking of him as much as possible.

She sent word to Ottercombe that she would like Sarah to be brought to her, assured her mother in her letter that she was much improved in spirits and that Aunt Harriet had offered her exactly the sort of diversion and refreshment that her soul required. The letter was sent and every day Jane anxiously awaited a reply.

'There's a letter for you, Jane,' said Aunt Harriet one morning, coming into the room. Jane looked up from her work.

'From Mamma?'

'Yes, my dear. Pray open it at once and let's see if she plans to come this week, for the other bed will have to be aired and it's difficult at this season.'

Jane opened the letter, but before she could attend to her mother's words another communication fell out, which had been enclosed. Instantly Jane thought it must be from Sir Thomas. Her heart leapt and she felt herself blush all over. Two seconds later, however, having turned the letter the right way about, she recognised in a flash the handwriting and very different feelings flooded into her heart. The letter was not from Sir Thomas, but from William Harris. 'This enclosure is from my husband,' she gasped.

'I thought so, my dear. I'll leave you in peace for a while.' Aunt Harriet hurried out and instructed Hannah to respond to this emergency by securing some fresh tea-leaves, for she had seen her niece's cheek mantle with blushes and grow pale, and assumed that extraordinary measures might be necessary to revive her.

42

La Rochelle, 15 October

My dear Jane,

More than two months have passed since the riot in Exeter forced us apart. I came to France, as I am sure you will have conjectured. I have heard through a third party that you returned safely to Ottercombe and are at your parents' house. I am sorry not to have written before. You must forgive me.

As you may guess I have not found it easy to address you, for guilt at my past conduct and indecision about the future have made me avoid pen and paper. First, I hope you are well, and that our daughter grows and flourishes. I can report myself in health, though I suppose that news of my death might have been more useful to you in your present situation.

I cannot adequately express my regret at having caused you a great deal of difficulty and sorrow. I had hoped, through our marriage, to find a place for myself in the common life from which I had always felt myself to be apart. You have read my pamphlet and I ask you to judge me by what I have written, rather than by my behaviour. I have always wanted life to be better for the generality of people.

Our society is vile as it is. The poor are required by unceasing labours to sustain the luxury of the mighty few. Hypocrisy, moral compromise and selfish exploitation characterise the lives of those among whom we found ourselves, though I exempt you from these censures. I have always thought you an exceptionally pure young woman, of high ideals and admirable impulses.

Marrying you, however, was a mistake. I should have accepted my solitude. I see now that it was required of me to offer a life of service and I have decided to submit this urge to the greatest challenge by taking ship for Martinique, in the West Indies. There, a society based on the abomination of slavery cries out for liberation and I am determined to make my contribution.

I do not expect to return to England. It is therefore unlikely that you will ever see me again. This is a most painful reflection, especially with regard to our daughter. Please accept that I would never have deserted you both had not the persecution of a tyrant state required my flight. I beg you, write to me, and have a likeness of Sarah taken and send it to me. We were but a sad couple when we were together, but I hope that by the tactful agency of the pen we might at length come to regard ourselves as friends.

I am aware that I leave you in most awkward circumstances. I myself have no desire for anything but a single life. You, however, must feel differently. In time, I am sure you will form an attachment and begin to resent our marriage as an uncomfortable impediment, if you do not do so already. I confess I do not know what to recommend in this case, nor do I understand the law of England, which I have been advised is sadly confused on the matter of divorce.

I cannot believe, however, that even a society so hypocritical and cruel would require you to drag out your days in a kind of limbo, neither wife nor widow. It is possible, perhaps even likely, that I shall not survive long in a tropical climate. But if I do, I wish you to know that I absolve you of all obligation whatever with regard to our marriage, beg your forgiveness for the injuries you have suffered as the result of my behaviour and will co-operate in any arrangements of a legal nature you may wish to make.

Please convey to your parents my deepest regrets for having caused them such anxiety and give to our child a kiss from the father she will never know, but who will think of her with tenderness every day of his life. Dear Jane, forgive me, and write to me, I beg, c/o M. Claude Julien at Fort-de-France, Martinique. I fear I shall be very lonely there.

Your very devoted,
William Harris

Jane put down the letter and reached for her handkerchief, for she found herself seized with the most bitter tears – not for herself, but for the sudden perspective she had been granted of the loneliness of her husband's life. Never to see his child again – perhaps to die alone in a foreign land, in the pursuit of his ideals – it was all very affecting. In weeping for him now, Jane recognised that she had somehow escaped from the resentment she had previously felt.

The possibility of not seeing him again distressed her greatly. She had cherished an obstinate hope that she and her husband might one day come to understand each other. This could be achieved by correspondence – more easily, perhaps. Jane reflected ruefully that she and William had always been uncomfortable in each other's company.

She could not write to him, however, until she had perused his pamphlet. If she were ever to understand him, that was the place to begin. Jane felt guilty that she had not read it yet, that she had lost her first copy and was not even sure of the whereabouts of the second one with which Mr Axton had recently supplied her.

She read over his letter again and was sorry not to find

there any enquiries about Mary, nor any greeting for Sir Thomas and his family. Instead, she recognised the intense preoccupation with himself and his own concerns which had always distinguished Mr Harris. Though his political and religious ideals could not have been more wide and sweeping, in his private life her husband had always suffered from a curious narrowness. She had not noticed this during their time together, being distracted and exhausted by the daily challenge of having to live with him, but she perceived it now. William Harris seemed oblivious to the ordinary pleasures of friendship. She felt very sad for him and cried again.

Half-way through her second salvo of tears she heard a loud knock at the front door below, and a hasty response as aunt and servant flew into a panic. She knew no visitors were awaited and that her aunt hated unexpected intrusion beyond anything. Jane was glad not to be in her own house. She was spared the responsibilities of hospitality and could perhaps lurk in her bedroom and escape the fatigues of conversation altogether. Her husband's letter had caused her such distress that she felt she would scarcely be able to utter a civil syllable to a stranger.

A minute later, however, she heard Hannah puffing up the stairs and understood her presence was required.

'A gentleman to see you, Madam – a Mr Burton?' Hannah saw that Jane had been crying and the horror with which her summons was received.

Jane leapt to her feet and ran to the window, almost as if she would jump out rather than oblige her visitor. She saw Sir Thomas's carriage standing in the road. The thought of him waiting below was unbearably shocking to a heart already so besieged by painful emotions. She could not see him. She could not. Her hands shook; her looks were wild.

'Are you not well, Madam? Shall I make your apologies to the gentleman?'

'No, no, Hannah. I must, I will come down – only ask him to grant me a few moments to compose myself.'

Hannah departed and Jane was left to endure an extraordinary attack of shivering. Eventually, however, she gathered up her courage and looked with disgust in the glass. Her eyes were swollen and her nose gleamed like a beacon, and yet she despised herself for caring about it. She ought to be perfectly indifferent to her brother-in-law's opinion of her looks. But despite the quiet days at Aunt Harriet's she was in agony at the thought of seeing him again.

She washed her face. Her fingers felt icy and her cheeks burned. She combed her hair and threw a shawl about her shoulders, but still could not fight off the shaking which yet racked her. At least she would not have to face him alone. Aunt Harriet would provide a sensible ground-bass of common observation about everyday things.

Jane went downstairs. Outside the drawing-room door she paused. She could hear her aunt inside talking in a peculiar public voice about her plans for a garden. Jane felt a surge of resentment that he should pursue her like this. If he asked for a private conversation she would say she was not well. She screwed up her courage now to a violent pitch and entered the room. But the dreaded countenance of Sir Thomas was nowhere to be seen. It was only dear Henry.

He rose and greeted her with rapture. Jane's face betrayed her great relief and pleasure to see him. He appeared quite recovered from his injury and looked remarkably handsome. Aunt Harriet beamed up at him. She was evidently not too much of an old maid to admire the stimulating sight of a dashing young man kissing her niece's hand.

They exchanged enquiries and received satisfactory assurances about the health of their relations. Jane admitted she had just received a letter from her mother and was hoping to receive a visit from her in the next few days, with little Sarah.

'Oh yes, preparations are coming forward and I believe

Mary will be one of the party too.' Henry smiled. 'Indeed, Mary was so mad to see you I could hardly persuade her to stay behind me. Only I could not have taken her back with me as I'm going on.'

'Going on?' enquired Jane uneasily. 'Not far, I hope?'

'Oh, to the ends of the earth, if necessary.' Henry waved his arms about expansively. 'Cheltenham first, to see an old cousin, then Oxford, then London, to stay with my sister and talk to any old admirals who happen to be kicking about, for I should like to get back to my ship. I've a great desire to have my head blown off by a French cannon.'

'I hope you will not do anything so careless,' cried Jane, dismayed to hear he was going away and struggling to conceal her agitation. 'The Navy has managed without you for so long and benefited from your absence, I'm sure. Your return could provoke an immediate naval defeat.'

'A rout, a rout!' Henry laughed.

Eventually Jane managed to express her real sorrow that he was going away. Aunt Harriet induced him to accept an invitation at least to stay for dinner and excused herself to the kitchen with the haunted air of one who knows that the moment has come to throw off the grudging economies of a lifetime and to provide a feast from a cupboard always kept judiciously bare.

Henry asked to see the garden and gave orders to the coachman to retire and refresh the horses for an hour or two. Jane put on her warmest cloak and bonnet, and soon they were walking through Aunt Harriet's gate into her precious wilderness.

'This is the piece of land', remarked Jane with a doubtful smile, 'which my aunt requires me to transform into a garden.'

'What a triumph of hope and vision over desolation!' cried Henry, looking about him at the rocks and brambles. 'The dear aunt! She is quite wasted on gardening. She should be in charge of the Navy. With a couple of bumboats, a punt and a coal-barge, I'm sure she could take

Cadiz and drive the French out of the West Indies – but my dear.' His attention was fixed suddenly upon her and his bantering air almost left him. 'What says the married man? You must go? Your aunt told me there was a letter from Mr Harris. Has he sent for you?'

'Oh no. He is in Martinique by now,' said Jane. 'He's gone to save souls and free slaves, if he can.'

Henry heard a sinew of resignation in her voice, which encouraged him. 'Admirable in him!' he cried. 'Liberation, yes. But dear Jane, I wish he would liberate you.'

'Oh, don't talk of that!' exclaimed Jane, walking away. 'I'm quite sick of it.'

'Forgive me. Let us walk further. I should like to see the fields beyond the town.'

Jane agreed. They left word with her aunt and soon found themselves in a lovely valley which the frost had transformed into a kind of faery kingdom. The trees sparkled like chandeliers, the dead grass looked like starched lace and uttered a crisp protest as they stepped upon it.

'I'll come to the point, Jane,' said Henry urgently. 'I'm a perverse fellow, so you must forgive me if I ask you once more to marry me. I've asked you before and to spare your-self the inconvenience of further solicitation you had best accept me at once.'

'Fool! I'm married already.'

'But if you were not, would you have me?'

'Certainly not. I would have nobody.'

'I can see you have enrolled yourself for a penitential period at Aunt Harriet's School for Old Maids. But after you have embroidered a few sheets, and planted a rose or two, I think you will grow tired of it. Yes. I think you would like a dear friend to take you on his knee now and then.'

Jane trembled secretly at the thought of Sir Thomas's knee. 'A friend?'

'You know my views on matrimony. I must marry a friend, not a woman who adores me. That vile poison of jealousy – possession – nothing is worse. Worse than daggers.'

Jane did not wish to consider this subject too closely. Her aunt's observations on her father's jealousies had convinced her that she must struggle with determination against anything of the kind with regard to Sir Thomas. She must not expose herself to his company again until she could see him with perfect composure. 'You're a silly fellow! Talk of something else. Tell me how Mary is.'

'Mary is well, though missing you dreadfully and all the more apprehensive because my sister Eliza is to go to Eleanor's after Christmas.'

'Why don't they all go?'

'My father is not quite in the mood for Bath.'

Here Jane had to endure an interesting pause. She waited, but Henry would not say more. Indeed he did not seem disposed to say anything on any subject, but amused himself by listening to a robin's whistle and answering it with satirical variations.

At last Jane could not contain her agitation, nor her curiosity. 'And what kind of mood is Sir Thomas in?' she burst out desperately.

'Oh, quite splendid,' said Henry, looking about him at the birds and occasionally casting an unexpected glance down at her anxious face. 'Between you and me, I think he's contemplating a little *amour*.'

Jane felt herself seized as if by an invisible trap. She could not speak any longer; she could not even walk, and Henry was obliged to pause in his ramble and fix her with his shrewdest look. 'Nothing serious, you understand – in his position, it's hardly surprising.'

'Who—?' Jane gasped, unable to hide her distress.

'Only a little dairymaid, pretty, adorable. He spends a lot of time in the dairy now. Indeed, I think he goes there every day to drop a sixpence in her churn and make the butter come.'

Jane began to shake again. She could not hide it. Tears of

dismay burst from her eyes. She reached out and caught Henry's hand.

'Don't cry, my dear,' he murmured quietly. 'Don't cry. It was only my little tease, my little joke.'

'What joke? What do you mean?' she cried in anguish. 'Is it true, or not?'

'Of course not. We have a dairymaid, indeed, but she cannot be regarded as a beauty, unless you have a taste for warts and a moustache. I've never seen my father in the dairy above once and then he was only looking for a dog which had run away.'

'Then why in God's name did you say so?' demanded Jane in a towering fury.

'But for a satisfaction of my thought,' said Henry lightly. 'No further harm. How eloquent Shakespeare is, is he not, my dear?' His look played upon her and there was an understanding in it which she could not bear.

Suddenly an old countryman came round a hedge and stood aside to let them pass. He was carrying the tools of a hedger: a billhook, an axe and some gauntlets. 'Good-day, sir!' he muttered.

'Good-day to you, my friend!' cried Henry, glad to be offered a distraction. 'We're admiring this valley here. What's it called?'

'Paradise, sir,' the fellow informed them sourly and passed on to his work.

'Paradise, eh?' mused Henry half to himself. 'I think to poor Jane it's more like hell.'

'I'm enjoying my walk very much,' said Jane defiantly. 'But I think we ought to make our way back to my aunt's. Dinner will be ready soon.'

'Yes, yes – give me your arm, it's steep here.' They walked in silence for a few minutes. 'I think you should go to Ottercombe as soon as you can,' he said suddenly.

'Is somebody ill?' asked Jane anxiously, alarmed by his tone.

'No. But there is a knot there which only you can untie.'

Jane felt herself to be so securely bound by invisible constraints she could hardly imagine being able to release
others. Henry's conjectures, moreover, had offended her. 'I
shall be very happy to visit Ottercombe,' she replied coldly,
'as soon as I have adequately discharged my obligations to
my aunt.'

'Why were you so upset at the thought of the dairymaid?'

'For my sister's sake,' replied Jane fiercely.

Henry only sighed and smiled. 'Poor Jane,' he said, as
they neared the house. 'Nature framed you for a turtle-
dove, but you will find you have to learn the behaviour of
the cuckoo. Indeed there has always been something of the
cuckoo in you, for you love to mock.'

'To be sure,' Jane conceded, as they reached the door, 'I
do love to mock you.'

'Tell me,' he asked in an urgent whisper, 'what's the skill
of your aunt's cook? Not that I care – a mutton-chop in your
company would be more delicious than ambrosia.'

'You'll be lucky to get a mutton-chop,' said Jane darkly.
In the event, however, Aunt Harriet had somehow managed to conjure up a roasted fowl and an apple tart – a sight
which filled Jane with astonishment and almost superstitious awe.

Afterwards she saw Henry to the gate. Her aunt, sensing some need for privacy, stayed in the house.

'Well, my dear,' Henry whispered, leaning out of the
carriage door for a last frenzied tête-à-tête, 'Remember I
shan't require your hand for seven years – you know my
marriage plans – and by then your own situation will no
doubt have received some clarification at law.'

'Seven years, Henry! We'll all be dead by then.'

'I trust not, my dear. We'll be just on the windward side
of thirty – a good age for matrimony, ripe but not rotten.
My father might by then be getting short of ammunition
and welcome reinforcements. Adieu!'

He tapped the coach with his cane. The coachman's lash
provoked the horses into motion and Jane was left dis-

turbed, as ever, by his profanities and attracted by his daring, and almost wished she could find it in her heart to fall in love with him. But that, of course, was the very last thing that he wished.

43

Jane felt perturbed by Henry's visit and downcast by his departure. She always enjoyed his company. When she had first made his acquaintance she had mistrusted his manner and his flamboyant gallantries could still irritate her.

'A most lively and engaging fellow,' conceded Aunt Harriet. 'Quite a heart-breaker, I should think?'

Jane shrugged off her aunt's curiosity with a smile. Henry had certainly inherited his mother's ability to fascinate and enthral. But Jane was beginning to suspect that his gaiety and wit concealed a mind very sensitive to others' happiness.

A few days brought a visit from Mr and Mrs Lockhart, with Mary and little Sarah, ably attended by Bessie. Jane received her babe with rapture, was encouraged to see Mary looking well and diverted by the unusual sight of her parents on an expedition together. John Lockhart had been persuaded to accompany his wife as far as Panswicke, as he wished to see the great garden at Panswicke House.

'I propose to go on to Cheltenham on Thursday,' announced Mrs Lockhart, 'and Papa will take Mary back to Sir Thomas.'

'How is Sir Thomas?' asked Jane swiftly, seizing the chance to mention his name without having to endure anxieties of preparation.

Mary seemed to flinch. 'Oh, very well. He sends his compliments.' Her answer was as curiously flat as Jane's enquiry had been hasty and they both turned awkwardly to other topics, principally the plan to go to Panswicke House the next day, if the weather was dry.

No rain arrived to thwart their plans, but Mrs Lockhart was more inclined to gossip with her sister than admire a garden in December, so she and Aunt Harriet stayed indoors, amusing themselves with the baby. Jane and Mary went with their father to see the garden, though neither he nor they were inclined to make a party. Jane was particularly anxious for privacy to hear Mary's account of herself and of Sir Thomas. But as they entered the garden through an arch in a wall, the great astonishment of the site broke upon her senses, quite distracting her for a moment from her thoughts.

The garden occupied a deep, romantic hollow, lofty and radiant on the right, rushing down to mysterious shadows on the left, sheltered and fringed about with hanging woods. The sky glittered here and there, reflected in several curious pools and mirrored in hollows by a persistent frost. Standing above the gulf, Jane was struck with the majesty of the situation. An elegant white building with Gothic pillars stood high up on their right, almost at the head of the garden.

'What is that?' she asked.

'That, my dear, is an exedra,' explained her father, taking out his notebook and pencil with an ostentatious air. 'If you would be kind enough to grant me half an hour for solitary observation I shall be glad to meet you both there.'

Mary and Jane gladly set off in the opposite direction down a melancholy walk fringed with beeches, towards a Gothic alcove. Beyond was a pleasing vista of fields and the pastoral sounds of sheep and bells reminded Jane very strongly of Ottercombe. Jane supposed that the loss of Mary's baby, and the prospect of never having any more, must oppress her sister's spirits dreadfully. She found it most affecting herself and, taking Mary's arm, led her off down a series of mazy paths which wandered through a glade.

'Look, Mary, the snowdrops are showing their leaves.

How brave they are! If I were a flower I should not have the courage to bloom in frost and snow.'

Mary was not tempted to pursue this thought. She did not pay much attention to the snowdrops, nor to four small coots which ran out from a bush.

'Here's a kind of Plunge Pool,' observed Jane. They had climbed out of the lower wooded garden and now stood upon a level which received the effusions of several springs, which in this limestone country were plentiful. 'Not very inviting!' Jane smiled. The surface of the pool was mantled with a faint membrane of ice. 'I should not care to bathe today.' This thought led irrevocably to Sir Thomas. Jane felt her own store of conversation shrink and began to fear the talk she had looked forward to with her sister might freeze into complete silence.

'How is . . . Sir Thomas?' she burst out. 'Does he . . . has he installed the furnace he was planning for his bathing pool? Does he ever . . . I don't suppose he bathes at this season.'

'Oh, yes.' Mary sounded preoccupied. 'It's a great success. He bathes every other day. I never go there. But he seems to like it.'

A stony silence ensued.

'Mary, dearest,' asked Jane in desperation. 'What's the matter?'

'Nothing!' Mary looked alarmed. 'Only I'm very concerned for you, Jane. You've had such a wretched time. Mr Harris going off and then nursing me in my illness until you were quite worn out, Mamma says. I feel so guilty! And having to stay here with Aunt Harriet – why did you come? So far away from all your friends. And her house is so cold.' Her lip trembled, and a tear stood out in her eye. 'None of my difficulties are anything to yours and I would not burden you with them.'

'What difficulties?' insisted Jane. 'Tell me, dearest. I can see you're unhappy and I'm quite composed enough myself to hear about them; indeed, I must.'

'It is . . . I wish you would come to Ottercombe and stay with us, Jane.' Mary held on to her sister's arm more tightly and they began to walk up the path towards the higher parts of the garden. 'Eliza is going to Bath after Christmas and Henry is gone, and that will leave me alone with Sir Thomas and that is the very thing I most dread.'

Jane heard this with a pang of pity and deep irony. Mary could enjoy an effortless intimacy with Sir Thomas whenever she wished, yet recoiled from the prospect. Jane counted the few precious moments she had spent with him as the sweetest of her life. 'But why, Mary? Is Sir Thomas not kind?'

'Oh, yes, very kind. But I feel I've been such a disappointment to him – losing the baby and being able to offer him no chance of any more—' Mary was weeping now, frankly, on her sister's shoulder.

'Sir Thomas has had plenty of babies,' soothed Jane. 'I think you should feel sorry for yourself, not him.'

'Oh, I don't mind at all,' sniffed Mary. 'I'd rather play with your Sarah than endure the anxieties of my own child. And I did not quite like . . . the private side of marriage. It was not at all as I had come to expect from my books.'

Jane understood that her sister had not enjoyed Sir Thomas's embraces, and was perhaps relieved that they had had to be curtailed. 'But I've seen you and Sir Thomas together, very playful and happy,' she said, smarting at the memory but determined to raise her sister's spirits. 'I'm sure he adores you.'

'No.' Mary paused in her walk to blow her nose and wipe her eyes. 'I must stop crying. There is Papa up ahead and if he sees me with red eyes he will be embarrassed.'

'We'll say it's the wind.'

'I dread Eliza going away. I feel I'm nothing much at all. Feeble, Jane. Inadequate. When Eliza goes I shall have such a struggle to stay cheerful. I shall always be thinking what a disappointment I am to him. I never know what to say. And he's been so distracted recently. Sometimes he comes into a room and does not even see me there. Oh, please come and be with me, Jane. As soon as you can. You always make me feel better.'

'Of course I will, dearest, as soon as I can decently excuse myself from Aunt Harriet.'

Jane embraced her sister lovingly, and they walked together to meet their father who was standing before the exedra contemplating the view.

'What do you think of it, Papa?' asked Jane, to divert attention from Mary's tear-stained face.

'I like the Red House very well – you've not been up that far, I think. It's a sort of retired shelter, almost hewn out of the rock. A hermitage.' Mr Lockhart looked back up towards the Red House almost with longing. 'But for the generality of the garden, I find it somewhat old-fashioned. The situation is very fine. As you can see, it is a coombe, with steepness of cliffs here, here gentleness of contour, as wild and natural as you might desire. But I don't like the way these formal plantings come rushing down the centre in rows. It's too obvious an imposition of man upon the wild exuberance of Nature.'

Jane found this opinion curious, coming from a man who had spent a lifetime subduing the wild exuberance of his own nature, but looking at the garden again she understood her father's opinion and in part agreed with it. The appearance of straight lines seemed an aberration, an intrusion of regularity and symmetry on what was wild and lovely. Mary was beginning to shiver, so they hastened back to Aunt Harriet's inadequate fire, to sponge their shoes and dress their chilblains.

'Mary looked rather thin, I thought,' remarked Aunt Harriet, as she sat down to work on a patchwork quilt after bidding her relatives farewell. 'She seems so frail, always. You're the strong one, Jane. You have twice her courage. I don't think poor Mary would have survived what you have had to bear.'

367

'I think Mary has had to endure worse,' replied Jane. 'The loss of her baby and the prospect of no others.' It was an awkward idea, for Aunt Harriet had none. Jane looked down into the cradle where Sarah was sleeping. Aunt Harriet had insisted that the baby and her nurse should stay. Bessie had been obliged to share Hannah's bed and suffer her snores, but was so glad to be with Jane again she was reconciled to the confinement and discomforts of Panswicke.

'Perhaps it's a blessing that she lost the child,' remarked the aunt. 'I can't imagine her being equal to the robust demands of family life. She seems so very timid. Perhaps it is just as well her husband is elderly.'

'He's not elderly at all!' cried Jane indignantly. Aunt Harriet looked surprised. Jane felt herself blush and bent down to attend to some imaginary discomfort of her shoe, in order to hide her face in her skirt. 'He's not above forty-five and as lively and vigorous as can be.'

Aunt Harriet was encouraged by the idea that somebody of forty-five could not be regarded as elderly and began to talk with animation of her garden.

Jane drew up extensive plans, but her aunt understood that as soon as the thaw came her niece must return to Ottercombe.

'I shall come back in the spring, Aunt, to see how the work is going on,' she promised.

'And bring the dear baby,' said Aunt Harriet, bouncing the child on her knee. 'This is the first child I have ever really taken to. She is an extraordinary beauty. And so sweet-natured!'

'She was lucky to have a handsome father.' Jane smiled and thought of Mr Harris for a moment or two almost with affection. It was easier in his absence.

Jane could not go to Ottercombe until January. A heavy snow prevented her earlier departure, though she spent many hours thinking about poor Mary and resolving to offer her as much love and support as she could muster.

The thaw came. The gutters ran with water all night and presently Sir Thomas's carriage arrived to take Jane back to Ottercombe. Her mother was still in Cheltenham and her father, alone at Newington, was pursuing thoughts of a hermitage hewn into the rock beneath the cliff. He did not want any more from his daughter than an occasional visit. It was quite settled that she was to stay at Ottercombe Park.

Jane spent the journey in increasing agitation and was grateful for the distractions supplied by Bessie and Sarah. Even a baby crawling and rampaging about, rather inconveniently awake for hour after hour, could not entirely remove her anxieties, however, and by the time they reached a certain familiar belt of elms, which stood but two miles distant from Ottercombe, Jane began to tremble at the thought that she must soon see Sir Thomas, that she must submit herself to the daily challenge of being in his company, without flinching. She was going to make Mary feel better. Nothing else mattered.

Jane had got over the superstitious conviction that her embraces in the churchyard with Sir Thomas had provoked Mary's miscarriage, like some portentous stroke of fate, but she felt very guilty that she had allowed herself to indulge a passion for her sister's husband, almost without ever stopping to consider what a disgraceful, what a painful wrong she was doing to Mary. She was determined to conquer her feelings, to cherish her sister and do everything she could to augment poor Mary's happiness.

The carriage arrived. A light flurry of snow kept Mary indoors, but Sir Thomas came out with his footman and helped her down. As he touched her, he looked directly into her eyes with an expression of frank tenderness completely unaltered by the weeks of separation. Jane felt with a flush of apprehension that nothing had changed between them: he kissed her cheek, she murmured a greeting, then broke from his arms and ran indoors to find Mary.

She found some relief in the turbulence of the arrival and having to deal with the baby. Sarah was to be accommodated in a beautiful little nursery, contrived with skill by Mary from a spare attic room, with a bed for Bessie, who was keenly anticipating a night without a snoring companion. Having satisfied herself as to her child's comfort and thanked her sister dearly for her loving preparations, Jane went down to the drawing-room.

It was easier than she had supposed. There was much to talk about – Eliza already gone to Bath, a letter from Henry in London and news from Mrs Lockhart in Cheltenham. Sir Thomas stood by the great fire, gazing most of the time into the flames and saying very little. Now and then, despite her best endeavours, Jane caught his eye and found there a more devouring blaze. She felt its power with the greatest agitation, prayed that Mary would not notice and wondered how she would ever find the strength to subdue her own feelings.

Mary talked with hectic speed, as if the arrival of her sister and niece offered the opportunity at last to release an almost hysterical accumulation of feelings. At length, supper was served and Jane found in the ceremonious comfort of Sir Thomas's dining-room, and in the refinement and skill of his cook, much relief after the frugal suppers at Aunt Harriet's. She was famished and ate heartily. Sir Thomas saw it with pleasure, though he took little himself.

A plate of roast venison, potatoes and parsnips, and a confection afterwards of apple and meringue, together with two glasses of claret, significantly soothed Jane's anxieties. Sir Thomas initiated a conversation about quiet everyday things: the state of the roads, the inconvenience of snow, and so on, which helped Jane to feel that she could talk calmly in his presence. The warmth of the room, its elegance, the glow everywhere of candles in their sconces, the gleam of mahogany, the fine linen, the sparkle of crystal, the exquisite arrangement in a silver bowl of

Christmas roses, all seemed to caress Jane's senses. She felt the knots of agitation leave her body.

Afterwards they returned to the drawing-room. The great fire had settled down to a decaying heat, more bearable now they had dined, and Jane began to feel very sleepy and begged to be excused. Mary conducted her to a room she had prepared, which offered every comfort including the great treat of a fire.

'Do you like your room, Jane?' enquired Mary, seeing her sister's pleasure in her face but wishing to hear it repeated.

'It is quite wonderful. I have never felt more comfortable. Ottercombe seems much warmer than Newington House. I suppose it is sheltered from the north wind.'

'Yes. Come and see. My room is just down there.' Mary pointed down the passage. 'And Sir Thomas's quarters are to the left.' She indicated an interesting door at the opposite end of the landing. 'Sleep well, dearest, get up when you like and always do as you please, for I want you to feel at home.'

Mary kissed her sister's cheek and left her to her reflections. Jane got into bed fearing she would be kept awake for hours by the confusion of her thoughts, but she fell asleep instantly and awoke nine hours later feeling she had travelled to exotic and unknown places, and met a host of puzzling strangers, but the moment her eyes opened all memory of her dreams perished.

Consciousness brought the pleasure of a beautiful room, the happiness to be with her sister and the challenge of living in the same house as Sir Thomas. For the first few days it seemed he made an effort to control the passion which, in the excitement of her arrival, he had not been able to hide. Now his behaviour was demure, his manner self-effacing. He did not tease or provoke her, as he had sometimes done. He seemed very considerate, not wishing to expose her to the least difficulty. Jane was grateful. She wanted to devote herself to Mary and she felt he understood it.

She was aware, however, that at the least brush of his clothes as he passed she experienced an intense arousal. She suspected he must feel the same. Jane maintained her composure, but wished the violent feelings he provoked would subside. Nothing would be worse than to feel herself drawn back into a series of accelerating intimacies with him, in her sister's house. She had felt a bitter sting of jealousy at the thought that Sir Thomas had caressed other women ten years ago or more. How much more agonising would be poor Mary's torment if she discovered that her husband and her sister were in love.

Jane was determined to spare her the possibility of that discovery. She remembered Aunt Harriet's opinion that she was blessed with a good deal more courage than Mary. It was her duty to protect, not wound, her sister. Jane suspected that Mary's perceptions were not as acute as her own. She herself was aware of every sigh of Sir Thomas's. No minute movement of his body escaped her notice. She always knew where his attention was fixed and felt she often sensed what he was thinking. Mary, having lived alongside him now for some time as a wife, would not be so observant.

Fortified with these hopes, Jane settled down to amuse and animate her sister, and restore her to her old gaiety. It could not be achieved without a great deal of suffering on her own part. Every day she had to witness Sir Thomas offering a caress or two to his wife. They were kind compliments, not the expression of a passion, but Jane had to look on, smiling, and subdue the longing to be touched by him herself.

One evening when she had been at Ottercombe for about ten days, Mary took her unawares by retiring suddenly to bed very early.

'I'm not ill, only very tired.' Mary smiled, kissing her sister. 'I've decided to award myself the treat of an early night. Good night, Sir Thomas.' She kissed the top of his head and went quickly out of the room, leaving its occupants in some embarrassment.

Jane had always been very careful to go to bed at the same time as Mary. She did not want to expose herself to a private conversation with Sir Thomas and had successfully avoided being alone with him for more than a week. Now, here they were together. Silence deepened around them. Jane looked steadily into the fire. She heard the ticking of the clock and beneath it, his breathing.

'Look at me, for God's sake, Jane,' he said quietly.

Jane got hastily to her feet. 'I think perhaps I'll go too,' she murmured.

Though Sir Thomas's habitual movements were slow, he was capable of swift action when required, and Jane found her path cut off, the door barred by his body and, feeling obliged to look into his face, saw there everything she loved.

'Don't run away,' he said. 'I hate it when you avoid me as if you feel I will harm you in some way. I only want to ask you one question.'

She stood back a little and prepared herself.

'Have you forgiven me yet, Jane? Last time we spoke alone together you ran from my company in disgust. I have passed the most painful weeks since then. Your coming back here has given me great joy, but much anguish also. I would never impose on you any attentions you would find disagreeable. I only wish to recover that understanding with you which has always been so sweet.

'But you avoid me. You look away. Is it the awkwardness of our situation here? Or have you not forgiven me for revealing what might have been better kept concealed? Tell me, Jane – I must know. Are your feelings unchanged?'

She could not speak.

He caught her hands and drew her to him. She felt his breath on her face. He was trembling all over. Looking into his eyes, she could not hide her despair and longing: he must know the answer. But there were more important things to say.

'I feel I must keep apart from you. Because of Mary.'

'Cannot we be together alone, then, ever? Can't we even enjoy a private conversation as we once did?' He seemed desperate.

She felt his arms close round her and broke away. 'Only . . . only if we can be quite ordinary together. I cannot offer such an insult to my sister.' She fought back her tears. If she wept, he would come closer.

'Quite ordinary?' Sir Thomas stared at her. 'Is that what you really want, my dearest girl?'

She nodded.

For a moment he stood and looked at her with the most solemn reflection, his eyes full of passion, but shadowed with dismay. Then his expression cleared and he appeared to reach some kind of conclusion. 'Very well,' he said briefly. 'Then I must bid you good-night.' He turned and walked out of the room.

Jane felt bereft. The suddenness of his departure shocked her. She wished he would come back, if only for a few seconds. A few minutes, perhaps, of private talk. She only wanted to look at his dear face a while longer. But she listened to his footsteps climbing the stair, heard him walk along the landing, pass through the interesting door to his quarters and close it firmly. She stood for some time alone, hearing only the quiet ticking of the clock and the settling of the fire, full of the most bitter regret.

44

The next morning Sir Thomas greeted Jane's arrival at breakfast with a serene smile, then turned his attention back to the newspapers. Mary announced that the first eggs were beginning to appear, for the fowls started to lay as soon as the darkness of December was past and now, in the middle of January, the days were already growing longer.

'Let me offer you a boiled egg, Jane, from my little Dorking hen. She's such a shabby little thing, but I can't help loving her. I got her from the farm. They'll be setting up the breeding pens soon.'

'I ought to go and see them all,' said Jane. 'I've neglected our neighbours since I came back. I've only been to see Papa twice.'

'We've been greedy and kept you all to ourselves. Haven't we, Sir Thomas?' Mary dragged her husband's attention from the columns of newsprint.

'What, my dear?'

'We've kept Jane all to ourselves and not permitted her to visit any of the neighbours.'

'You could both go, if the weather is fair. It would do you good to get out, Mary. I'm sure Parson would be very glad to see you, or the Axtons.' Sir Thomas rose, yawned and looked out of the window to consult the weather.

'I can't go down to the Axtons' yet,' faltered Jane. 'Mr Axton lent me a copy of William's pamphlet, for I confessed

375

I had not had the opportunity to read it and I still have not – indeed I'm not quite sure where it is.'

'I think I've seen it lying about somewhere,' mused Sir Thomas. 'It will come to light, I'm sure. Well, ladies – I shall be in my library, answering letters all day, and not to be disturbed.'

'Answering letters indeed!' cried Mary, with a rare return of her old playfulness. 'You will be dozing in your great chair.'

He acknowledged her tease with a smile and a bow, and went out.

'He looks in rather better spirits,' said Mary anxiously, watching him go. 'What do you think, Jane?'

'He seems more settled,' admitted Jane. It was what she had wanted and she ought to be glad. 'I expect he's encouraged to see you are so much better.'

'Oh, I'm better now you're here, Jane. And if I'm happy, I'm sure Sir Thomas will be more content. But you – are you happier here? Even though we keep you prisoner, like a maiden in a dark tower?'

'Oh yes!' cried Jane with a determined smile. 'Very much happier now, dear, for being here with you.'

The days passed, and signs of spring began to appear. The spirits of the company seemed buoyant enough. There was never any want of agreeable conversation at dinner and supper. Sir Thomas seemed particularly tranquil. He became preoccupied with a scheme of repairs to his tenants' cottages and was absent many mornings until dinner. He spent the afternoons at his bathhouse and in the evenings after supper he could sometimes be prevailed upon by Mary to join them in a game of cards.

Jane received from him only the most affable smiles and open and friendly looks appropriate to a brother-in-law. She discerned no buried torment beneath his easy manners, rather the suggestion of a comfortable indifference. Jane needed all her resolution to welcome this development. In company she managed to sustain a pleasant, light-hearted manner, but her private hours were very painful. Her appetite began to desert her and she awoke in the mornings earlier and earlier, tormented by despondent thoughts, and found it impossible to go back to sleep.

Apart from playing with her baby, only solitary walks seemed to relieve her feelings. She indulged herself in a ramble now and again, for Mary was inclined to sleep in the afternoons and there was no danger of meeting Sir Thomas, for he was always closeted at that hour of the day in his bathhouse.

The thought of her own mortality continued to haunt her from time to time over the next few weeks. To cheer Mary, she remarked with pleasure on the appearance of the earliest flowers, but her own delight in them seemed dimmed. Sir Thomas came in one afternoon, looking very clean from his bathe, and holding a bunch of violets.

'I rambled about the hedges for a while just now,' he said, 'and saw these peeping out, where I gathered them once before. Who will take them?'

Mary was sewing a small shift for Sarah. Her hands were full. 'Take them, Jane,' she said. 'There's that little Italian vase of Lady Charlotte's, on the spinet – the tiny one – that will do very well for them. Thank you, Sir Thomas.'

Jane got up and approached him. Her heart was full of the most vivid recollection. A year ago, just after Sarah's birth, he had sent her a note of congratulation, with a bunch of violets, and said he had seen them peeping under a hedge when he had been thinking of her. She had kissed the violets, crushed the letter to her heart and had felt the milk burst from her breasts, so powerful was the feeling aroused by his words. Now she took the violets from him without a look or a touch, struggling for the most elementary smile. Tears threatened to burst from her now, as milk had then.

He turned away and strolled off to his chair by the window, humming a tune to himself. Jane escaped to the kitchen to fetch water and wept for five minutes in the pantry while she was arranging the flowers, though five seconds would have sufficed for the work. She knew he must have recalled the previous year's gift as vividly as she did, but his steady hand, casual manner and, above all, that cruel humming, betrayed a mind not half so agitated by remembrance or regret.

This event was added to the catalogue of her torments, which, when she awoke early every day, she would turn over in her mind. Since their last private conversation Sir Thomas had provided daily evidence that he was quite capable of offering her an ordinary acquaintance. It was what she had asked for. But she began to feel it was like a poison, killing her by degrees.

The spring unfurled gently outdoors and indoors Jane withered. She knew she had got thin. Her dresses hung upon her. Still she managed to provide cheerful company for her sister. Jokes helped sustain her, but they were hard work now. Her reward was to see Mary flourish.

'I'm fatter than you now, Jane,' observed Mary one morning in April. 'We must exchange gowns. I shall ask cook to make a plum-pudding. I don't like to see you so thin.'

'It's only the season,' said Jane. 'I'm always thin in the spring.'

Mary looked sceptical, for she had never observed anything of the kind.

A week later Jane awoke as usual very early. As it got light, she heard an unaccustomed twittering song about the eaves of the house and realised the swallows were come at last. This, of all moments, had the power to rouse her from her torpor. She rushed to the window, saw their shining bodies swooping and soaring in the early sunlight and, determined to admire them outdoors at once, flung on her old shawl and slippers, ran downstairs and out into the air.

She stood for some time on the terrace, admiring their exquisite motion and feeling almost happy for the first time for months. Then she heard a step and turned to find Sir Thomas beside her. Shock, and embarrassment to be in her nightclothes, together with an impulse of delight at his arrival which she knew she must instantly smother, all conspired to render her speechless. They stood for a while, silently watching the birds, in particular one pair which seemed to take a giddy joy in each other's company, flirting and teasing in an ecstatic courtship of the air.

'It is sad', observed Sir Thomas quietly, 'to think we shall never be able to fly.'

The vividness of her dream returned instantly into her mind and she knew exactly what he meant. However, his remark was so delicately expressed as to offer her the chance of an ordinary response, if she required.

Shaking all over, Jane seized on the escape. 'All human beings must reconcile themselves to that,' she replied, in a voice scarcely louder than a whisper. She heard Sir Thomas sigh.

'True enough,' he acknowledged, walked away down the steps and was lost behind a yew hedge.

Jane's dejection was so overwhelming she could scarcely say a word at breakfast and Sir Thomas was very quiet too. Mary seemed not to notice, however, and chattered happily about her pots of lilies in the glasshouse and, as soon as Sir Thomas had excused himself and gone to his library, Mary asked Jane to come and admire her tender plants, and Jane was glad enough to comply.

The atmosphere in the glasshouse was moist and warm. Water dripped upon the old brick floor. The smell of healthy young leaves revived Jane so far as to make her wonder for an instant how Aunt Harriet's garden was progressing, and to resolve to write and enquire very soon.

'Thank you, John,' said Mary to a young gardener who was watering the pots. 'Leave us now, for I want to show everything off to my sister and pretend it is all my own work.' The young man obliged and Mary closed the door carefully behind him. Jane admired the thrusting buds of the lilies breaking the surface of their soil like the snouts of dolphins bursting from the deep. But once Mary was sure they were alone her manner changed and an expression crept into her face which alarmed Jane exceedingly.

'I have something to say, Jane, which is not easy.' Mary's tone was determined, but she walked to the other end of the glasshouse and turned her back on her sister, looking out towards the kitchen and other offices, where busy servants could occasionally be seen. Jane felt exceedingly apprehensive at Mary's challenging air.

'Jane ... will you be sure and tell me the truth, without any hesitation? Have you ever felt anything beyond an ordinary sisterly affection for Sir Thomas?'

Jane recoiled in terror. Here was the moment she had tried so desperately to prevent. Mary had grown suspicious, was perhaps even now in the grip of a dreadful jealousy and might at any moment succumb to an hysterical attack which could endanger her fragile health, perhaps even her life.

'No!' cried Jane, wishing only to protect her sister from what she knew would prove the most painful of wounds. 'I've never had anything beyond a common regard for him. He's a delightful fellow and I enjoy his company. That's all.' Her hectic manner and an absurd nervous stammer had betrayed her, she was sure. She was furious not to have managed a more convincing answer, but she had been so surprised by Mary's sudden enquiry she had had no time to prepare herself.

'You astonish me exceedingly,' she added, trying to excuse the raggedness of her first reply. 'How could you think such a thing? He loves you, Mary, you know that. He's your husband and no sister would encroach on the sanctity of that tie, even if she could permit herself illicit feelings for him.' She finished her assurances on a wavering note, praying that Mary's timid and feverish sensibility would accept her words as convincing, and she waited in the greatest uncertainty for Mary's reaction.

Her sister's shoulders rose a little, but she did not reveal her face. 'You don't love him? You've never loved him? Not the slightest bit? And he does not love you either?'

'No. Never. I assure you. Don't torture yourself with these jealousies.'

Mary turned at last and Jane endeavoured to receive her look without flinching. She did not look at all timid or feverish. Her eyes were calm. 'That's unfortunate.' Jane was astonished and puzzled in the extreme. 'I rather thought', Mary went on, 'that I'd noticed particular signs of your affection long ago. Before I ever married him. Before you ever married Mr Harris.'

'Affection, to be sure – yes, certainly.'

'And when we met you in Bath, on our way back from Italy, and he came back and told me he had danced all night with you – I was sure he loved you then. I saw it in his face.'

Jane could not help blushing deeply, but still struggled to reassure her sister. 'Don't torment yourself, Mary.'

'I'm not tormenting myself, Jane!' cried her sister with healthy indignation. 'I think I'm the only person in the house not tormenting myself. We live together here in perfect misery. I feel your unhappiness, and his unhappiness, every hour of the day. Please do me the kindness of admitting that you love each other. I'm not a child, or an invalid. I require the truth.'

Jane hung her head. 'I've tried very hard to subdue my feelings,' she admitted.

'Well stop subduing them,' said Mary with firm resolution. 'Love him and let him love you. I want nothing else.'

'What?' Jane gasped. 'But how can I?'

'Very easily, I think.' Mary smiled. 'I saw how affected you were when he gave you the violets. I've seen you similarly agitated on a thousand occasions and I don't wish to see you suffer any more, dear Jane.'

'But—'

'Don't ask me what people will think – I don't care tuppence for them. It's hateful that we try always to impose conformity on ourselves, at no matter what cost to our feelings. I don't know if there is a God, but if there is, I'm sure he did not create us to be unhappy; and if he did he is not worth obeying. Those are my opinions and I don't repent of them one bit.'

'But—' Jane was staggered by her sister's confidence. Mary was not weak or in the least hysterical. Courage and generosity shone in her eye. She seemed to know exactly what she wanted and to require Jane's assent. 'But how did you come to think in this way?' asked Jane.

'It was your husband's pamphlet!' Mary laughed. 'I found it and read it, and you ought to, for besides the attacks he makes upon kings, there is a great deal there about liberty, which brought my mind the greatest relief. When I examined my life in the light of your husband's observations I began to believe I could make myself and my dear ones happy, if only I ignored all the old rules invented to make us obedient.

'Anyone who sees you together will know that you and Sir Thomas are in love. I've done a great deal of research on the subject – in novels!' She laughed again, in rare good humour and, coming across now and embracing her sister, concluded her extraordinary address with the most emphatic of kisses. 'Dear Jane, be happy. I married Sir Thomas on a whim. He's now only a kind of dear old friend to me. It's your birthday next month. Take him as a gift! And be sure I shall be most offended if he's not well treasured and put to good use every day.'

Jane was dazed by her sister's words. It had brought Mary an almost intoxicating lightness of heart to reveal her feelings. But Jane was too shocked almost to comprehend what Mary had offered, much less to frame a reply.

'I shall say no more about this,' whispered Mary, taking up a watering can and beginning to admire her young plants. 'And of course I've not spoken to Sir Thomas on the matter. You must settle it between you.'

Private reflection convinced Jane that her sister's

account of her feelings was genuine. There could be no mistaking the relief which now shone in Mary's face. But even supposing she could find the opportunity or the words to initiate any conversation on the subject with Sir Thomas, Jane doubted whether he would co-operate in Mary's revolutionary design.

There had been something, recently, in the ordinariness of his manners towards her which suggested he was glad to have escaped the torments of passion. His remark about the swallows had seemed like a last opportunity for her to acknowledge their long-buried understanding; and in her emphatic rejection of his overture, and his prompt departure, Jane feared she might have seen the last breath of a passion already exhausted and quite spent.

45

Jane had been used to think of herself as the spirited sister, but she had to admit that she would never have found the courage for such an initiative. Indeed, it seemed, as she later reflected on her past conduct, that she had often been peculiarly intimidated by authority and more inclined to conform than Mary, who had made her own world out of her imagination.

Jane had enjoyed a rumbustious life out of doors as a girl, had even been thought to be something of a hoyden, but indoors – in the arena of social behaviour – she had only wished to please, to avoid giving offence.

Her marriage had seen the disastrous consequences of such an acquiescent temperament. She had found herself with a husband she could never please; indeed, one whom she could not avoid offending, despite the most strenuous exertions. There was one person, however, whom she had never indulged. In no part of her history could she see any evidence of a desire to please herself. And when at last pleasure had arrived in her life, in Sir Thomas's admiration, she had felt unable to welcome it.

Jane emerged from her reflections knowing only that she loved and respected her sister more than she could express, and that she must free herself from her condition of suffering for Mary's sake if not for her own.... For Mary's sake! There it was again. Mary had told Jane to give herself some happiness and here she was once more supposing it her duty to oblige others. She could not help smiling at the trap she had made for herself, from the best of intentions.

She escaped the trap as usual by running out of doors. The world seemed full of light. It was now five o'clock and a warm afternoon. Bessie and Sarah were sitting on a rug under a tree. Seeing her mother approach, the child laboured to her feet and stood rocking uncertainly, her arms outstretched, her face full of delight.

Jane embraced her with gladness and felt the tiny arms wind with passion about her neck. She vowed not to encumber her child with the anxieties which had so disfigured her own will. She would try to make Sarah feel that she pleased others simply by being herself. 'Dear Sarah!' she murmured. 'You must grow up into a better woman than your mother.'

'Why do you reproach yourself, Madam?' asked Bessie indignantly.

'Oh, I'm just now feeling such a poor thing, Bessie. I feel inferior to my sister in so many ways. She's so much the more intelligent and brave and generous and strong. I used to think she was the weaker one, who needed my protection. But the opposite is true.'

'Don't punish yourself so.' Bessie frowned. 'Life has punished you quite enough as it is and you have borne things which would have broken most folks' hearts. Your only weakness, if I may say so Madam, is not thinking well enough of yourself.'

Sir Thomas suddenly appeared, walking back to the house from his bathing place.

'Come and sit with us here!' called Jane, suddenly reckless. He hesitated for an instant, surprised.

'You must excuse me, my dear – I have some letters to attend to.' He waved and went on his way. Jane felt crushed.

'Sir Thomas would not wish to sit outdoors after his bath, Madam,' said Bessie quickly. 'He could catch cold. And he knows Miss Sarah is always fretful at this hour. Look! She'll be walking soon.' Bessie provided a distraction in the child's determined tumblings.

'And soon after, running,' said Jane. 'And exercising her will more and more strongly.'

'Ah yes – she's a determined character.' Bessie laughed. 'Just like you, Madam.' Jane looked at her child, but she could see only Mr Harris in the high, pale brow and the clear eyes. Delighted to be admired, the infant seized her mother's hand and attempted to bite off her fingers, then launched into a series of impatient screams. Jane sighed. This wild creature could not simply be told she must be herself and please herself. She required stern discipline, to be taught duty, compliance and obedience. Otherwise, Jane feared, she might kill everybody with her terrible new teeth.

Jane went to bed early, exhausted by the day's events. But sleep eluded her. Despite Mary's declaration, Jane still felt uneasy. All her education had enforced the view that such a passion as she felt for Sir Thomas was wrong. She began to long for some sign of supernatural advice, though she knew it was absurd. At dawn she got out of bed and spent some time at prayer. She endeavoured to empty her mind of all distracting thoughts, so that the Almighty might drop into the receptive vacancy some luminous verdict on her situation. But she emerged from her devotions with nothing more useful than a pair of sore knees.

Light was now touching the topmost slopes of the valley. She dressed, for sleep was impossible, and began to feel an inclination to walk out to the church. It lay but a few yards beyond Sir Thomas's garden wall and she had hardly been there since the night when she had kissed him by the tower and Mary had been taken ill. Some resolution might await her there. The house seemed utterly still. Even the servants were not yet stirring as Jane tiptoed out and passed along the dewy walk.

The birds were awake, however, and filling the valley with their discordant threads of sound. Not a breath of wind stirred. It seemed a morning most auspicious for divine advice. As she walked through the gate to the churchyard, Jane prayed for a message. She recalled that when she had first heard of William Harris it had been said he could see angels standing among the congregation. The hairs on the back of her neck seemed to crawl at the thought.

She wound her way around tombs and tussocks of grass to the door. Her heart began to beat with apprehension. 'Send me an angel, Lord,' she whispered, 'send me a sign of Thy will.'

The latch was stiff, the door heavy, but she heaved it open and found obscurity and shadows. Jane stood for an instant just inside the door, hesitating. A strange fear gripped her senses, a feeling she was not alone. Ottercombe Church was small enough for her to see the whole of the nave. It was empty. But a faint sound could be heard, like the stirring of feathers. Suddenly a harsh scream rang out, she felt the beating of wings and something flew almost directly into her face.

Jane cried out and threw herself to one side. A cock pheasant flew out, followed by his two hens. They had somehow been shut in the church and now seized their chance for escape. Jane flung herself into a pew and lay there panting with shock and laughing. At length her heart slowed back to its regular rhythm, and she knelt down and tried to pray. However, she could only think how hungry she felt and smile again at the loud cries her stomach gave out for food, like an impatient baby, echoing in the empty building.

At length she abandoned her solicitations and walked back to the house. She met Mary in the hall, who noticed her unusual expression.

'Where have you been, Jane? And what are you laughing at?'

Jane told her the whole story, which Mary listened to with amusement and some impatience.

'And how many pheasants were there?'

'A cock and two hens.'

'A cock and two hens? Why, there's your sign, Jane. What could be clearer?'

Mary provided some breakfast for her sister and brought her the pamphlet Mr Harris had written.

'This will put more fire in your belly, Jane, than a hundred prayers. Really it is disgraceful that you have not read it yet – and Mr Harris your husband, too!' she scolded playfully.

Jane took the document back to her own room to read and spent most of the morning absorbed in it. She was interested to find Mr Harris more ardently engaged in plans for transforming society than for saving souls. Jane found herself greatly moved by the power and passion of his words. Mr Harris wanted a world where every man and woman, no matter how humble, would enjoy rights and responsibilities equal to the mightiest. Indeed, he wanted a world where there were no longer the humble and the mighty, but all were brothers and sisters in comradeship, as all were equal before God.

His compassion and his humanity shone in every page of the work and Jane read it with growing excitement. The eloquence and idealism she had first admired in him were vividly before her again. She felt her admiration of him restored and the sufferings she had experienced in her marriage purged from her soul. He convinced her of the justice of his argument. But the words worked upon her in a more personal way.

Mr Harris's pamphlet was so expressed as to be almost a call to arms. He urged the reader to believe that it was in the hands of every man and woman to control his or her own destiny; that there was no oppressive condition which could not be thrown off, with a sinew of self-belief. To live in misery was an offence against nature. Happiness was a right. It must be fought for. As she read, Jane felt physical sensations of thrilling excitement and power. She began to feel she could do anything and, though social revolution was at present unlikely in Ottercombe, she could at least take action to transform her own life and bring happiness to herself and those she loved.

She put down the pamphlet with a profound sigh. She could understand how reading it had changed Mary. Resolution had flooded into her with her husband's words. Some transforming consummation had at last been enacted and though her husband had not been able to make her happy himself, he had given her the means to release her joys and desires with another. In his presence he had blighted her soul like a frost; now in his absence he had helped her into bloom.

She decided to walk down to the Axtons in the valley to return the pamphlet, told Mary she would not be in for dinner, and departed. The poet and his sister were very glad to see her and pleased to find she shared their admiration for Mr Harris's work. They invited her to partake of their dinner of bread and cheese and a soup made of young nettles, and at length, about the middle of the afternoon, Jane bade them farewell and began the walk back up to Ottercombe.

It was a mild day in early May and, as it had been a frosty spring, it was only now that exquisite season had arrived when the leaves are not fully unfurled, but have begun to peep. Every tree seemed freckled in a different shade of green and Jane noticed as she walked primroses and violets in every hedge. The climb was steep. She grew hot. She paused to remove her shawl and, as there was nobody about, her stockings also. She walked on, feeling the air about her shoulders and up her legs, enjoying every sensation, even the steepness of the way, while her mind seemed to hang in happy suspension, not attempting thought.

The road climbed sharply through a belt of trees.

Sunlight slanted down between the branches and the westering light seemed full of whirling atoms. She paused for a moment to get her breath back and to admire the movement of the particles on the air. They wandered, sank, rose and spiralled here and there apparently without any aim, only letting themselves be. Then a sound floated across the valley. It was the cuckoo's haunting call.

Jane recognised it with a shock and half remembered something Henry had said, which she had not entirely understood. The direction of the call changed. The bird must have flown over her head, for at first it had echoed from the west. Now it seemed to be calling her from somewhere behind Ottercombe Park. Perhaps it had perched on the church tower. There must have been cuckoos calling here long before the church tower was built seven hundred years ago.

Jane did not pursue these enigmas. She found a little gate leading into Sir Thomas's grounds and saw his bathhouse directly ahead of her, some three hundred yards away. She felt able now to approach it. Anticipation, not apprehension, ran across her skin. It was the middle of the afternoon. He would certainly be here.

As she got nearer she heard the splash of water. She prayed there would be no servant present. Her heart was racing, for she could not imagine how she could find the necessary words. She opened the door and went in. Sir Thomas was facing her and looked up in some surprise, but said nothing. He was alone.

Turning to close the door, Jane found a sturdy bolt and drew it firmly across. Privacy was assured. She turned back and saw that in her small action he had found a meaning. He smiled at her now with alert curiosity and waited. Jane kicked off her shoes. Sir Thomas leaned back against the edge of the pool, cocked his head to one side and watched her. Light danced on the surface of the water and the skin of his shoulders and arms shone. The air glowed between them.

Jane felt at last there was no more need to be hasty. Slowly she unlaced her gown. It was easily done, for it was one of her old nursing gowns which opened at the front. It dropped from her shoulders and she kicked it aside, standing only in her shift. She looked constantly into his eyes, in which a sparkling delight and a dark longing alternately blazed and dimmed. Her shift was but a loose thing, held on her shoulders by two strings, the knots untied in a moment. The garment crumpled to her feet and she stood naked, showing herself to him with awkward delight.

She felt the air caressing her body all over and the sunlight mantling her shoulders. His eyes explored her with rapture. At length he stirred and shook his head in amazement, as if he had seen an angel.

'Well, Jane,' he said at last, with a sigh, 'I take it my indifference is no longer required.' She inclined her head with a smile. 'I was wondering whether to drown myself, but since you've come, I might leave it till tomorrow.'

An envious breeze ruffled her hair and a rash of goosepimples fled across her skin. She shivered.

'Come, you will catch cold.' He held out his arms.

Jane stepped down into the clear green water. It was warm, but not as warm as Sir Thomas.

Jane and Sir Thomas found themselves as happily matched in their bodies as in their minds. A passion long suppressed was now explored at leisure. Mary retired to rest for three hours every afternoon and always went to bed early in the evenings, and in these hours Jane discovered unimagined joys in Sir Thomas's sensitive and delicate attentions. Despite Mary's encouragement of their union, out of respect to her their association retained a clandestine element which intensified their pleasure and satisfied the requirements of society.

The radiance of a mutual passion is hard to hide, however, and in due course Mr and Mrs Lockhart began to suspect that their daughters enjoyed a domestic situation very different from what was usual in Gloucestershire. Mr Lockhart proposed to escape by taking his wife on a trip to Italy. He had the misfortune, however, to contract typhoid fever in Rome and died there.

Mrs Lockhart insisted that the best mason in Rome was engaged to provide her husband with a funeral monument of fitting elegance and she turned at last from it with a smile glinting amongst her tears at the thought that now her husband must be happy to have arrived in a place where he would never be exposed to emotion, or required to make conversation.

She returned to Ottercombe to find a baby on Mary's knee. The child was called Frederick, and rejoiced in the attentions of a pair of mothers. Mrs Lockhart did not enquire into the obstetric details of this happy event and a year or so later, when little Fred was learning to call Mary Mamma, Mrs Lockhart noticed that Jane was beginning to look stout and decided to go and spend several months with her sister in Cheltenham.

Thus tactfully did Mrs Lockhart avoid witnessing Jane's pregnancies at too close quarters. She was a practical soul before anything and, finding only happiness in the faces of both her daughters, marvelled at the ingenuity with which they had managed to patch together a vibrant life out of the scraps and relics of two mistaken marriages. She occasionally received impertinent remarks on the subject, for Cheltenham was full of barbed tongues, but Mrs Lockhart defended her daughters with indignant pride and enjoyed their company whole-heartedly for a few weeks every summer.

There were of course many conjectures as to the parentage of Frederick and the second baby, Susannah. The London gossips liked to think that the mother was Lady Mary, and the father John the gardener who watered her lilies with such devotion, but local opinion settled around the likelihood of Jane being the mother, and the father either Sir Thomas or Henry Burton, who had returned from the sea with the best sort of injury: one that did not curtail pleasure, only forbid duty.

Mary was fulfilled. She saw her sister and her husband profoundly happy. For herself there could be no greater treat than to be surrounded by children without the fatigues and dangers of pregnancy. Sarah grew up tall and beautiful like Mr Harris, but rejoiced in her mother's ardent nature and delighted in being an older sister to Frederick and Susannah.

A most amicable correspondence grew up between Jane and Mr Harris in Martinique. When after some years he returned from the West Indies to teach and study in Paris, William Harris was overjoyed to receive a visit from the daughter he had last seen as a baby, now transformed into a lovely young woman. Sarah was escorted on this occasion by her Uncle Henry, for Jane did not wish to risk the affection which had sprung up between herself and Mr Harris by the awkwardness of a meeting.

Sir Thomas's only anxiety was for Miss Eliza, who, after several flirtations with lieutenants, attached herself to an even wealthier and older man than her own father and transferred her tyrannies conveniently to him. Henry developed an interest in agriculture and often irritated the tenant farmers with his advice. They always enjoyed a joke with him, however, for this was really Henry's gift and he made use of it relentlessly.

Mary was always singled out for a special nostalgic flirtation when Henry was about, but her heart was secure. As mistress of Ottercombe Park she had everything she could have wished for and found a safer exercise for her passions in her books than in the dangerous company of men. He never left off proposing to Jane and encouraging her to believe that Mr Harris would acquiesce in a suit of Criminal Conversation. But Jane always declined his kind offers very firmly, for in Sir Thomas she had her heart's desire and was quite happy to remain neither wife nor widow, only a scandalous anomaly.

The new century was to see an increase in that piety, allied to a zeal for social justice, which Mr Harris had espoused with such ardour. However, the parish of Ottercombe, being so remote, remained a hidden outpost of old-fashioned compromise and ease. Jane was busy, occupied with her children by two different fathers. But proposals to improve the conditions of the poor received her ardent support. However, she no longer felt guilty at enjoying some happiness of her own, because others might be suffering. She still had a conscience, but she had ceased to be persecuted by it.

After the trials of her early life, Jane was satisfied and fulfilled and grateful for her good fortune, though never quite sure what gods, if any, heard her murmured thanks. In her worst moments she had felt that the Church offered its absolutes without a trace of pity, and society its expectations without a hint of escape. She had found herself thwarted and trapped, and had only been able at last to express her joys and desires by contrivances which many found scandalous and disgraceful.

She enjoyed in maturity the exercise of her assertiveness and wit, which too severe an authority in her youth had almost crushed out of her. Many found her domestic arrangements a hideous sin and her forthright character unbecoming in a woman. Gossip and disapproval could always hurt her. But whenever she stole a rare moment of repose in which to admire her valley with its tumbling woods, blue depths and floating drifts of light, it seemed to her that the sun shone as generously upon her as if she and her family were peculiarly blessed; more like the redeemed and the forgiven than the ruined and the damned.